MIDNIGHT
IN CAIRO

MIDNIGHT IN CAIRO

The Divas of Egypt's Roaring '20s

Raphael Cormack

W. W. NORTON & COMPANY
Independent Publishers Since 1923

MIDNIGHT IN CAIRO
Copyright © 2021 by Raphael Cormack

Published by arrangement with Saqi Books 2021

Frontispiece photo courtesy of Lucie Ryzova
Map by Chris Robinson

For information about special discounts for bulk purchases, please contact
W. W. Norton Special Sales at specialsales@wwnorton.com or 800-233-4830

Manufacturing by LSC Communications, Harrisonburg
Production manager: Lauren Abbate

Library of Congress Cataloging-in-Publication Data

Names: Cormack, Raph, author.
Title: Midnight in Cairo : the divas of Egypt's roaring '20s /
Raphael Cormack.
Description: First edition. | New York, NY : W. W. Norton & Company, 2021. |
Includes bibliographical references and index.
Identifiers: LCCN 2020047125 | ISBN 9780393541137 (hardcover) |
ISBN 9780393541144 (epub)
Subjects: LCSH: Women—Egypt—Cairo—Social life and customs—20th
century. | Nightlife—Egypt—Cairo—History—20th century. | Cairo
(Egypt)—Social life and customs—20th century. | Cairo (Egypt)—
Civilization—20th century. | Egypt—History—1919–1952.
Classification: LCC HQ1793.Z9 C67 2021 | DDC 305.40962/16—dc23
LC record available at https://lccn.loc.gov/2020047125

W. W. Norton & Company, Inc., 500 Fifth Avenue, New York, N.Y. 10110
www.wwnorton.com

W. W. Norton & Company Ltd., 15 Carlisle Street, London W1D 3BS

1 2 3 4 5 6 7 8 9 0

CONTENTS

If you visit a city during the day, you cannot claim to know it. You have to see its nightlife.

—JEANETTE TAGHER,
Les Cabarets du Caire dans la Seconde Moitié du XIXe Siècle

MIDNIGHT
IN CAIRO

To the Bosphore Casino

Badia Masabni's Sala
Majestic Theatre
Egyptiana/ New Printania
Bijou Palace
Casino de Paris

Queen Nazli Street

Kantaret al-Dikka Street

American
Cosmograph
Cinema

Ramses
Theatre

Clot Bey Street

Tawfiq Street

Emad al-Din Street

Wish al-Birka Street

Kursaal
Music Hall

Shepheard's
Hotel

Alhambra
Music Hall

Old Eldorado
Music Hall

Alfi Bey Street

al-Ginaina Street

Old Printania/
Basque Pelota

al-Busta Street

Fouad I Street

Kamel Street

EZBEKIYYA

GARDENS

Street

al-Maghraby Street

al-Madabigh Street

al-Manakh Street

Tiyatru Street

Thousand and One
Nights Music Hall

Opera
House

Qasr al-Nil Street

Abd al-Aziz Street

Mohamed Ali Street

0   100   200
Metres

Ezbekiyya in the 1920s.

Introduction

THE PAST IS A SET OF OLD CLOTHES

IN THE LATE 1980S, the Egyptian writer Louis Awad looked back on his student days in Cairo between the wars. In particular, he remembered the nights he spent in the cafés of Cairo's nightlife district, Ezbekiyya.

> All you had to do was sit in one of the bars or cafés that looked out onto Alfi Bey Street, like the Parisiana or the Taverna, and tens of different salesmen would come up to you, one selling lottery tickets, another selling newspapers, another selling eggs and simit bread, another selling combs and shaving cream, the next shining shoes, and the next offering pistachios. There were also people who would play a game "Odds or Evens," performing monkeys, clowns, men with pianolas who performed with their wives, fire eaters, and people impersonating Charlie Chaplin's walk. Among all these, there was always someone trying to convince you that he would bring you to the most beautiful girl in the world, who was only a few steps away.[1]

In the 1920s and 1930s, the centre of nightlife in Ezbekiyya was Emad al-Din Street—long and wide, with a tram line down the middle

Emad al-Din Street looking north

running north to the suburbs of Shubra and Abbasiyya. The intersection with Alfi Bey Street, where Louis Awad used to sit in the bars and cafés, was at the southern end of the action. There stood the grand Kursaal music hall, owned by the Italian impresario Augusto Dalbagni, its two-storey entrance topped with stars and crescent moons to imitate Egypt's flag, where touring European acts and local Egyptians alike performed. Down into Alfi Bey Street was an ever-changing series of venues, which in the early days of this area's prominence included the grand Printania Theatre and, beside it, the Abbaye des Roses music hall. In the mid-1920s a new form of entertainment emerged when the venue became a court where the Basque sport of pelota—a ball game similar to squash or fives—was a popular late-night attraction, with the main match starting at midnight.

Farther north up Emad al-Din Street, the four grand domes of the khedivial buildings, finished in 1910, towered over the street from both sides. In this complex of apartments and offices, the Greek poet George Seferis used to work in the 1940s. In one of his poems he recalled the "car horns, trams, rumbling of car engines and screech of brakes" that used to greet him on his walks.[2] The street was lined with cinemas: the American Cosmograph, Empire, Obelisk, Violet, and more. In the 1910s and '20s they ran a selection of foreign films with intertitles (aka title cards) in French, English, Arabic, and Greek and, sometimes, with live musical accompaniment—the Gaumont Palace featured a small orchestra led by the famous violinist Naoum Poliakine. Just before the junction with Kantaret al-Dikka, the street that led towards the red-light district to the east, was Youssef Wahbi's Ramses Theatre, where his troupe put on a selection of Arabic tragedy, comedy, and melodrama.

Across Kantaret al-Dikka, on the other side of the junction, was the European-style Casino de Paris cabaret. One Egyptian journal described it enthusiastically in 1923 as offering "exquisite Parisian girls, who come on stage to interpret the latest numbers from Paris, an agreeable atmosphere, fine champagne, and nothing lacking to give a total illusion of one of the Montmartre cabarets." A more cynical writer said that "with its walls hung with pink paper, its stage which is not much more than platform, and its bar of varnished wood . . . the Casino de Paris, in fact, much more resembled one of those small clubs that flourish in austere provincial towns, to the terror of the virtuous bourgeoisie." This notorious venue was run by Marcelle Langlois, a Frenchwoman with strikingly dyed red hair, who was notorious among anti-prostitution campaigners as a "procurer" of chorus girls for wealthy clients. Her activities, both in and out of sight, earned her enough money to buy a large chateau in France.[3]

Just past this European-style cabaret were a series of music halls and theatres that showed, in the words of one American journalist, "continuous three to five hour shows in Arabic and English . . . heavily peppered with bawdy jokes" and catered to local Egyptians and occasional tourists. There was the Majestic, the Bijou Palace, and the Egyptiana. In these theatres and music halls, the Franco-Arab revue flourished. It was a uniquely Cairene genre: a selection of short farces, songs, and dances, all in a mixture of Arabic and French, bringing together in one night of entertainment Egyptian actors and dancers with performers from the music halls of Europe.[4]

Today, Emad al-Din Street has retained only traces of this world. There is just one theatre still working on the street, a derelict cinema stands on the site of the Casino de Paris, and the Scheherazade is the only major cabaret still operating in the area; the others have either moved out to Giza or behind nondescript doorways in the side streets of downtown Cairo. But in its heyday, Cairo's nightlife could rival that in Paris, London, or Berlin. Any resident of Egypt's capital city in the early twentieth century could have claimed, with justification, to be living in one of the great cities of the world, at the centre of many different cultures.

The city's population had come from an amazing variety of places across Europe, Africa, and Asia. Some people (mostly the Europeans) enjoyed pampered lives with lucrative jobs in Africa's latest boom town. Others struggled, working in menial jobs or negotiating the growing criminal underworld, trying anything to stay afloat. People seeking better opportunities lived alongside refugees from Europe who came in the wake of the First World War. Spies and political agitators from as far away as Russia and Japan crossed the paths of sybaritic aristocrats, who whiled away their afternoons in hotel bars.

This history of cosmopolitan Egypt is memorably recorded in the novels, poems, and memoirs of Europeans, most of them living in

Alexandria. From the Greek poet Constantine Cavafy's melancholy evocations of Mediterranean café life to the rich, chocolate-cake prose of Lawrence Durrell's epic *Alexandria Quartet*, these writers created some of the most enduring images of twentieth-century Egypt. But, far from the elite literary salons of Alexandria, another story unfolded— less well known but just as exciting—in the Arabic theatres, cafés, and clubs of Cairo. In the transgressive nightlife of central Cairo, with all the freedom that came with performing for an audience of strangers, rigid identities and conventional barriers that separated different nationalities were more fluid than anywhere else.

Even a cursory attempt to list the stars of this period reveals the huge variety of their backgrounds, whether religious, national, or cultural. Some became legends, others have been forgotten, but they all played their part. There were Egyptians of all kinds. Many of the earliest star actresses, like Nazla Mizrahi or the Dayan sisters, were Jewish; others were Christian or Muslim. Some performers came from farther up the Nile. One dance hall in the 1930s boasted a troupe of Sudanese dancers, and among the many young actresses trying to break into the big time in the 1920s was Aida al-Habashiyya, who, to judge from her name, must have been of either Ethiopian or Sudanese descent (*Habasha* is the Arabic word for that part of sub-Saharan Africa). Other dancers, singers, and actors came to Cairo from all over the Arab world to perform on its stages. Europeans, too, populated this primarily Arabic-speaking world. One of the most famous dancers of the 1920s was the Englishwoman Dolly Smith, who worked as a choreographer for the biggest theatrical companies in Cairo. Then there was the French Madame Langlois, the influential cabaret impresario and owner of Cairo's Casino de Paris. The life of the stage proved a magnet for ambitious misfits of all kinds. They found ample possibilities in the nightlife district of Ezbekiyya, where the refined opera house and expensive hotels sat alongside smoky bars, hashish dens, and nightclubs; where Greek waiters served their artistic patrons coffee, wine, and *zabib* (a potent Egyptian version of arak); where singing and dancing lasted long into the night.

The story of this world from the late nineteenth century to the 1950s is often mythologised in Egypt but largely overlooked in the West, where the Middle East is usually seen only as a political problem to be solved. Yet it is full of surprises. It includes, at different points, a gay English Arts and Crafts designer, several cross-dressing actresses, a belly dancer involved in underground left-wing politics, and an unsuccessful attempt to make a film version of the life of the prophet Mohammed, directed by the man who went on to make *Casablanca*. Offstage, the action is punctuated by lawsuits, murder, and revolution.

It should come as no surprise that early twentieth-century Cairo was full of so much drama. Egypt, at the time, was a country on the verge of huge social and political change. In 1919 a generation-defining series of events was set into motion; Egyptians had revolted against British colonial rule and, as a result, Egypt became officially independent (albeit with significant British control remaining, as we shall see). After this, they began to ask themselves what they wanted their country to be and what their future could look like as new beliefs and ideologies jostled for space.

The new generation debated big political ideas: liberalism, communism, atheism, and more. In a 1941 film called *Intisar al-Shabab* (The triumph of youth), the main character caught the mood of the times: "That past is a set of old clothes; take it off and throw it away." Everywhere people were talking about this *Nahda* or "renaissance" and the new opportunities it was heralding. The 1920s and 1930s were an exciting time to be alive in Egypt.

It was in this atmosphere of revolutionary ideas and change that the feminist movement in Egypt grew and expanded. In the early twentieth century, a number of organisations and unions were set up to support women's rights; magazines were established that gave women space to discuss the issues that affected them directly; books on female progress and liberation were published. Egyptian women became part of a movement for change that took advantage of new technologies and a new feeling of internationalism to promote these ideas across the globe.

The conventional history of early twentieth-century Egyptian feminism usually runs through a list of prominent female activists, most (if not all) from middle- or upper-class backgrounds—Hoda Shaarawi, Nabawiyya Musa, May Ziadeh, Ceza Nabarawi, and the Egyptian Feminist Union. The brand of progress they advocated was cautious and incremental. They published magazines, attended international conferences, promoted women's education, and campaigned for women's political rights, but they were careful not to make men too uncomfortable. Men, in turn, gave lip service to these new feminist ideals but maintained and protected their own male spheres of influence. High politics remained almost exclusively a male domain, as did high literature. Literary men professed their commitment to equality but spent their long evenings in the cafés, pontificating about art and beauty without any women present. The few female writers to enter these closed literary circles were exceptional.

However, outside this world, another history of Egyptian feminism was being written on the stages of Cairo's nightclubs, theatres, and cabarets. The women's movement in Egypt is not usually seen from the perspective of music hall singers, dancers, and actresses. They lived in the margins of so-called decency, and hardly anyone who saw themselves as respectable wanted to be publicly associated with them.

British visitors, missionaries, and colonial administrators saw these women as embodiments of all the old stereotypes they had about Egyptian society—primitive, exotic, and pleasure-obsessed—further evidence that Egypt was not yet a nation capable of ruling itself and either dangerously erotic or there to be saved. Meanwhile, members of Egypt's elite class of modernising nationalist politicians and intellectuals, who were trying to show that they were capable of self-governance, were no more pleased than the British with the dance halls and nightclubs in their capital. They saw them, though, not as signs of their country's own backwardness but as one of the many corrupting forces imported from the West. The bars, cafés, and dance halls of Cairo, and particularly the female entertainers who filled them, were dragging the nation down and bringing the bright prospects of a new generation down with them.

Yet, in these disparaged music halls and theatres, women were defining their own place in the new century. They had a lot to fight against, from the disapproval of conservative society to men who thought they could do what they wanted with an actress or night-club singer. But the lucky ones who managed to navigate their way through this world achieved significant personal and financial independence. Female singers commanded large audiences; actresses were in high demand; women owned dance halls, wrote and directed films, and recorded hit songs. In 1915, eight years before the founding of the Egyptian Feminist Union, the singer and actress Mounira al-Mahdiyya formed her own theatrical troupe.

These women who did so much to create modern Egyptian culture were not part of the elite. They frequently grew up in poverty, and many had little formal education—often they had to learn how to read just to be able to understand the scripts for plays they were supposed to act in. Nonetheless, telling the history of Egyptian culture—of Egypt itself—would be impossible without them. They chose what to perform and the Egypt they wanted to show. This is the story of a parallel women's movement, one that happened in the demi-monde, late at night after the high-class critics had gone to bed.

Despite their lack of respectability (or perhaps because of it), these women soon became the first modern Egyptian celebrities. In the 1920s a series of popular entertainment magazines came into being, all of them catering to fans obsessed with these female stars. Journalists dissected everything about them, publishing countless photos, interviews, and articles, feeding the public demand for details of their favourite stars' lives. Later in life, many of these women also published their own memoirs of this period, often casting themselves in the best light or settling old scores. In this celebrity story-mill, fuelled by gossip, romanticism, and myth, tales often took on a life of their own— the more flamboyant the better. Yet at its core, this was a group of women demanding to be heard as they asserted their wishes, claimed their rights, and made space for themselves.

Women offered a perspective on this world that men could not— and it was one in which men often came across quite badly. In 1951 a veteran actress called Fatima Rushdi wrote an article explaining why she loved acting parts written for men. She argued that such roles as Romeo, Hamlet, Napoleon, and Don Juan "suit a woman's nature because they have a universal character. They have a certain subtlety and intelligence that only she can succeed in capturing." Women, she argued, with their sensitivity to the world around them, just make better actors—whether the part be male or female. "Men have been luckier than women in the acting profession, but women are better actors," she said, contending that "only a woman can really get to the depths of the characters." She concluded that, "to put it plainly, women can give a performance that is more complete and successful than any man."[5]

Since my first visit to Egypt in 2009, I have gone back and forth more times than I can count—first to learn Arabic, then to work on a PhD on adaptations of Sophocles' tragedy *Oedipus Rex* in modern Egyptian theatre, and finally to research this book. Cairo is a city whose history feels, physically, very present—from the tombs around Imam al-Shafii's mausoleum to the mosques and madrasas of the old walled city. I have always gravitated towards downtown, the heart of the modern city away from the historic centre, and wondered what stories also lurk there. What would it have been like to walk the same streets a hundred years ago?

While writing my PhD, I discovered that an abundant, animated, and spirited entertainment press existed in 1920s and 1930s Egypt.

Some of these magazines are still well known in Egypt; others seem to exist only in the collections of the National Library of Egypt; all of them are filled with bizarre and offbeat stories of Cairo's wild night-life and the stars of its entertainment world. There was, as one might expect, a good amount of gossip and rumour; but it was enough to send me on a mission to find out more. I soon discovered that a lot of the celebrities from that period had written memoirs (some had written more than one set) that were equally full of amusement and intrigue. After reading some more academic works of history on the period and searching through archives across the world, I managed to build a history of Cairo's modern, cosmopolitan nightlife, a scene that was enticing and seductive but also exploitative and dangerous.

This book is my attempt to shine a light on that history and to show how Cairo became one of the most exciting cities in the world for anyone to spend a night in the early twentieth century. This is a theatrical story in three acts. The first act tells the eventful modern history of Egypt's nightlife from the late nineteenth century until the 1920s, alongside the wider context of colonialism, war, and revolution. The stars of the second act are a few of the most important, successful, and influential women of Cairo's 1920s entertainment industry. With careers that often lasted several decades, spanning theatre, music, cabaret, film, and journalism, their lives were entangled and intertwined both professionally and personally. Delving into the complex, well-lived lives of these seven exceptional women, this act returns them to the limelight after almost a century. The final act recounts Ezbekiyya's journey through the Second World War to its final days as the centre of Cairo's nightlife as Egypt moved into a new, post-colonial era with Nasser's revolution in 1952. Together, these three acts tell an overlooked story of theatre, song, and dance that shows the modern Middle East from a different angle—not one dominated by wars, "intellectuals," "great men," or high politics, but by late nights in cabarets, wild music, and women calling for change.

Act 1

SETTING THE SCENE

Chapter 1

"PARDON ME,
I'M DRUNK"

IN THE CLASSIC EGYPTIAN PLAY *The Phantom*, the main characters are having dinner soon after a particularly harsh government crackdown on vice—brothels have been closed, the wine shops shuttered, and Cairo's hashish supplies cast into the fires. One disappointed character consoles the assembled guests with an "Elegy to Satan," in which he describes the city's debauched nightlife in earlier days, a demi-monde of drunkards, musicians, hashish-heads, clowns, and prostitutes. "From now on," his poem laments, "no more hugging, no more fucking, no more kissing"; the good times have come to an end.[1]

This scene is not from modern Egypt. It was written for shadow puppets in the thirteenth century CE by Ibn Daniyal, an eye doctor originally from Mosul but based in Cairo. He composed his poem under the administration of the Mamluk Sultan Baibars, who is best known for his military victories against the crusaders and the Mongols but also, according to Ibn Daniyal's play, started a moral crusade of his own at home. One of his three extant shadow plays, *The Phantom* is among the earliest dramatic scripts in Arabic to survive from Egypt and a rare medieval example of the genre, in which a huge range of elegant and finely made leather puppets acted out bawdy and often unapologetically obscene dramas. Light on plot—but stuffed full of songs and short sketches—the plays seem designed to show off the poet's wit and the puppeteer's skill while painting a vivid picture of the city's culture and entertainment. Another of Ibn Daniyal's shadow plays, *Strange and Amazing*, consists of a procession of characters who enter briefly to perform short skits and then leave. He populated Mamluk Egypt with an array of oddballs, acrobats, preachers, magicians, animal tamers, tricksters, tattooists, and sword swallowers.

For centuries afterwards, shadow plays continued to be performed on the streets of Egypt and at religious festivals. Later surviving manuscripts include *The Crocodile*, in which a fisherman is eaten by a crocodile as a Nubian and a North African compete to save him from its stomach, and *The Café*, in which two characters debate the relative merits of homosexuality and heterosexuality. The proponent of heterosexuality wins the argument but loses the war because the former proponent of homosexuality promptly has an affair with his wife. As late as 1911, the German Orientalist scholar (and later spy) Curt Prüfer described the shadow plays that he had seen:

> The player sets up his *kushk*, a movable wooden booth, wherever he wishes it; there he sits behind a tightly stretched muslin curtain, which is lighted from behind by a primitive oil lamp, and presses the transparent leather figures against the curtain by means of wooden sticks fastened to figures at the back, and serving at the same time to move their limbs. The player is supported by his troupe, who help him in the manipulation of the figures and in reciting the different roles.[2]

At the beginning of the 1800s, some six hundred years after Ibn Daniyal's plays were first performed, many different public entertainment traditions existed alongside shadow plays. There was, for instance, another kind of puppet show called Aragoz, an Egyptian version of the Turkish shadow plays called Karagoz, that used hand puppets like a

Punch and Judy show but kept the stock characters, slapstick humour, and dirty jokes characteristic of the shadow theatre. As well as puppet shows, itinerant farce players (usually called *Muhabbazin*) were a regular feature at weddings, religious ceremonies, and private parties. Their sketches, often concerned with contemporary rulers or the plight of the downtrodden, managed to mock both the strong and weak. "It is chiefly by vulgar jests, and indecent actions, that they amuse, and obtain applause," the traveller and Orientalist Edward Lane wrote in the 1830s. Performances like these were not based on a precise script and had considerable room for improvisation and audience interaction. For the most part, details about the shows come from the (not always reliable) accounts of European travellers.[3]

In the cafés, storytellers recited oral epics, sometimes with musical backing and sometimes without. The most popular tales in the early nineteenth century were *al-Sira al-Hilaliyya*, the epic story of the migration of the Beni Hilal tribe from the Arabian Peninsula to North Africa; *Sirat Antar*, a tale about Antar, the son of a slave who became a great poet and warrior in pre-Islamic Arabia; and *al-Sira al-Zahiriyya*, an epic about the life of the Sultan Baibars (whose reforms Ibn Daniyal had mocked centuries before).

Then there were the singers and dancers. According to Lane, still a major source for nineteenth-century entertainment history (even if used a little cautiously), Egyptians were, in comparison to the British, "excessively fond of music." He divided musical entertainers into three main types. The first was the *alatee*, a male musician who sang and accompanied himself on an instrument such as the oud (lute). Lane viewed these as "people of very dissolute habits," however he remarked that they were "hired at most grand entertainments, to amuse the company; and on these occasions they are usually supplied with brandy, or other spirituous liquors, which they sometimes drink until they can no longer sing, nor strike a chord." The second type was the *almeh*, a female singer who almost exclusively performed in the houses of the elite. Lane said these women were often very skilled, writing their own poetry and receiving large sums for their performances. The third kind of musical entertainer, in Lane's early nineteenth-century categorisation, was the *ghawazee*, a dancing girl who performed either in public streets or at the private parties of ordinary people. He considered their dancing to be inelegant and more highly sexualised than the dances he had seen in wealthy houses, but he admitted that "women, as well as men, take delight in witnessing their performances" even if "many persons among the higher classes, and the more religious, disapprove of them."[4]

For the residents of Cairo at the beginning of the nineteenth century, the city had a rich cultural life. But the coming decades would transform Egypt—and its nightlife—almost beyond recognition. Over this time, Egypt would develop from a largely unremarkable province of the Ottoman Empire into a flourishing, politically important modern state; a booming economic powerhouse; and before long, a (semi-formal) protectorate of the British Empire. As a new Egypt took shape, theatres, cinemas, cabarets, and music halls—like those that were popular around the world—would take over Cairo. By the end of the century, Cairo's nightlife would converge around the district of Ezbekiyya, named after an old Mamluk emir called Ezbek who once had a palace there. The district boasted at least thirteen large entertainment venues and innumerable smaller bars and cafés. Many of these places offered shows by singers or dancers in rooms heavy with smoke and alcohol, and they also housed gambling halls, hashish dens, and more. This was Cairo's equivalent of Montmartre, Broadway, or Soho.

Alongside the nightlife venues were several hotels that catered to European travellers. Most prominent among them was Shepheard's with its renowned terrace where, in the winter season, the world's elite thronged. According to an article in *Harper's Bazaar* in 1884, "In olden days, before the canal diverted the course of travel between India and Egypt, Shepheard's Hotel was the spot where the streams from the East and West met."[5] These hotels, combined with the new French-style buildings springing up in this part of Cairo, led people to call Ezbekiyya the European Quarter. More was going on there, however, than that name indicates. To the north of the gardens was St. Mark's Cathedral, seat of the Coptic Patriarchate and one of the most important sites of Egyptian Christianity. To the east was Mouski, a historic area with Arabic architecture and narrow streets leading to the heart of the Fatimid old city, which Europeans viewed as hugely exotic. Ezbekiyya, far from being just a tourists' hotspot, was *the* place for pleasure-seeking Cairenes to go out at night.

The story of Ezbekiyya is also the story of modern Egypt. In most history books, the year 1798 is singled out as the beginning of a new phase in the country's history. In that year, Napoleon led his armies across the Mediterranean and conquered Egypt, defeating the Ottoman armies at the Battle of the Pyramids. Living out a fantasy in which he played a cross between Mohammed and Alexander the Great, the French emperor took Cairo by storm, accompanied by thousands of soldiers and a team of 151 savants tasked with a minute analysis of the history, culture, and geography of this "antique land." The French army took up residence all around Cairo, including Ezbekiyya—then a neighbourhood of only middling importance—where they set up a temporary theatre to entertain the troops with dramatic performances including Voltaire's *Death of Caesar* and a new opera (*The Two Millers*) written by two members of the expedition.

Many people have been tempted to see the French invasion as a decisive turning point in Egypt's history and the beginning of modernity in the country—for this reason, many books on modern

Egyptian history begin in 1798. However, in reality, Napoleon's short but romanticised Middle Eastern campaign (which lasted only until 1801) probably had more of an impact on the European imagination than anything else. The most important result of the French invasion came about totally by chance. In 1801 Mohammed Ali, an Albanian military commander, arrived from Kavala in modern-day Greece as second-in-command of a small contingent of soldiers—one small part of the joint Ottoman–British army that defeated the French. But by 1805 Mohammed Ali had skilfully managed to manipulate the political chaos and make himself the Ottoman governor of Egypt. In 1811, he took complete control of the country by comprehensively defeating his powerful rivals—a caste of warrior-slaves called the Mamluks, who had been the Ottoman vassals in Egypt before the French invasion. In a brutal and now legendary ploy, he invited hundreds of the most powerful Mamluks to a party in Cairo's citadel; once they were inside, he shut the gates and had them all killed.

From the 1810s to the 1840s, Mohammed Ali turned Egypt into a de facto self-governing state, establishing a dynasty of his own only nominally under the control of the Ottoman Empire. He instigated a huge programme of modernisation, professionalising the army, bringing in European advisors to help with state-building projects, and setting up a printing press, hospitals, and educational institutes. He also set about the work of transforming Ezbekiyya into something new. In the early days of his reign, the area had been an elite enclave consisting of sumptuous palaces built around a small lake. The lake was drained and then turned into a garden, and soon hotels, small ramshackle bars, billiard rooms, and music halls all started popping up around it.

By the time Mohammed Ali died in 1849, he had established a dynasty that his sons and grandsons continued with varying degrees of success for almost 150 years. After a brief period of rule by Mohammed Ali's sons Ibrahim and Said and his grandson Abbas, "Ismail the Magnificent," another grandson of Mohammed Ali, became the khedive (viceroy) of Egypt in 1863 (though the Ottomans did not let him formally use the title until 1867). More than anyone else, Ismail turned Ezbekiyya (and downtown Cairo more generally) into the centre of Egypt's cultural life. In the 1860s, because of the American Civil War, cotton was in high demand globally, and Egypt capitalised on this. The crop, which had only recently been introduced to the country by Mohammed Ali, became a gold mine, and Ismail suddenly found he had huge amounts of money to spend on his passion for building. He spent lavishly on public works and private extravagances across the country, including the Gezira Palace that now houses the Marriott Hotel in Zamalek.

Ismail also began to design a whole new centre for Cairo. His workers knocked down crumbling old palaces to build new streets. He employed Jean-Pierre Barillet-Deschamps, the former chief gardener of Paris who had planned the Bois de Boulogne, to lay out the new Ezbekiyya Gardens on the spot where Mohammed Ali had drained the old lake. Around the new gardens, Ismail ordered the construction of a series of luxury entertainment venues. Between 1869 and 1872, a "French theatre," a circus, a hippodrome, a "garden theatre," and an Italian-style opera house all sprang up. As pride of place in his building project, he erected a large bronze equestrian statue of his own illustrious father, the successful General Ibrahim Pasha, by the French sculptor Charles Cordier. Ibrahim Pasha's statue pointed its finger to the horizon in a triumphal pose, befitting a general who had won decisive victories for his father, Mohammed Ali, in the Arabian Peninsula, Greece, and Syria.

In Ismail's Ezbekiyya, modern Egyptian nightlife and entertainment was born and went on to thrive. Clowns, acrobats, farce players, and animal trainers carried on as they had done for centuries—a shadow theatre existed in Ezbekiyya until 1909, when authorities shut

Opera Square, Ez bekiyya
(Library of Congress, Prints & Photographs Division, [LC-DIG-matpc-17901])

it down because they considered it too raunchy—but new attractions were now on the rise too.

The Khedive Ismail's vision for Cairo's new entertainment district was dominated by theatre and opera, largely following European models in European languages. He wanted to show his court and his most elite subjects the best examples of those genres that existed, in order to glorify his rule. With the vast sums of money available to him as the ruler of Egypt, this goal was within his reach. In 1869, he inaugurated the Théâtre Français with a production of his favourite opera, *La Belle Hélène*. Two years later, Ismail realised one of his great triumphs when he persuaded the highly sought-after Italian composer Giuseppe Verdi, helped along by the vast sum of 150,000 gold francs, to write him an opera to be performed at his new opera house. The opera was *Aida*, the story of an Ethiopian princess in Pharaonic Egypt, and it premiered in Cairo in 1871. A long-standing myth holds that the opera was commissioned to celebrate the inauguration of the Suez Canal but was delayed. This is not, strictly speaking, true; but Ismail did use *Aida* in the same way that he used such large public works as the Suez Canal: to project an image of a powerful global leader.

Although not commissioned directly by Ismail, an Arabic-speaking dramatic movement soon emerged in Ezbekiyya to follow these European classics. The colourful and eccentric figure Yaqub Sanua, who went by the name of James, is now usually considered to be the father of Arabic theatre in Egypt. He was the son of an Egyptian Jewish mother and a Sephardic Jewish father from the Tuscan port of Livorno who worked as an advisor to a minor member of the khedivial family in Cairo. Over the next seventy years the Jewish population of Egypt would increase many-fold, but in the mid-nineteenth century it was not huge. In Cairo, as the London Society for Promoting Christianity amongst the Jews estimated in 1856, there were around 4,000 Jews in a population of about 300,000. A number of prominent Sephardic families had some power and influence, but most of the Jewish population led ordinary lives, though not free from discrimination or prejudice.

James himself was a dreamer, a visionary, and a prolific self-publicist. He was also a committed Egyptian nationalist and an enthusiastic promoter of Arabic-language culture. As a teenager he was sent to study in Livorno on a government scholarship. On his return he worked for a while as a tutor to the children of the khedivial court before landing an appointment in 1868 at the École Polytechnique, an institute in Cairo for the study of engineering and architecture.

While enjoying this comfortable bourgeois existence in the summer of 1870, James saw two touring theatrical companies—one French, one Italian—performing at Ismail's new open-air theatre in Ezbe-kiyya Gardens. He might have seen drama of this kind in Livorno, but he had almost certainly never been to a play in Cairo before. He approached the companies and asked if he could help with their pro-duction. They both welcomed assistance from this enterprising young Egyptian and invited him to join the troupes temporarily (it is unclear whether he acted with them or helped in some other way). In his later recollections, James identified this as the precise moment that his pas-sion for theatre was sparked.

Once these touring troupes had left Cairo, James quickly got to work forming a theatrical company that would put on his own plays in Arabic. He gathered and trained a group of actors, wrote a script, and was ready for his opening night by the next summer. In a speech in Paris more than thirty years later, James could still remember the moment. He described, perhaps with a degree of poetic licence, the vast audience of 3,000 people gathered around the stage—men and women of all colours, including some government ministers and Euro-pean ambassadors. "A thunder of applause welcomed us and cries of bravo in all the languages of the Tower of Babel," James reminisced proudly. Backstage, the actors had been buoyed by the gift of a bottle of three-star Cognac from a wealthy Egyptian fan and, when they came onstage, delivered an assured performance of the newly written script.[6]

That day the troupe performed a one-act farce known sometimes as *The Harem* and sometimes as *The Bowman*. Usually considered the first piece of modern Egyptian drama, this short comedy mocked both the increasingly outdated, elite Egyptian system of the harem, in which the wives and concubines of the wealthy lived together in a separate area of the house, as well as the obsession that foreign visitors had with these harems (and myths that had grown around them). The story begins with a visiting European prince who is desperate to have an authentic illicit experience in a genuine Arab harem. He makes a bet of 1,000 Egyptian pounds with the son of a well-connected young Egyptian noble. Within a month, the prince says, he will be able to smuggle himself inside the women's quarters of some local pasha (an Ottoman noble title whose closest equivalent in English may be "lord").

Just a few days later, the prince receives good news. A letter arrives for him from a woman who (she says) has seen him from the harem as he was visiting her house, and his blue eyes have pierced her heart. The letter tells him to wait that night at the foot of the Sphinx, where a eunuch will pick him up and take him to her. After nightfall he goes to the agreed spot—and, sure enough, the eunuch soon appears. The prince is blindfolded and driven in secret to the palace, where he is smuggled into the women's rooms.

Now that they have the European prince at their mercy, the women of the harem play a cruel trick on him. They dress an attractive sixteen-year-old Syrian boy in women's clothes and pretend that he is the pasha's favourite out of all of them. They lead the prince into a secluded spot where he removes his blindfold. Seeing the boy in front of him, he is captivated and attempts to woo what he thinks is the young girl. He declares his love, and she reciprocates. As the two lovers are on the verge of a passionate embrace, the old, bearded pasha bursts into the room, interrupting their tryst.

Scandalised by the breach of his inner sanctum, he threatens to punish both of the transgressors by putting them in a sack and feeding them to the crocodiles. The holidaying prince pleads for mercy, even offering to give the pasha all of the 1,000 Egyptian pounds that he stands to win in his bet. At this point the characters remove their different disguises. The pasha takes off his white beard to reveal himself as the young man who had taken the prince's wager at the beginning of the play. The boy takes off his women's clothing to reveal himself as a young military officer, no doubt the bowman that the play is named after. Then a group of the prince's friends all emerge, laughing, from the next room, and the play ends with a sumptuous dinner in the palace gardens.

Over the next two years, James's company went on to produce thirty-two different plays. His repertoire mostly consisted of one-act farces or comedies of manners, similar to the first play he had written, with evocative names like *The Dandy of Cairo*, *The Alexandrian Princess*, and *The Tourist and the Donkey Boy*. Characters in the plays were drawn from the many different communities that lived in Egypt at the time—Nubian, Armenian, French, Greek, Arab, and English. There were frequent appearances from comic stock characters, among whom were the hashish-addled servant, the foreigner out of his or her depth, and the upper-crust Egyptian who tries, with comic incompetence, to ape European culture. This kind of thing later became the bread-and-butter of Egyptian comedy for many decades, and James's dramatic style may well have owed an unacknowledged debt to the shadow plays or travelling farce players of nineteenth-century Cairo.

Ultimately, James's theatrical career did not last long; by the end of 1872, his troupe had stopped performing. The Khedive Ismail was originally very supportive of the company—he was not against Arabic theatre, as long as it served his aims. But James later said that he fell out of favour with Ismail, who forced him to end his theatrical activities and eventually get out of Egypt; James suspected that his rivals, some *"gros bonnets"* and "sworn enemies of progress and civilisation" were whispering poisonous words to Egypt's ruler, trying to persuade him that James was hiding anti-government messages in his plays. An 1879 article in the *Saturday Review* claimed that "the wrongs of the Fellah ['peasant'] and the corruption of Ismail's government were treated by him in terms that quickly brought upon him the displeasure of the authorities." James himself later circulated the story that his play *The Two Wives*, which criticised the practice of taking more than one wife, offended Ismail, who had several wives. The khedive's riposte to James was, "If you don't have stout enough kidneys to please more than one woman, that's no reason to put others off."[7]

James may also have had more prosaic reasons for drifting away from the theatre in the 1870s. The money was running out. The cotton boom of the 1860s was starting to wane. And Ismail's extravagance was starting to catch up with him. He had borrowed heavily from European creditors and—alongside his disastrous decision to wage a war in Ethiopia—his spending was unsustainable. Finally, in 1876, a debt-ridden Egypt went bankrupt and, after long negotiations, British and French experts were brought into a new ministry created to supervise the country's finances on behalf of foreign lenders.

Politically, the late 1870s were extremely charged. Britain, in particular, began to exert more influence in Egypt; as this happened, James Sanua turned his attention towards more conventional politics, becoming a vocal critic of the khedive's compliance with further European expansion and playing a minor part in big political changes to come. In 1878 he started a fiercely anti-colonial and anti-Ismail satirical magazine called *Abou Naddara Zarqa* (The man with the blue glasses), whose circulation soon reached 50,000 copies in a population of around 6 million. Before the year was over, the magazine was bringing James unwanted kinds of attention and, after enduring two assassination attempts, he decided to leave Egypt for self-imposed exile in Paris. There he found a new permanent home for his journal, now simply called *Abou Naddara* omitting the adjective *zarqa* ("blue"), in Paris's Rue du Caire. Under this new name, and with the protection of exile, he began to publish more savage attacks on both the British and Egyptian ruling elite.

The European powers, however, did not stop their meddling in Egypt. Despite the agreements they had come to a few years before, in 1879 they decided to remove the Khedive Ismail from Egypt's throne and appoint his son Tawfiq as khedive in his place. But this did not stop the turmoil; in 1881 an Egyptian army officer called Ahmed

Urabi led a revolt based on a new constitution, which he had drafted, and called for parliamentary government. James Sanua's satirical journal got behind this new movement from Paris, filling the magazine with flattering cartoons of the Egyptian rebel. The British were so worried about the possibility that Urabi could take control of Egypt that they launched a military invasion to quash his uprising, which they painted as fanatical and dangerous. In 1882, claiming to be worried on behalf of foreign creditors and the European population of Egypt, the British installed Evelyn Baring (Lord Cromer) as their new consul general. Although the Khedive Tawfiq was kept on the throne and Egypt officially remained in the Ottoman Empire, Cromer and the British were now in effective control of the country.

James Sanua continued publishing magazines in Paris until the 1910s. He also became something of a celebrity in France, performing comic monologues at conferences and walking around with medals on his chest of fourteen grand orders of chivalry—which he claimed he had been awarded by governments across the world, including those of Persia, Tunisia, and the important Indian Ocean trading stations of Obock, Zanzibar, and Grande Comore. In these later years he wrote an autobiographical play, which he extravagantly named *The Sufferings of Egypt's Molière*. This dramatised account of his theatrical experiment of the early 1870s was published in Paris in the early twentieth century. In 1912 James died in Paris and now lies buried in the Montparnasse Cemetery.

After the lull of theatrical activities in the 1870s and then the political turmoil of 1882, Arabic drama seemed to be on a downward trajectory in Egypt (after the British invasion of 1882 there is no record of any dramatic productions in Arabic until 1884). The theatre scene was only saved by a wave of theatrical companies coming in from the Levant (*al-Sham* in Arabic, an area that encompasses what is today Syria, Lebanon, and Israel-Palestine). Arabic drama had existed there since at least 1848, when a troupe in Beirut had performed a play inspired by Molière's *L'Avare*, and in the 1880s several thriving companies were plying their trade to the East of the Mediterranean.

By the mid-1880s, Cairo was again looking like an attractive place to come—politically and economically stable, at least for the moment—and at the same time, poverty, hunger, and sometimes repressive Ottoman policies were pushing people away from the Levant. Refugees from the area were starting to travel across the world. Some of them ended up as far away as the Americas, but many came to Egypt, where the theatrically minded flocked to Ezbekiyya and started giving their own performances to Egyptian audiences hungry for Arabic plays. Ismail's ambitious theatre schemes were faltering; two decades after the khedive had begun four grand projects in Ezbekiyya—the opera house, the French theatre, the circus, and the hippodrome—only one, the opera house, remained. But these experienced Arabic-speaking actors, who had already been performing in Beirut and Damascus, started a new revolution in Arabic-language theatre in Cairo.

The Levantine troupes soon found enthusiastic support from Egyptians. One "group of patriots" clubbed together to build a theatre for the Levantine director Sulayman al-Qardahi; it was located to the north of Ezbekiyya Gardens, close to the Grand Bar. Two of these recent immigrants from across the Mediterranean moved into theatres across the road from one another, in a square near the opera house called Ataba al-Khadra. One of the theatres burned down in 1900, but the other continued to prosper for years.

These theatrical troupes had eclectic repertoires. They often performed their own Arabic versions of the classics of European drama—works by Racine, Corneille, and Shakespeare were among the most popular. There was good money to be made as a translator, and a cottage industry of multi-lingual writers formed which could meet the demand for new scripts. They often lightly adapted plays for local tastes, sometimes changing names and places, sometimes changing the plot itself, and *always* adding songs and musical interludes to the action (when one company tried to perform a version of *Hamlet* without singing, the audience complained so much that the troupe never repeated the experiment). The titles gave clues about what audience members should expect, since many of them would have been unfamiliar with the originals. So, *Romeo and Juliet* became "The Martyrs of Passion," *Othello* was given the title "The Moroccan Commander" or "The Schemes of Women," and Corneille's *Le Cid* was known as "Passion and Revenge."

But the troupes did not only rework European classics. In these early days, Arabic theatre took influences from anywhere it could find them. Some performances were based on stories taken from Islamic history and vignettes from the *Arabian Nights*. Legends about the Abbasid Caliph Harun al-Rashid were particularly popular sources for plays, as was the life of the pre-Islamic hero Antar ibn Shaddad, whose epic was still being sung by storytellers in Cairo's cafés.

Before long, some Egyptian writers also began to write their own plays and stage them. This group included one young lawyer, Ismail Asim, who gave up his lucrative profession to join the new dramatic movement. His most famous play was called *Brotherly Truth* and focused on the story of a young libertine called Nadim. He has been squandering his life in the bars and gambling dens of Ezbekiyya, but he is eventually redeemed after his father dies—he gives up his dissolute existence, becoming a successful merchant and ensuring the family's survival.

At first, the expanding world of the theatre was overwhelmingly male. In these early days, female roles in plays were often taken by boys, because women could not be found to play them. As is so often the case, *actress* in Egypt was coming to be seen as a byword for immorality, even prostitution, and was not considered a respectable profession for women. Most of the women who broke this taboo came from the Levant. When Sulayman al-Qardahi's Syrian troupe first arrived in Egypt in the 1880s, his wife, Christine, appeared onstage, as did at least one other actress, known as "Leila the Jewess."[8] Muslim women did not usually act onstage in this early period, a phenomenon often noted but seldom explained. It may have been because Muslims at the time had stricter views about the appearance of women in public than did Jews and Christians. Or the concerns may have been more general ones of maintaining propriety; minority religions, already outside the mainstream, might have been less worried by such niceties than were Muslims, who made up around 90 percent of the population.

Audiences at the time would also have been predominantly male. Women were certainly present at the performances of most plays, but they were in the minority and usually segregated. Ismail's opera house had separate boxes, concealed by a kind of latticework that female patrons could look out of without being seen. We cannot be certain that every single theatre was like this—elite Egyptians in the late nineteenth century placed much more emphasis on female "seclusion" than other classes did—but it is likely that comparable sex segregation was practised in most theatres in the late nineteenth century.

It is perhaps surprising, therefore, that perhaps the most in-depth autobiographical accounts of a member of one of these Levantine theatre troupes in Egypt was written by a woman. In an article published in 1915 in *al-Ahram* newspaper, one of the biggest female stars of early Egyptian theatre, Mariam Sumat, was given the chance to tell the story of her career. "I have stood on Arabic stages and acted different historical scenes to the generous Egyptian public for twenty-five years and I have won the respect of troupe leaders and actors," she said. Finally, after all that time, she was going to tell her readers about "the stages that acting went through, from its foundation to where it is now, and the changes that happened to it along the way."[9]

Like many others, Mariam had a family connection to the stage.

Her father had been a merchant in Syria, trading in jewels and precious stones. Then one day in the late 1880s, for reasons she does not fully explain, he decided to pack it all in and try his luck as an actor in Egypt. His first real break occurred after he became friendly with the Levantine troupe leader Iskandar Farah, who started to give him roles in his plays. It was also this friendship that gave Mariam her own path to the stage. Once, when Iskandar was visiting the family house, he encouraged her father to let Mariam start acting. He talked at great length about the lofty glories that actresses around the world had attained. Apparently persuaded by the speech, Mariam's father allowed her to join the profession and she soon made her acting debut in a small troupe called the Society of Learning. Her first play was an Arabic adaptation of Jean Racine's *Mithridate*, a tragedy about the ancient King of Pontus, one of the great enemies of Rome in the first century BCE. Mariam played Monime, Mithridate's fiancée, who ends the play pledging to take vengeance for Mithridate's death with his son Xiphares, her new lover.

As the theatre boom of the late nineteenth century continued, more troupes sprang into life. Mariam was part of a generation of young actresses that included Labiba Manoli and her sister Mariam, Milia Dayan, and the Estati sisters, Ibriz and Almaz, whose names translate as "gold" and "diamond," respectively. They moved back and forth between troupes, competing for good roles. Unfortunately, because of scant information about the lives of these women and only short notices in newspapers to identify them, they remain largely a parade of names on the edges of the historical record.

The life of a jobbing actress in this period, judging from Mariam's memoirs, was almost impossibly complicated. She herself changed troupes frequently and, as well as recounting successes in Cairo, she recalled her tours in the countryside of Egypt and even as far as Damascus and Beirut. Theatrical companies had to do what they could to stand out. In addition to the play itself, theatrical notices at the time also advertised short comic skits and "pantomimes," as well as lots of singing and dancing. Singing was such a crucial part of what people expected from live entertainment that troupes would have to add their own songs to the action of the plays that had no singing parts. On Cairo's stages, every play became a musical and every actor a singer. As the 1890s continued, more and more ploys were invented to boost ticket sales. Some companies advertised that there would be a raffle before the performance. With the advent of new technology such as the cinematograph, short films also became part of the night's attractions.

Problems of funding and power struggles at the top of troupes followed wherever Mariam went, as did arguments and jealousy between the ordinary members. All this left Mariam upset with the pettiness of her fellow actors and actresses. In her view, the early days of Egyptian theatre would have produced much better work if not for the envy, jealousy, and ambition of others. "Oh greed!" she lamented, "corrupter of success, sure path to ruin, and destroyer of noble work."[10]

As these theatre troupes thrived in 1880s and 1890s Ezbekiyya, many other forms of entertainment were becoming available. Even before Ismail's opera house opened, small bars and cafés in the area gave people places to play billiards and listen to music. Now a huge number of bars appeared, capitalising on the late-night life of the area. In the 1890s the most famous establishments were the Splendid Bar and the New Bar, under the same ownership, as well as the Bodega and the Mahrousa Bar; but many other smaller drinking spots existed in and around Ezbekiyya. The (mostly male) clientele included a mix of classes and nationalities, from the Greek merchants to the Egyptian *omdas*—village mayors—whose debauched sprees in the bars of the big city soon became a cliché in Cairo.

One especially popular new pastime was gambling, and the press was full of stories and warnings about people who had lost fortunes after long nights out in Ezbekiyya. Some even wrote poems exhorting people not to throw their money away on the pleasures of the nightlife:

> *So many times I have seen the elites—omdas and famous names*
> *Gamble their property and lands, mess it up and end up paupers*
> *I've seen omdas sell their possessions and pour all that money*
>   *down the drain*
> *Spending it on cognac and dance halls, what a waste!*[11]

There were enough Christians, Jews, and foreigners in this predominantly Muslim country to support bars on their own; however, there were also many Muslim customers. In the early twentieth century, an English writer described "a succession of cafés, most of them filled with Arabs consuming strong liquors indirectly forbidden by their religion." He surmised that "the Arab who wishes to break these ordinances without defying them, assures himself that champagne is a mineral water, and that spirits and ale and stout are not wines."[12] In fact, in 1902 the Islamic scholar Rashid Rida published a strange story in his religious journal *al-Manar*. He claimed to have walked past a bar that advertised itself as Egypt's "only Islamic bar." Outside, he saw a man drinking a toast to the popular Sufi saint al-Sayyid al-Badawi. When Rida asked this man if the Prophet had commanded him to do this, the man replied, "He'd forgive me."[13]

In 1898, the writer Mohammed al-Muwaylihi started to serialise a canonical comic fantasy story in the newspaper *Misbah al-Sharq*. The tale, *What Isa ibn Hisham Told Us*, begins with the resurrection of an old nobleman, or pasha, from the early nineteenth century. He finds himself in an unfamiliar Cairo of the 1890s, then effectively under British occupation. The narrator, Isa ibn Hisham, comes across this reborn pasha in a cemetery and takes it upon himself to guide the horrified old man around the city, showing him everything that has changed over the course of the century—and this turns out to have been rather a lot. When Isa takes the old pasha to Ezbekiyya, he is appalled by the scenes that confront him.

As they stroll through the recently laid-out Ezbekiyya Gardens, Isa and the pasha happen to run into three men who are also taking some fresh air—a dissipated libertine, a merchant, and an *omda* on a visit to Cairo. The two men get dragged along with new acquaintances on a raucous pub crawl through all the local pleasure spots that have sprung up since the pasha was last alive. The evening described in the narrative begins with drinks and billiards in the Opera Bar, followed by dinner and more drinks at the New Bar and then even more drinks in the Bodega.

Now suitably intoxicated, the libertine drags his cohorts into another kind of venue that was springing up in large numbers in late nineteenth-century Ezbekiyya: the dance hall. The first large, long-lived dance hall established in the area, the Old Eldorado, had been popular as early as the 1860s. However, by the 1890s the area teemed with different places including the Thousand and One Nights, the Alcazar Parisien, and the Café Égyptien, which had an all-female band of musicians brought in from Europe. These dance halls soon became the preferred venues for the kind of performers that the traveller Edward Lane had seen dancing in public in the early nineteenth century; they rivalled the district's theatres in popularity.

These music halls stayed open much later at night than the theatres did. Each night would include a succession of different singers and dancers, who mixed with the audience after their shows. The performers were paid according to how many drinks they could get the clients to buy, whether beer, cognac, or champagne, so the levels of drunkenness in the clubs were very high. When, in this comic story, the young libertine takes his group of friends and new acquaintances to end the night at a nearby dance hall, the reader is offered a tour of these new, decadent places that everyone had been talking about.

Dancers at the Old Eldorado music hall

As the group walks through the door, a sordid scene opens up before them. The air is heavy with alcohol, tobacco, and hashish smoke and an unidentified but unpleasant smell is coming from the vicinity of the toilets. During their short stay, the group witnesses a series of fights breaking out among the customers; at the bar, a senior policeman sits with his girlfriend and calmly watches the scene without intervening. When they arrive at the club a singer is onstage, entertaining the crowd. Her place is soon taken by a dancer, her face covered in thick makeup, her body adorned with heavy bracelets and jewellery. Moving like a snake, she contorts herself into all kinds of shapes, taking breaks only to guzzle glasses of alcohol bought for her (at a huge mark-up) by the admiring audience. At the end of each dance, she makes a series of saucy and suggestive comments to the audience before wiping the sweat off her brow with a handkerchief.

The narrator of the story lets his fascinated disgust at the woman onstage spill over several paragraphs. He particularly resents the power that the dancer holds over the country's elite, whom she seduces and whose money she takes. "She has destroyed prosperous houses and corrupted noble lineages," he laments. She has also left in her wake a succession of rich, gullible men, now penniless and humiliated; a turbaned old sheikh in the audience is so infatuated with her that he behaves like a randy teenager. The narrator is, of course, largely worried about the corruption of the nobility. The crowds at these clubs would have come from all social classes, but he either does not care about the poor or assumes they are already corrupted.[14]

As the tale continues, the narrator's depiction of the dancer becomes ever more misogynistic, from his insistence on her ugliness to his resentment of the way the audience is charmed by her. The power that she wields bothers him most of all. This concern was, no doubt, shared by many men at the time. Dancers and singers in this period earned their own money (sometimes quite a lot of it) and wooed influential admirers. The dance halls and cabarets in turn-of-the-century Cairo were not an uncomplicated space of women's liberation—they were obviously predicated on the commodification and exploitation of female bodies—but certain women managed to exploit the system to their advantage and ended up with considerable control over their own lives and influence over others.

Foreign visitors to Cairo also left descriptions of the cabarets of 1890s Ezbekiyya, and they were just as disgusted as Mohammed al-Muwaylihi. One British writer described a dance hall he visited in Cairo as "a veritable place of torture. Weird instruments, driven to despair by the hands or lungs of untiring performers, emit wild and unearthly sounds, and to the accompaniment of these a band of singers give vent to doleful strains suggestive of untold internal sufferings."

Observing the dancer, the writer said she was "attired in loose drapery over a tight-fitting flesh-colored jersey, the whole surmounted by necklaces of jingling coins," and her act consisted of "hideous contortions." All the dancers, he noticed, "when not actually engaged in distorting their bodies, puff away with enjoyment at the ubiquitous cigarette." The only person he did seem to like was the "Mutaib, the peripatetic claquer of the Arab 'halls,'" whose job was to drum up enthusiasm for the performers: "He calls on all there assembled to bear witness to the magnificence of the entertainment they are enjoying, to the skill of the musicians, the sweet voices of the singers and the proficiency of the beauteous maiden in the dance." The foreign customer dryly comments, "That he earns his pay, there can be no doubt."[15]

But not everyone was so vehemently opposed to the music halls. One correspondent for the English-language version of the Egyptian National Party's official organ, *The Egyptian Standard*, made a night out in a Cairene music hall seem like more fun. He described a trip he had made in the first years of the twentieth century to the popular Theatre Elias, the kind of venue that people referred to as a *café chantant*. "The café is gaily, though gaudily decorated with hanging lamps, chandeliers, flowers, reflecting globes, etc. The walls are covered with large mirrors and colored prints—the latter we regret to say, not of high artistic quality. At one end a marble fountain plays continually and freshens the atmosphere. Pretty girls in abundance—artistes doubtless—are moving about."

On the night when the correspondent went to the Theatre Elias, the main attraction was a Syrian woman called Muntahah. She had recently returned from New York, where she danced under the name "Bella Rosa" and could perform the belly dance (*danse du ventre*) as well as "other marvellous feats which baffle description." The writer was quite taken with her skill: "She was a revelation of possibilities of the human body in the way of suppleness, dexterity and grace." He advised that all visitors to Egypt should see a performance like this for themselves. The audience, he said, was almost entirely Egyptian, but he assured foreigners that they would not feel unwelcome. "The visitor will find that the weird, sensuous music and the slow graceful movements of the dancer's body all produce an indefinable sense of an Oriental somewhat [*sic*]."[16]

In the early twentieth century, one Egyptian songwriter published a short book extolling the pleasures of these nightclubs. In it, he reproduced pictures of seven famous dancers of the period as well as lyrics to the songs that played as they performed. These were mostly light and often playful, talking about late nights out on the town and love affairs (sometimes both—one song describes a wedding taking place in a dance hall). The uproarious atmosphere of the clubs themselves is captured in many of the tunes, including one that gives a comic roll call of the whole band, each line punctuated by shouts of "Allah, Allah":

> *The oud player is generous and poured me a glass of wine*
> *The qanun player is a drunkard and lives in the alley of the*
> *   unbelievers*
>
> . . .
>
> *The drummer took his donkey and went to loiter in the red-light*
> *   district.*[17]

The queen of these music hall stages in the 1890s was, without question, the dancer and singer Shafiqa al-Qibtiyya; she ran her own dance hall, had a reputation for seducing Egypt's upper crust, and made enough money to buy several houses of her own. In the early twentieth century, she was immortalised by the singer Bahiyya al-Mahallawiyya in a parody record called *Raqs Shafiqa* (Shafiqa's dance). Now an obscure collectors' item, the record was a huge hit when it was released; at least three different versions were produced, each with subtly different lyrics and their own B-sides, including one evocatively titled "Come on Baby, Let's Get Drunk."

For three minutes, the singer gently mocks Shafiqa, portraying her as a coquettish, hiccupping, flirtatious drunk. The different recorded versions of this song always begin with the same scene: Shafiqa is having a conversation with a customer in her nightclub and, already noticeably intoxicated, she asks him to buy her another drink before she goes onstage. In one version she asks for beer, and in another she asks for champagne and hashish. Unfortunately for her, before the waiter can bring over the order, she is thrust onstage and forced to start a haphazard performance, accompanied by a flute, an oud, and the clapping of hands. Feeling the effects of the smoking and drinking, she interrupts her singing and dancing with frequent giggles and apologies of, "Pardon me, I'm drunk," or "I can't!"[18] Shafiqa al-Qibtiyya's life, often shrouded in myth, ran in parallel to Mariam Sumat's, but in a seedier world where the parties went on until early morning and entertainers made a lot of their money by persuading customers to buy the overpriced drinks.

Shafiqa's story, in particular, is a strange one, in that she gained a modern celebrity status sometime after her death. Thanks to a steadily accumulated series of fables, which culminated in the 1963 film *Shafiqa al-Qibtiyya*, her name is now a byword for the glamorous decadence of late-nineteenth-century Cairo's nightlife. This film, above all, has turned Shafiqa into something of a myth, making her a magnet for stories of enormous talent coupled with extreme personal flamboyance and rendering the task of prizing apart the fact and fiction of her life almost impossible. Her own side of her story has not survived.

She was born, it is usually said, in 1851, to a Christian family in Cairo. According to one article published in the Egyptian press in the mid-twentieth century, her big break came in 1871. A dancer called Shawq had come to perform at a wedding that Shafiqa was attending in the neighbourhood. Shawq was performing for the women, who were gathered together in a different place from the men—as was usual for weddings of that time—and everyone started to dance. Shafiqa showed off some of her own moves, and Shawq was so impressed with the girl's natural talent that she offered to train her to become a professional dancer. Shafiqa's worried mother, who was very religious, overheard this proposal and immediately forbade any more talk of dancing. The family could not countenance her entering this shameful profession.

Shafiqa would not be dissuaded so easily. She started to take secret dance classes with Shawq on Sundays, telling her parents she was going to pray at the local church. One day, after showing progress in her lessons, she decided that she wanted to work as a dancer full-time. To do this, she knew, would mean running away from home. She fled to the Mediterranean coast and started performing at saints' festivals (known as *moulids*) there. After this brief apprenticeship in the countryside, she moved back to join Shawq's troupe in Cairo, where they performed together at weddings and private parties. Her distraught parents were still trying to bring her back home. They sent a priest to talk with her; he begged Shafiqa to come back and give up this immoral life, but she refused. She had been dancing with Shawq for only six months when her teacher and mentor died. Shafiqa was now forced to make it alone, so she headed for the dance halls of Ezbekiyya, where she became a star.

A completely different story also circulates about her first forays into the dance world. She was married, it is said, to a ticket inspector on the Egyptian railways. The man was a lazy drunk and spent a lot of time boozing at home with his friends. When he saw that Shafiqa could dance, he first made her perform for his friends and then, eventually, forced her to work in Cairo's cabarets to earn money and support his destructive lifestyle.

The truth may be something entirely different.

If Shafiqa's early life remains a little obscure, more detailed stories about her began to proliferate once she reached the dance halls clustered around Ezbekiyya Gardens. Known for her skill and innovative choreography, she was credited with inventing two different dances. The first, the "candlestick dance," involved dancing with a large candelabrum balanced on her head. The second required her to balance several full glasses of liquid on her stomach, while lying backwards and making them rattle against each other. In some accounts, these two dances are combined into one gravity-defying performance in which the performer had to balance the candelabrum on her head and the glasses on her belly at the same time.

Her show attracted the Egyptian elite of wealthy landowners and politicians, who showered her with money and gifts. Many of the tales about Shafiqa involve different creative uses of champagne. Her wealthy admirers washed her feet with the drink. One man was said to be so infatuated with her that he gave it to her horses. Pictures of nightclubs at the time show tables piled high with bottles of it.

Her reputation for lavish spending was as famous as her colourful lifestyle. She dressed in clothes threaded with gold, wore diamond-encrusted, golden-soled shoes, and lived in a large villa just south of Ezbekiyya, not far from the royal Abdeen Palace. At a time when only nobles and the aristocracy rode around in their own private carriages, she had two made for herself—a white one pulled by white horses for the day, and a black one pulled by black horses for the night. In another apparent dig at the Egyptian upper class, who overwhelmingly relied on Sudanese and Nubian domestic labour, she hired a staff of Italians and dressed them in the finest tailored suits. She is also remembered for her wild generosity with money, especially towards Cairo's poorer residents. If people could not afford to pay for her to dance at their wedding, she would do so for free, and give them enough money to pay for a luxurious honeymoon.

In the 1960s an Egyptian writer, Galil al-Bindari, developed a small obsession with Shafiqa, writing not only the script for a 1963 film but also a stage play and a novelisation of her life. His version of events solidified a particular image of Shafiqa in the Egyptian consciousness. Many of the tales about her have a feeling of poetic exaggeration. The tales of champagne, elegance, and excess were a familiar trope across the world and could be applied to almost any performer. Some of the stories also seem to drift into the realms of metaphor. It is hard not to imagine that her fabled golden-soled shoes, for example, represented the vast wealth that was cast at her feet.

No matter which mythologised version of Shafiqa's life you hear, there is invariably a tragic ending. Her popularity waned in the early twentieth century and in the final years before her death (sometime between 1926 and 1935), she lived penniless and alone. In the words of one obituary, "She died in a tiny room in Darb al-Barqi, one of the winding alleys off Clot Bey Street, poor and miserable. . . . None of those who enjoyed her dancing and knew the beguiling secret of her art attended her funeral."[19]

But there is another way to tell the story of the dance-hall queen, Shafiqa al-Qibtiyya. It can be found, if you look hard enough, in contemporary sources about her life, before such a powerful legend had been born. In later stories she is portrayed as a unique woman, a star who rose above everyone else; but earlier reports show her as a participant in a larger world of female dancers and singers, not just as a woman on her own. This story still has many of the same features— the dancing, the late nights, the opulence—but it shows her in a different light.

These traces and echoes of Shafiqa's life are found in some unusual places. Browsing through the catalogue of the National Library of Egypt, I found some 78 rpm records that she made with the Gramophone Company in the early twentieth century, after the pinnacle of her career. These records have not yet been added to the digital system, so it is not possible to hear them, but the evocative titles—"Patience," "It's Never Like That," and "Me and Barhoum Are a Great Match"— give some idea of their content. Like most cabaret singers at the time, she sang about love or the sad loss of it.

Shafiqa's name also turns up in a different kind of record: secret police records. She and her nightclub feature prominently in a set of covert reports that were sent to Abbas Hilmi II, the khedive in the 1890s, by a network of spies. Even at that early date, the authorities were becoming concerned about the nocturnal revels of Ezbekiyya. If people were drinking and carousing until the early hours of the morning, it was felt that the khedive ought to know the details. So, a censorious police officer called Mohammed Said Shimi set up a team to investigate. From 1894 onwards, Shimi and his team of spies compiled several years of reports for the khedive.[20]

These communiques give a vivid account of nights of excessive drinking, dancing, and parties—one strikingly similar to the experience of the resurrected pasha's in Mohammed al-Muwaylihi's fictionalised account of Ezbekiyya nightlife. Groups of men moved between bars, getting drunk and starting fights over their favourite singers and dancers. The police spy was outraged by much of what he saw. He, like al-Muwaylihi, was particularly worried about the corruption of the Egyptian upper class. A list was kept of the elite Egyptians— particularly government and army employees—who went to the dance halls, bars, and gambling dens.

The reports show a world in which the normal rules of society did not apply—sometimes in a very appealing way. One thing that particularly annoyed Mohammed Shimi was the free mixing between religions that went on in these bars. He reported seeing well-educated Muslim men drinking with foreigners, Jews, and Christians. He told the khedive that in these places, "You see a Muslim drink a glass to the health of some Christian as if the Noble Quran had allowed him to drink wine just like the Christian religion does."[21] The Ottoman system of government gave religious minorities much freedom, safety, and power; but in the eyes of traditionalists, it also required these groups to keep largely to themselves and concern themselves with their own communal interests. Ezbekiyya, with its blurring of the old boundaries of faith and sect, was a sign of things to come. For some this was inspiring, but for others, like Mohammed Said Shimi, it was deeply worrying.

Shafiqa al-Qibtiyya herself was a repeated target of this surveillance because she ran one of the most popular dance halls in Ezbekiyya at the time. Gratifyingly, the stories about her high-ranking admirers are confirmed in these flustered reports sent back to the palace. Shimi's lists of perceived undesirables going to Shafiqa's cabaret included several military officers and upper-class patrons bearing the noble titles of pasha or bey. One such elite customer, Ahmed Nashaat Pasha, was reported in 1894 to have spent a large number of his nights and evenings in Shafiqa's dance hall with a group of people described as being "in an immoral state of raucous drunkenness."[22] He had previously held a number of government posts, including the prestigious role of director of the Daira Sanieh, which put him in charge of the khedive's vast landholdings. After the 1890s, though, Nashaat held no significant positions— perhaps, in part, because of his fondness for Cairo's nightlife.

These secret reports show another side to Shafiqa: not just a charismatic performer but also a savvy operator, manipulating the authorities to her own advantage. During the 1890s, as well as running a music hall, she was also conducting a love affair with Ellis Mansfield, the British assistant to the commandant of Cairo Police. He was an influential friend to have and was later promoted to commandant himself. Mansfield was said to have been besotted with Shafiqa, and she convinced him to put a number of his own men at her disposal, serving as a private mini-police force. The local spies frequently saw her walking into the Ezbekiyya police station and spending all day there. It must have been useful for the owner of a potentially suspect dance hall to walk in and out of the local police station as if she owned it.

Mansfield was not Shafiqa's only contact within the police. The area police superintendent, Mohammed Abaza, was also a regular customer at her dance hall, and she made good use of this relationship too. The secret police reports suggest that he used to go around other dance halls (the popular Thousand and One Nights was a particular target) and arrest dancers for minor infractions, thus eliminating Shafiqa's competition. Plagued with corruption at all levels, the Ezbekiyya police force was ripe for her exploitation. Some of the more minor officers caused a scandal in 1895 by running their own quasi-brothel, in which they held parties and provided prostitutes for the guests.

In 1900, Shafiqa's name appeared in another unexpected place—not in Egypt this time, but in France. At the Théâtre Égyptien in the 1900 Paris Exposition Universelle, a group of dancers performed: "Their stomachs rolled, rocked, and turned as their bodies stayed immobile, just as eyes move in a stationary face; their stomachs whirled around liked animals in a cage." Among the performers was a woman called Chafika (the French spelling of Shafiqa). The "tireless" dancer had, according to one observer, "a profound gaze," and her contortions "gave you vertigo." Reports of the show described the same dances that Shafiqa was famous for in Egypt. One newspaper printed a picture of a woman dancing with a candelabrum on her head, just as Shafiqa was said to have done. Other publications showed pictures of dancers smoking shisha pipes that were balanced on their heads. Another report was illustrated with images of that hard-to-visualise dance of the teetering glasses. A dancer named Samha was shown lying on her back, lifting her belly off the ground as she balanced four or five glasses on it. According to one observer, "The rhythm of her belly made them tremble with a harmonious jangle."[23]

In later stories about Shafiqa's life, the trip to Paris took on huge importance as being the moment her act went global. But the tale, even if based on some truth, has probably gained in exaggeration with every telling. If she really was the dancer called Chafika (likely, but still only an assumption), she was there as part of a larger group of dancers and her role was not as central or influential as some have claimed. Now, however, Shafiqa has come to represent a whole generation of Cairo's dancers. Through her story, the nightclubs of the 1890s come alive.

One other form of nightlife prospered in Ezbekiyya alongside the bars, theatres, and music halls: the brothels. Generally, when members of the British colonial administration arrived at any place, they sought to impose their own order. When they occupied Egypt in 1882, one of the targets for reform was the sex trade. The approach to prostitution in Egypt before the 1880s had generally been one of regulation rather than prohibition, but the British codified it more strictly, just as they had done in India earlier in the nineteenth century. Two streets in Ezbekiyya—Clot Bey and Wish al-Birka—became an officially sanctioned red-light district. In part this was an attempt to ensure the sexual health of British military and administrative forces in the country. Women who worked in the brothels were supposed to be issued with permits and submitted to regular health check-ups—even if a combination of official loopholes, unofficial evasion, and illicit bordellos meant this was not always the case.

For those who were already worried about the lax morals of Ezbekiyya, these brothels must have confirmed their worst fears. For the people (particularly women) who worked in the entertainment business, brothels were a blot on their own reputations. A few sections of Mariam Sumat's memoirs recall, with growing irritation, the rumours and allegations that were thrown against dramatic troupes in Egypt in their very early days. Though she was putting on serious plays, "There were some who accused the theatre of being a house of vice, dissipation and prostitution," she recounted in disbelief. To defend the honour of her fellow performers, Mariam responded in part by blaming the women who came to watch the plays and condemning the way they dressed. "This isn't the fault of the theatre or those who work in it," she told her readers, "the responsibility lies on those women's lack of modesty, extravagantly doing themselves up and appearing in their finery without their veils. This is what has cast doubt and uncertainty into the minds of the well-meaning writers and delighted those with diseased hearts." Still, she insisted to her readers, the theatre was a place for pure entertainment, art, and moral improvement not to be confused with whatever happened in the red-light district.[24]

In only a few decades—from the 1860s to the 1890s—Ezbekiyya had been totally transformed. With the opening of a tram terminal there in 1896, the district could well claim to be the centre of modern Cairo. By night, though, it was a complex patchwork of different entertainment spots, and a hierarchy of shame began to emerge. Respectable theatre sat on the top, followed by the more licentious music halls and then by brothels on the bottom rung. Those higher up in this system of ranking made constant efforts to separate themselves from those lower down. Actors and actresses insisted that they were not cabaret singers or dancers; cabaret singers and dancers insisted that they were not prostitutes. However, the boundaries between the three were more fluid than many wanted to admit. One person's entertainment, after all, is another's debauchery. Theatre troupes used singers and dancers to entice audiences. In the dance halls there may well have been pressure from wealthy patrons who expected that the dancers would repay their generosity with sexual favours.

Efforts to stress the district's own respectability, however, fell on deaf ears, and by the 1890s Ezbekiyya became known as much for its seedy demi-monde as it was for its opera house or theatres. It became a byword for carousing, revelry, and misspent youth. Ibn Daniyal had lamented Satan's departure from Cairo in the thirteenth century, but by the late nineteenth century, the devil was back in town.

Chapter 2

FROM QUEEN OF TARAB TO PRIMA DONNA

O NE DAY IN EARLY 1917, at a small village south of Cairo, a play was being put on for the Egyptian spring festival of Shem al-Nessim. An unlikely spectator was in the crowd: the British writer, designer, architect, town planner, and Arts and Crafts devotee C. R. Ashbee. During the First World War, he had come to Egypt to work at a teacher training college for post-secondary school students. It was to be an unexpectedly short-lived posting, for it soon became clear to the British authorities that they had made a big mistake in hiring him. A flurry of worried exchanges between British officials commented on his many "faults," both in his manner and his politics. He was "a socialist without any sense of discipline" or "an ultra-socialist" in the eyes of some; for others, he was "practically a communist." "His methods were subversive of discipline: he openly ridiculed regulations and authority." His opinions on the war and on Egyptian nationalism proved especially disturbing. One person had overheard Ashbee saying that the Allies were conducting the war just to satisfy their cupidity and also believed that he was secretly passing anti-government newspapers to his Egyptian friends. Besides all this, his mother was German, which meant the British also suspected him of pro-German sympathies.

In addition to Ashbee's political views, his unorthodox and undisciplined teaching methods became an explicit target for his detractors (he later published a pamphlet defending his views on education). But his homosexuality may also have been behind some of the hostile reactions. Ashbee was greatly influenced by his friend at Cambridge University, Edward Carpenter, who was an early advocate of gay rights (or homogenic love, to use his terminology), and although he did have a "comrade wife," Janet Ashbee, his sexuality was an open secret. Perhaps, then, there was a homophobic subtext in one letter exchanged between British officials complaining that "he is very conceited and prides himself on being an eccentric" and in MI5 accounts in his file in the National Archives that called him "a crank, and a strange fellow, the object of suspicion to some of his neighbours."[1]

When he attended the spring festival, Ashbee was still new in Egypt, before these troubles had begun. Some of his students had brought him to that village to see the theatrical performance, which was acted on a makeshift stage. Theatrical troupes often travelled in the Egyptian countryside, carrying a bundle of brightly coloured fabrics and tent poles, which they could erect in any large public space to form a temporary performance area. They would roll into town, announcing their arrival with much pomp and ceremony, hoping to drum up a level of excitement that would inspire the locals to pay a small fee and watch one of their plays. Then, just as quickly as the troupes had come, they would move on to the next town. After witnessing a scene like this, Ashbee described it with awe, painting a picture that was rather different from the raucousness of Cairo's theatres and music halls. He was a follower of the William Morris style of socialism, idealising pre-industrial forms of art and industry that had not been corrupted by capitalism. In his eyes, this was an enchanting survival from an unspoilt age:

> I've seen real living Shakespearean popular drama—Tragedy—as
> it must have been played in Europe 250 years ago. Bernard Shaw,

Masefield and Barker would give their eyes for it. . . . The hang-
ings were of gorgeous colours in bright Arabic patterns; they were
fastened to great masts and hung on 4 huge palm trees through
the open tops of which you saw the stars and the moon as the evening wore on. . . . All the audience, some 600 men, were dressed
in their national costume, the majority in gorgeous silks . . . with
turbans and red tarbooshes. . . . All this national colour and
beauty is the essence of what followed.

On that spring day in 1917, Ashbee had seen a touring theatrical
troupe performing an old Egyptian favourite that had been popular
for a couple of decades: *The Victim of Seduction*. The play was written
in the style of earlier European dramas, but its details appear to be an
Egyptian invention. It opens with a young prince onstage, promising
a dying king not to marry the royal ward, called Charlotte. But the
audience soon learns the reason for this promise: Charlotte is the king's
illegitimate daughter and thus the prince's sister, although the king
has kept this a secret. The king dies and, as might be expected, the
prince soon forgets the promise. He proposes to Charlotte, who refuses
because, as these stories often go, she loves another man, called Raoul.
The prince resorts to the classic ploy of sending her to a nunnery in the
hope that she will change her mind, but it fails. A competition between
Raoul and the prince to win the love of Charlotte ensues, which ends
with Raoul killing the prince in a duel and Charlotte dying in the nunnery. In a final graveside lament, Charlotte's ghost appears and bids
Raoul to come with her to the next world. The play ends with the lovers' last embrace, and Raoul is carried away.

Ashbee, excitedly watching Egyptian drama for the first time, was
impressed by the female leader of the troupe, who acted in the star
role of wronged lover, Raoul. He was rather surprised that this woman
was playing the part of a man who spent much of the play singing
heartfelt laments to his absent lover. However, Ashbee was even more

struck when, after the play had concluded, she came onstage to give an encore, singing two well-received solos of her own. He had his students give him a translated summary of one song that was particularly popular, in which the actress celebrated her professional move from a singer in a nightclub to a star of theatrical stage:

> I have sung all my life on the music hall stage—the *café chantant* where cheap Arab love lyrics are retailed to you—I want to do better. That's why I do this—give you drama. I'm glad you liked it, I want to lead you to greater things.[2]

The next year, British authorities moved Ashbee on to the newly captured city of Jerusalem, where he was appointed as a "civic advisor." In his new role he founded—along with the British governor of Jerusalem, Ronald Storrs—the Pro-Jerusalem Society, which was committed to restoring and conserving the city's historic sites.

Had Ashbee stayed in Cairo longer, or had he been less committed to the idea that Egyptian theatre was untouched by modernity, he might have discovered that the troupe he had seen was at the forefront of a theatrical revolution taking place in Cairo in the 1910s, and that the woman who played the part of Raoul was Mounira al-Mahdiyya, the new sensation of Ezbekiyya nightlife. Among Cairo's music lovers and theatregoers, she was one of the most famous leading ladies in the new age of revue theatre that was just taking off in Egypt, combining singing, dancing, comedy, and drama into one long night of entertainment. Mounira had come to Cairo a decade previously and, less than two years before this performance, had made her name as the first woman to lead her own theatrical troupe as well as the inventor of Arabic opera.

Mounira's life was spent on the stage, and her early career was shaped by the changes and innovations in Cairo's nightlife over the first two decades of the twentieth century. Because she performed well into the 1930s, she had (unlike the stars of the 1980s) the chance to tell the story of her early life herself in interviews she gave in the press. It is generally accepted that she was born in 1885 somewhere in the Nile Delta, though the exact place is disputed: some say she came from a village called Mahdiyya, some claim it was the larger town of Zagazig, and others say it was Alexandria. In an interview with a journalist in 1927, Mounira recalled one vivid incident from her childhood.

The journalist, condescendingly, asked if she could read when he noticed her flicking through the pages of a newspaper. Of course, Mounira told him, she could both read and write and advised him to print the story of how she came to learn. Wiping a tear from her eye, she took him back to the days of her childhood in Alexandria, to the time before, as she dramatically put it, her struggles had started to wear her down, before work had sapped her strength and constant worries troubled her mind.

After her father's death, Mounira told the journalist, her older sister had been put in charge of the family (she did not mention her mother at all in the story). Even as a child, Mounira had a stubborn will and little interest in the boring lessons at school. She had much more fun playing with her friends and constantly tried to come up with differ-ent tricks to escape the drudgery of school. Her favourite ploy was to walk out of the house in the morning, dressed in her school uniform as if she was on her way to school as normal. Once she was out of her sister's sight, she took off her uniform and hid it, changed into a set of ordinary clothes, and went to find her friends. After a day spent doing whatever she wanted, Mounira recovered her uniform and then went to a local shop, where she spattered her fingers with ink, and returned home looking like she had been studying all day.

This ruse went on for some time, until the school contacted Mouni-ra's sister to ask about her absences. Her sister, who had no education herself but was committed to ensuring that Mounira would have some schooling, was confused by this revelation. She asked her truant sister what was going on and Mounira, casting about for a strategy, began to cry and then claimed she did not want to go to school because she was being bullied. She said the other children were jealous of her because she was much cleverer than they.

Mounira's sister, not entirely convinced by this story, decided to test it. She asked Mounira to tell her what she had learned at school. Reaching back into her memory, Mounira grabbed the first thing that came into her head. She was able to recite a Christian prayer that the school had taught non-Muslim students—even though she was Muslim herself, it had somehow stuck in her head. In Mounira's recollection, her sister was so impressed with her recitation of the prayer that she accepted her story about being bullied.

Her sister, perhaps calling Mounira's bluff, insisted on transferring her to another school where she would not be bullied. This time, she took the girl all the way to the school gates so she could not skip away. The beleaguered older sister kept up this routine until she was sure that Mounira could read and write. Once this accomplishment was safely complete, Mounira left school.

Mounira later recalled this as an important and formative experience in her life, one in which she demonstrated qualities she would later rely on in her career: wilfulness and rebellion, as well as an early attraction to transgression. But she also told the journalist she was proud of her older sister, who managed to be the head of a large family and even force the young, headstrong Mounira to learn to read and write. As Mounira would later find out, hard work was also a necessary part of success.

In Mounira's version of her early life, it was while she was at her second school that she realised a career in singing was calling her. She claimed that during the breaks between lessons, when all the children were playing together, she would start to sing. Whenever she did, everyone immediately crowded around her. After school, her walks home became jubilant parades through the neighbourhood. As she sang, children flocked to her and were pulled into the procession; the

windows of the houses along the road flew open, and people came out
to their balconies to discover where such a beautiful voice was coming
from—it was a scene that conjured images of her later stage success.[3]

Just out of school and still a young girl, Mounira did indeed enter
the world of early twentieth-century Egyptian popular music. At first
she performed around the small towns of the Delta, singing at local
festivals and in little cafés. She sang a style of music usually referred to
as *tarab*, and she sang it so well that she was soon known as the Queen
of Tarab (or *Sultanat al-Tarab*). *Tarab* is a central tenet of Arabic music,
but the word is almost untranslatable; everyone seems to have their
own definition. It literally means something close to "ecstasy," "joy," or
"rapture" and is often used to describe the state a listener enters while
listening to a particularly moving performance. The word has since
come to mean any music or singing that could induce this state in its
listeners and is usually applied to a particular kind of traditional music
popular in the early twentieth century—on the stages of the nightclubs
of Ezbekiyya, among other places.

Tarab, as a kind of music, featured a male or female singer accompanied by an ensemble called a *takht* (from the Persian word for the
platform on which the musicians sat), usually singing deeply emotionally charged lyrics. This *takht* was traditionally made up of an oud, a
harp-like instrument called a *qanun*, a flute, and a violin, accompanied
by a percussion section featuring a number of small drums or tambourines. In its full form, this music came together powerfully with a
driving beat of the drums, resonant strumming of the oud, and pierc-
ing melodies of the violin, *qanun*, and flute. But not every *takht* had
all these elements. Sometimes a singer would be accompanied by only
an oud and drums; at others, the music was played by something close
to a small orchestra. Audiences were immersed in long performances
played with a steady beat, the evocative quarter-tone intervals that are a
feature of Arabic music, and drawn-out vocal lines.

After some years of touring in the countryside, Mounira had her big break. According to a recent biography by Ratiba al-Hifni, it took place in 1905, when a café owner in Cairo happened to see her perform as he passed through the town of Zagazig. His venue in Cairo featured nightly singing acts, and the story is that when he saw and heard Mounira, he immediately offered her a job. She, in turn, jumped at the chance to move from small countryside stages to Egypt's capital. After her first job at that café, Mounira moved on to the larger, more central music halls and quickly found success performing at some of the famous clubs of pre–First World War Cairo. She sang in the Eldorado, where Shafiqa al-Qibtiyya was said to have sung before her. She started to earn decent money. At the Alhambra, she was paid 124 Egyptian pounds a month for a set that lasted around 40 minutes (somewhere between 7,500 to 9,000 pounds sterling in today's money).[4]

The atmosphere at one of Mounira's sets in the 1910s would not have substantially differed from that in the Ezbekiyya music halls of the 1890s. As a major star, she would have come onstage after midnight and played to crowds that were almost exclusively male—many of them quite drunk, to say the least. The only women likely to have been there were fellow performers who were circulating around the tables and having drinks bought for them. It was expected that the spectators and the performers would constantly interact. These venues were often called dance halls, but the audiences did not dance; they came to watch performers dance and sing. The women onstage would often banter with the crowds, telling jokes or making witty comments. The spectators, in turn, had a variety of ways to show their appreciation. If a particular line or couplet went down especially well, for instance, the crowd might cry out "Allah!" or "*kaman!*" ("again!") and sometimes throw in the performer's name for good measure. Audiences were known to get too enthusiastic and sometimes cross the line. One songwriter complained that he hated it when drunk people in the clubs grabbed onto the oud as it was being played and made requests for specific songs.

But there was an important difference between Cairo's music scene in the early twentieth century and the late nineteenth: the arrival of 78 rpm records. Starting in the 1900s and 1910s, European record companies like Gramophone and Odeon began to flood into the country. Bringing new technology, they recorded songs by local artists in an attempt to crack the potentially lucrative Middle Eastern market. They released as many discs as they could, signing up established stars and new talent. The public bought these records in a variety of ways, ordering from catalogues, directly from the label, or from shops; throughout the early twentieth century, gramophones and musical discs were sold alongside watches and clocks. Some entrepreneurs also started making money as travelling jukeboxes; they "carried a phonograph from one public place to another, playing discs upon request and charging a certain fee per playing."[5] As the business grew, Arabic competitors also entered the market to claim their own piece of the moneymaking pie. Two new companies were formed: Baidaphon, run by the Lebanese Baida family, and Setrak Mechian, a one-man operation named after its founder and located on the outskirts of Ezbekiyya.

Mounira found herself in the right place at the right time to ride this musical wave. In the 1900s and 1910s she recorded singles with all three of the major companies working in Egypt—Gramophone, Odeon, Baidaphon—and became one of the most popular recording artists of the time. She was a major player in a booming world of popular music where the nights were just as long and raucous as they were in the dance halls. One record company executive describes the hedonistic, nocturnal lifestyle of the musicians he met on his trips around the Middle East from 1910 onwards. His account, part boastful, part cliché, still gives a sense of the atmosphere at a recording session:

> The amount of raw spirits, cocaine and other drugs absorbed by the artistes and their *entourage* throughout sessions lasting from early evening to two and three in the morning (I could never get them to work during the daytime) rather alarmed me until I got used to it. No wonder they sleep most of the day! I remember one obese lady consuming the best part of a bottle (full-sized) of Martell's Three Star Brandy at a single session, neat, mind you. What a capacity![6]

As so often happens with new technologies, there was a symbiotic relationship between these new records and the kind of music recorded on them. The 78 rpm discs led to the rise of a new genre called the *taqtuqa*, which, in its most basic definition, was simply a form of light popular song, often with a romantic theme. It is thought to have originated in wedding ceremonies, where it was sung by women and usually celebrated the beauty of the bride or the pleasures of the wedding night. In the early twentieth century, *taqtuqas* began to move from weddings to the stages of Cairo's nightclubs. Still almost exclusively sung by women, the *taqtuqa* had by then expanded to include different kinds of love songs or romantic ditties. The short, light *taqtuqa* was the perfect kind of song to put on a record; it fitted on a 78 rpm disc (either on one side or across both), and its wide appeal made marketing easy. While *taqtuqas* boosted the popularity of the records, the thrill of the new technology meant that the *taqtuqas*, in turn, were associated with this new era.

The songs that Mounira recorded can help reconstruct her nightclub repertoire from the early twentieth century. Often suggestive and sexually charged, the material is almost exclusively romantic *taqtuqas*. Her hits included numbers like "Come Here, My Duckie," "Beautiful Girl," and "Why Can't the Night Be Longer?" Some titles like "The Bridal Procession" and "The Bride Is Beautiful as the Moon" suggest that the *taqtuqa*'s origin as a wedding song was not totally forgotten.

As in New York's Tin Pan Alley, Cairo's record companies hired professionals who wrote most of the music and lyrics —sometimes with specific singers in mind. Mounira, for instance, frequently worked with the poet Mohammed Yunus al-Qadi, who became a sought-after composer thanks partly to his work for her. Unlike many other singers of the time, Mounira was also able to write her own music and improvise around a melody, occasionally adding some words of her own to the songs.

Her biggest hit of this period was *Asmar Malak Ruhi* (A dark-skinned man rules my soul). A short, simple song imploring an absent lover not to neglect her, it began with these words:

> *A dark-skinned man rules my soul*
> *My lover*
> *Come here quickly*
> *Where are you going?*[7]

This song, which continues in its pleas for the lover not to leave, soon became Mounira's signature tune; she recorded several different versions of it, re-releasing new versions into the 1920s.

The lyricist's identity is unknown—perhaps it was Mounira herself. Its popularity certainly reveals something important about her image as a performer. Although not explicitly political, this song and its celebration of a "dark-skinned" lover was making a scarcely concealed and quite radical statement. The word *asmar* can refer to a wide range of skin colours, encompassing both *black* and *brown* in English. However, in the early twentieth century it could be used to distinguish the ordinary people of Egypt from the Ottoman (and increasingly European) rulers of the country, who were known for their lighter skin. In this hit record Mounira was stressing her connection to the average Egyptian, to a more working-class lover, and to her own identity as an average rural woman, distinct from the urban elite. Off the stage, she also cultivated this image. There are many stories of people being shocked to see Mounira dressed in a flowing black robe and a veil like an ordinary village woman. They often failed to recognise that they were face-to-face with Ezbekiyya's most famous music hall singer.

By the early 1910s, she had reached the height of her music hall career and moved to a nightclub called *Nuzhat al-Nufus* (an evocative name, meaning something like "entertaining the spirits") on Wish al-Birka Street, on the edge of the red-light district, where she used to sing almost every night. Mounira also agreed to an exclusive contract with Baidaphon, which made her the most important and well-known female artist on that label. Her songs became so popular that others started to imitate them.

Around this time, according to some stories, Mustafa Kemal Ataturk, best known later as the founder of modern Turkey, saw Mounira's show in Cairo. Although this story seems a little too good to be true—urban legends often put two famous people together in the same place—it is not impossible. Ataturk certainly was in Cairo in 1912, after the Ottoman forces he was commanding were defeated by the Italians in Libya. Ezbekiyya was also known to be a hangout for members of the Young Turk movement, in which he played an important role. In 1905 Ahmed Saib Bey—a Daghestani army officer who was head of the Young Turks in Cairo, where he also published an opposition journal—was arrested while having a drink in the Splendid Bar, a few steps from Ezbekiyya Gardens.[8] So maybe the young Ataturk did go to Ezbekiyya and see her perform.

In 1914, just as Mounira was coming to dominate Cairo's nightlife, the First World War began; and although Egypt saw no serious military action in this period, it was totally transformed by the British war effort. Until that time, the British had maintained a lack of clarity about exactly who was in charge in the country, and that served their purposes well. They had allowed Egypt to remain part of the Ottoman Empire and kept the khedive—officially, at least—on the throne while they pulled the strings. But when the Ottoman Empire had become an enemy combatant, they could not leave the question of who was running Egypt unanswered. So, they asserted their power in no uncertain terms. They deposed the Khedive Abbas Hilmi II and turned the country into an official protectorate. They created a new title, Sultan of Egypt, to rival the Ottoman sultan and installed Abbas Hilmi II's uncle, Hussein Kamel, as their puppet.

In Ezbekiyya, the more punishing effects of the war stayed at arm's length, but the district changed in other ways. The influx of huge numbers of soldiers from the British Empire, including Australia, New Zealand, India, and the West Indies as well as Britain, brought an entirely new clientele and atmosphere. Insulated from any actual combat, Cairo had become a kind of operations base and a place for soldiers on leave to relax, staying at hotels and army barracks across the city. For many, taking a break meant heading towards Ezbekiyya at nights in search of exotic entertainment and drinks. The red-light district was a particular draw, and soldiers on leave in Cairo soon got a bad—perhaps justified—reputation for drinking and fighting their way through the legalised brothels on Clot Bey Street and the Wish al-Birka, colloquially known by the soldiers as the Wazza (sometimes called Wassaa, Wazzir, or Wozzer). As one soldier wrote in his memoirs, "You don't find many troopers lounging about the headquarters in Cairo . . . and there is no street quite so amusing as the Wazza."[9]

Sometimes these amusements spiralled out of control and turned violent. In 1915, British and Australian soldiers started two major riots, jokingly referred to as the First and Second Battles of the Wazza. They started fires, smashed up shops, and in one case pushed a piano from a second-floor window. The First Battle of the Wazza allegedly began when a soldier from Manchester found his sister, who had been sent to

Egypt as a domestic servant, working in one of the "can-can halls." He tried to get her out, but her employer refused and threw him out of a window, sending him to hospital. After recovering he came back, on Good Friday, with a group of about five hundred friends. They grabbed his sister and burned down the brothel she was working in, along with much of the rest of the street. The fighting raged from about four in the afternoon until midnight. One observer, in a letter home to his family, described the memorable (we might say appalling) sight of the Westminster Dragoons, swords flashing, charging their horses through the fires of the red-light district to clear it out and stop the riots.[10]

In the wake of this destruction, the military authorities were determined to impose order on the city. At the end of June 1915, the head of the British Armed Forces in Egypt, General John Maxwell, issued a decree concerning bars and clubs. It declared, firstly, that no alcohol could be served anywhere after 10:00 p.m. Secondly (to prevent nightclubs finding a loophole to stay open late by not serving alcohol after 10:00 p.m.), it decreed that any place that served alcohol at all had to close by 10:00 p.m. The new law, designed to keep the soldiers under control, was obviously catastrophic for many businesses in Ezbekiyya. Mounira's show, which always began well after 10:00, could not survive in that climate; her music hall, *Nuzhat al-Nufus*, was forced to close, along with many other venues.

After effectively being banned from performing in nightclubs, Mounira had to come up with an alternative, quickly. Her next decision was bold and turned out to be hugely successful: She moved away from the music hall stages and into the theatre. It was a shift that went down in history—the first time, people have claimed, that an Egyptian Muslim woman had acted onstage.

On 26 August 1915, just two months after the British edict that forced so many clubs to close, Mounira made her acting debut. She appeared as the character William in a few scenes from the play *Saladin*, an Arabic theatrical adaptation of Walter Scott's novel *The Talis-*

man, about Richard the Lionheart and Saladin in the Third Crusade. It was a night of variety in the Printania Theatre on Alfi Bey Street: It began with Mounira singing a 20-minute song that had been specially composed for the occasion. Then, to formally inaugurate her career as an actress, she performed in the third act of the play. The evening closed with a performance by Troupe for Arab Comedy of an Arabic version of the French farce *Mademoiselle Josette, Ma Femme*. Variety evenings like these were becoming increasingly popular among Cairo's audiences.

Mounira had already released a recording of a lament by the main character of the play, William (Kenneth in Walter Scott's version), the bearer of Richard's standard, who is in love with Richard's sister Julia (Edith in Scott). It was a song of sorrow and separation, making it a suitably romantic addition to Mounira's set, that she then repurposed for her dramatic debut:

> *In the army I bore the standard*
> *And in your love I bear only pain*
>
> . . .
>
> *I spend my lonely nights away from you,*
> *awake in the company of the moon and the darkness.*[11]

After these first steps into the theatre, Mounira was determined to keep her momentum going. She drew up an agreement the following month with two actors, Ali Youssef and Hussein Hassan, to form the Egyptian Acting Company. Mounira was the obvious leader of the troupe as her two partners were minor figures in the Egyptian dramatic scene. Hussein Hassan was barely known, and Ali Youssef was more famous as an impresario than an actor—he arranged tours for theatrical troupes across the Egyptian countryside. Mounira signed a contract, including an exclusivity deal: for the next two years, she could appear onstage (whether to sing or to act) only with this company or at one-off charitable events. The three partners immediately set to work developing a repertoire.

At first, Mounira's new troupe borrowed most of its plays from veteran Egyptian actor and singer Sheikh Salama Higazi. Since the 1890s, Sheikh Salama had been one of the biggest stars of the Cairo stage, loved for his beautiful singing voice and for performing musical versions of classic European plays. He came out of the same dramatic tradition as Mariam Sumat and the Levantine troupes that came to Egypt at the end of the nineteenth century, though he himself was an Egyptian. Born and raised in Alexandria, Sheikh Salama began his career there as a Quran reciter before moving into modern theatre. His plays included an astonishing mix of influences: from the Crusader drama *Saladin* to the Arabic version of Romeo and Juliet, *Martyrs of Passion*, and *Anis al-Jalis*, a popular dramatisation of a story from *The Arabian Nights*. These plays made a perfect basis for Mounira to quickly start her own theatrical troupe.

After an autumn spent preparing its material, the company was ready to start performing for an audience by January 1916. In the months between forming the company and starting its operation, Mounira had been pushed (or had pushed herself) to the front. The name Egyptian Acting Company had been dropped, and the troupe was known simply as Mounira al-Mahdiyya's Troupe, or the Troupe of the Egyptian Actress.[12] Mounira was keen to promote her troupe in any way she could. She performed in the modern theatres of Cairo and Alexandria. She also performed in travelling shows like the one that British artist and architect C. R. Ashbee saw in 1917. Taking out adverts in the newspapers, she announced that she was available to perform for any charitable organisation, of any religious affiliation, as long as it gave 10 days' notice. She embraced anything that raised her profile or put her name in the public eye.

Mounira's troupe is now remembered as the first female-led theatrical company in Egypt, even though strictly speaking at least two other female-led troupes had been in Egypt before. The first was in 1910, when an all-female acting troupe performed a version of Racine's *Mithridate*—a popular play in early twentieth-century Egypt and the same one Mariam Sumat had debuted in. Then, in 1914, another all-female troupe presented an evening of entertainment that included a new play called *The Three Lovers*, as well as humourous monologues, poems, and a comic sketch by Andronike (a famous Greek comedienne). But in a world where firsts, mythical or not, count for a lot, Mounira claimed the accolade of first female troupe leader for herself, and she also claimed the title of first Egyptian Muslim woman to act onstage.

Perhaps the most striking thing about the troupe's early plays was that, in all of them, Mounira would appear onstage as a man, playing the same roles that Sheikh Salama had already made famous. She had good reason to want these parts: they almost always had the best songs. However, theatregoers regarded one of Egypt's most famous cabaret singers' decision to appear onstage as a man as unusual. They were used to men dressing as women to play female parts, but not the opposite. Notices in newspapers for the performances would often entice the audiences by announcing that "Mounira al-Mahdiyya is appearing in men's clothes."[13]

Arabic performances have a long history of male-to-female transvestism, likely going back at least to the Prophet Mohammed's time. In Egypt, the modern popularity of this practice is often traced back to 1834, when Mohammed Ali, the first khedive of Egypt, issued an edict that banished female dancers from Cairo. What exactly pushed him to enact this rule is still debated (he always had to weigh the tax revenue he got from the dancers against the public accusations of indecency), but it lasted only a couple of decades. If it was indeed aimed at curbing public dance performances, it was only partially successful. In the absence of women, the dance-starved populace of Cairo instead turned to young men imitating women—referred to by the Arabic word *kha-wal* or the Turkish word *gink*.

Foreign visitors to Egypt in the nineteenth and twentieth centuries often had strong (and confused) reactions to these cross-dressing performers. The French romantic poet and writer Gérard de Nerval saw three of these male dancers perform when he visited Cairo in the 1840s. At first, he was captivated: "Now, came the *Almées* [singer-dancers] who appeared in a cloud of dust and tobacco smoke . . . their hips quivered in a sensuous movement; their bodies looked naked under the muslin that hung in the gap between their vests and their fine belts, which hung loose and low like Venus' girdle." But after noticing that one of the dancers had a week of beard growth, he looked more closely and determined that all of the dancers were, in fact, men. He took away the gold coins he had been preparing as a tip and replaced them with small change. His view of what he had seen changed totally. He no longer rhapsodised about their seductive moves. Instead, he mocked the performance as "dances by effeminate looking men . . . who so deplorably parody the half-veiled charms of the dancing-girls."[14]

Most Europeans' accounts of these dancers revealed a combination of excitement about seeing this act of transgression coupled with the worrying possibility that they might mistake these men for women. One British police officer, Joseph McPherson, wrote about an experience he had with a dancer in the mid-twentieth century. In describing the all-important moment when the dancer revealed himself as a man, McPherson said, "He danced always in the dress, ornaments, hair, lipstick, and manners of a woman, and people who watched for the umpteenth time could hardly be made to believe he was not what he appeared." However, at the end of the performance, the dancer would pass around a card advertising himself (in the masculine gender) as "The Famous Egyptian Dancer, Hussein Fouad." The policeman became a fan of this dancer and invited him to perform at his parties for the titillation of guests. At one of these parties he organised a fake raid, convincing several guests that they were about to be dragged off to prison.[15]

For the Egyptian audience, these drag acts seldom raised an eyebrow. One of the few mentions of dancing men like these provoking any consternation came when a group of eight men dressed as orthodox priests were onstage giving an interpretation of a royal dream. Instead of just walking offstage, they made their exit by performing an elaborate belly dance. The audience, feeling that a line of religious sensibility had been crossed, hissed at the stage. Mounira, however, did something new—she turned these old conventions on their head and became the first Egyptian actress to make her name dressing as a man onstage.

In 1916, Mounira was entering a theatrical world in the midst of radical change. The great symbol of the old era of Egyptian drama, Sheikh Salama Higazi, whose plays Mounira was performing, was nearing the end of his career. A serious neurological condition that left him barely able to walk was slowly wearing Sheikh Salama down, and illness soon undermined his performances. By the end, he often had to be wheeled onstage on a stretcher to play his parts. Sheikh Salama Higazi died in 1917, just days after his final performance as Romeo in *Martyrs of Passion*.

In Cairo, a new kind of entertainment was emerging: revue theatre. The music halls had closed, and drama was becoming rowdier and more boisterous. Then Mounira had to compete not just with the serious Arabic theatrical companies inspired by classic European drama, but with the new vaudeville boom. Shows lasted late into the night, and as well as the advertised plays, they included dancers, magicians, acrobats, comic sketches, wrestling matches, and short films. Spectators were often an active part of the performance, commenting on what was happening or inserting themselves into the action.

One Australian soldier, Captain Hector Dinning, was in Cairo during the First World War and later recalled his nights out at revue shows. He described the physical space of the theatre, where largely foreign residents—Syrian, French, and Italian—occupied the stalls, often with their wives; middle-class Egyptians sat on benches behind the stalls; and there was a "large and high rear gallery for the herd." He also wrote about the sellers circulating through the crowds, offering coffee, cakes, and lemonade. But he was most impressed by the way the audience followed the play, constantly shouting at performers, giving them their opinion of the events unfolding. The soldier was particularly surprised when some boys brought donkeys onstage as part of the act, and members of the audience jumped up to ride them. Besides words, audience members tossed other things at the actors and actresses:

> Small bouquets are shied as marks of appreciation; these missiles are being hurled all the evening. There are boys in the crowd who hawk nothing else. Hurled with vigour they are: the degree of vigour marks the degree of appreciation. I have seen a girl become a casualty on the stage through being hit in the eye with an admirer's bouquet.[16]

In Ezbekiyya during the war, as up-and-coming Egyptian actors mixed with European cabaret acts, the uniquely Cairene form of entertainment known as the Franco-Arab revue was born. Performed in a mix of Arabic and French and featuring European and Arab actors, dancers, and singers, it featured short farces as well as set pieces consisting of song-and-dance acts. The genre was inspired by European variety acts and by the older Egyptian farces or puppet shows that were common in the streets and cafés of early nineteenth-century Cairo. This strange fusion symbolised the city's new cultural mix in the 1910s.

The most important pioneer of the Franco-Arab revue was Naguib al-Rihani, born in Egypt to an Iraqi Christian father. In 1916, at the Abbaye des Roses music hall, he first showcased his popular and enduring comic character Kish-Kish Bey, who was at the centre of his revue show from then on. In most of the plays, loosely based around French farces, Kish-Kish Bey acted the part of a hapless village *omda*—or mayor—who comes to Cairo with his pockets full of money from the cotton harvest. Unaccustomed to life in the big city, he is quickly seduced by its bars, gambling dens, cabarets, and women. As the *omda* pours away his money, the plays, which usually followed similar trajectories, simultaneously mocked his countryside ignorance as well as the strange behaviour of Cairo's cosmopolitan residents. By the end of most of the plays, Kish-Kish's small-town common sense has managed to see him through the tricks and cunning of the city slickers—or (as was often the case) to get one up on his mother-in-law, who often appeared as another common stock character.

Within a few years, Naguib al-Rihani had turned Kish-Kish into a national hero. At the height of his productivity, he was writing a new play for Kish-Kish Bey every couple of weeks and his theatres were packed. The style was silly and slapstick, often relying on puns, comic misunderstandings, and light-hearted mockery. The plots were populated with Egyptian characters, drawn from the streets of Ezbekiyya: dancers, actors, pimps, and café owners. During these plays, which had lyrical titles like *Hizz ya Wizz* (Shake it baby), *Bukra fi-l-Mishmish* (In your dreams), and *Balash Awanta* (Enough rubbish), performers were expected to enter into a kind of comic dialogue with audience members. The dialogues were interspersed with clever wordplay, known as *qafiyya* and referred to by the British critic and playwright H. R. Barbor after a visit to Egypt as "proverb-exchange." Mixed into the action were several catchy song-and-dance numbers designed to entertain the raucous audiences.[17] Revue shows proved to be so successful that in 1917, Naguib al-Rihani opened his own Egyptiana Theatre on Emad al-Din Street; the theatre became Kish-Kish Bey's new home and welcomed a huge mix of Cairo's residents.

Before long, imitators were offering their own brand of Franco-

Arab revue. Naguib al-Rihani's biggest rival was the troupe leader Ali al-Kassar, who had created a comic character of his own: Osman Abd al-Basit "al-Barbari" (the Berber), who was half-Nubian and half-Sudanese. Ali al-Kassar blackened his face to play this part, and he starred in a series of plays including *al-Barbari in the Army*, *al-Barbari the Philosopher*, and *al-Barbari in Monte Carlo*. Like Naguib al-Rihani's farces, these plays were performed in a mix of Arabic and French, had a similar mix of stock characters and suggestive jokes, and ended with the eventual triumph of the underdog star.

Blackface soon became Ali al-Kassar's signature, and he used it in roles where it made little sense. When he took the main part in an Arabic adaptation of the cross-dressing British farce *Charley's Aunt*, he did it in blackface. He sometimes used this character to address racism and the place of Nubians and Sudanese in Egyptian society or to lionise al-Barbari as a true hero of Egyptian nationalism. However, many of these plays also made dark-skinned Nubians the butt of racial jokes, mocking their speech or their unrefined manners. This depiction, which reflected the condescending and paternalistic opinions of many Egyptians in Cairo at the time, was not entirely unlike the attitudes of the British towards the Egyptians. Traditions of blackface in Cairo had grown independently of Western ones; but Egypt, too, had its own history of sub-Saharan African slavery. After Mohammed Ali's invasion of Sudan in the early nineteenth century, thousands of slaves came to Egypt and were forced into hard labour, domestic service, or the military. Ali al-Kassar's revue did not have the same historical background as a Western-style blackface minstrel show, but it was similarly troubling.

Along with this new style of theatre there came a new geography of Ezbekiyya. The old nineteenth-century music halls to the east of Ezbekiyya Gardens started giving way to the modern twentieth-century buildings on Emad al-Din Street, which would later be dubbed "Egypt's Broadway." At the beginning of the century, much of the street had been owned by the Egyptian khedivial family and was sparsely developed. However, the 1900s and 1910s saw a flurry of new construction, including luxury apartment buildings, cabarets, cinemas, cafés, and several new theatres—one for Naguib al-Rihani's troupe and another for Ali al-Kassar's. The Printania Theatre, where Mounira made her stage debut in 1915, was inaugurated in 1908 and, presumably, named after the short-lived Printania concert venue in Paris. There was also Augusto Dalbagni's Kursaal music hall, the Casino de Paris, and much more. The farces and singing of the Franco-Arab revue had found its place.

A host of hopeful new entertainers started flocking to the street. One of the most animated accounts of what it was like for an ambitious young person taking their first steps into the entertainment business comes from the memoirs of Youssef Wahbi. He later became a great star of the Egyptian stage; but during the First World War, he was still just a teenager born into the Egyptian elite. As a young boy living with his family in the Upper Egypt town of Sohag, he first began to dream of a life onstage after seeing a performance of *Othello*. As soon as he could, Youssef went to Cairo, straight to the centre of the theatre scene on Emad al-Din Street.

He hung out in the cafés and bars where actors and actresses sat and drank alongside young writers and critics. He submitted scripts to some of the people he got to know there, achieving only limited success at first. He was not picky about what he would do. In Ezbekiyya there were all kinds of entertainment, and Youssef's first proper gig was not as an actor but as a wrestler in a circus—though when asked to wrestle in the persona of a mute Armenian, he might have felt he was practicing his acting skills. His prominent jaw and broad shoulders gave him the ideal physique to play the part of a wrestler. Soon after playing the mute Armenian, he was asked to wrestle as a Turk against an Australian soldier—a reference to recent events at Gallipoli, where in 1915 troops from Australia and New Zealand had fought a bloody and ultimately unsuccessful battle against the Ottoman Empire.

The modern atmosphere of Emad al-Din Street, which was less sleazy than the music halls to the east of Ezbekiyya Gardens, offered a host of new chances for female stars. In his memoirs of those early years, Youssef recalled his first meetings with female performers of Ezbekiyya. He remembered a Greek dancer called Beba, who lived particularly wildly and was using large amounts of a new drug, cocaine, that had recently come to Egypt. Beba, according to Youssef at least, was eventually deported from Egypt after stealing 500 Egyptian pounds from another lover to fund her drug habit. An Armenian actress, Ihsan Kamel, introduced Youssef to wine and his first puff of hashish in her apartment. He would have had sex with her too, he claimed, if her ex-husband, a Cypriot-Armenian drug dealer, had not forced the door open in a rage and attacked them both. Youssef fought the man off, got his clothes, and left. When he got home, Youssef told his mother that a gang of Australian soldiers had attacked him. Later, Youssef read in the paper that Ihsan was recovering in hospital, and her ex-husband had been arrested. Ihsan went on to make her own mark in history as one of the most popular actresses in 1920s Cairo, and her face was often on the cover of theatrical magazines.

During the war, Youssef also met the woman he called his first love—an aspiring Greek cabaret dancer named Calliope. After meeting her in a café in Ezbekiyya, Youssef had somehow managed to convince her to leave her fiancé and move into a flat he was renting. But if Calliope was hoping that a relationship with the son of a wealthy man would give her a lavish lifestyle, she was soon disappointed. Youssef's father hated his wayward son's interest in acting and gave him very little money. In tough times, Calliope was forced to pawn her sewing machine and wardrobe to support them both. In the end, one of the few things that Youssef actually paid for was a secret abortion from a Cypriot doctor in Ezbekiyya (and even that was with stolen money).

In his memoirs Youssef described this relationship in grandiose terms, but it did not last long. Soon after meeting Calliope, he decided to go and train as an actor in Italy. When her mother became ill and there was no money to pay for treatment, she went back to her former fiancé, who had offered to cover the costs. Unlike Ihsan Kamel, Calliope never became a star and instead sank into obscurity. By the 1930s, some newspapers speculated that she had been caught up in a drug-dealing ring in Alexandria. They were forced to issue a retraction after it became clear that the Calliope who had been arrested in the bust was a different woman with the same first name.

Youssef's memoirs, with its series of heroic transgressions and sexual conquests (or near misses), are clearly told from his triumphalist, male perspective. Still, they paint a vivid picture of the new world of Arabic entertainment that emerged during the First World War and hint at the place that women occupied in it. But many questions remain about the other side of Youssef's stories. If his little tryst with Ihsan Kamel actually did happen and was not just an optimistic piece of wish fulfilment inserted into Youssef's memoirs, it would be fascinating to know how she saw it. Was it a moment of sexual liberation, or something else? Was the teenaged Youssef Wahbi as irresistible as he thought? And, as for Calliope, was her time with Youssef a love story or merely a cautionary tale of lust and betrayal?

Mounira al-Mahdiyya's new venture into theatre was shaped by its competition with these modern revues, but she also contributed a great deal to this new form of entertainment herself. From the beginning, she infused her performances with her music hall sensibilities. In one of her plays, she enticed the audience by putting on a large musical set piece including a chorus of sixteen dancers. In addition to the advertised play, she performed her own hit songs for the audience between acts or at the end of the play, accompanied by the *takht* ensemble that appeared at her nightclub.

However, after over a year of performing someone else's plays, Mounira wanted her troupe to have its own recognizable material. She wanted scripts that could compete with those of the new revue troupes, but she had a few false starts before finding the right ingredients. Her troupe briefly experimented with a translation of Alfred de Vigny's play *Chatterton* (subtitled *The Misery of a Poet*). It was a tragedy about the English poet and forger Thomas Chatterton, who committed suicide at age seventeen, but it never became a regular offering for the troupe. Then she tried out an Arabic translation of the French playwright Henri Bernstein's 1906 work, *The Thief*; that too failed to take off. One Egyptian playwright at the time remembered seeing posters announcing the play's imminent debut but lamented that he never managed to find any actual dates for the play: "I waited for a performance of *The Thief* until I got bored with waiting any longer."[18]

After these unsuccessful trial runs, Mounira finally began her troupe's new era in early 1917—not a with play, but an opera. A translation of Bizet's *Carmen* by the popular novelist, playwright, and early Arab socialist Farah Antun had been doing the rounds of theatrical troupes for a few years. No company, though, had successfully produced this nineteenth-century Spanish classic about a seductive, free-spirited Gypsy girl. Before Mounira got her hands on Antun's translation, other troupes had found it particularly difficult to adapt Bizet's original score for the tastes of Egyptian audiences, who were not used to European classical music. When another troupe tried to adapt the opera, the composer originally hired to produce the score had been completely overwhelmed; so overwhelmed, in fact, that he left the musical trade altogether. In 1917, he could be seen on the streets and in the cafés of Cairo with a shoeshine box under one arm, plying his new trade. His only company was a cat called Farfura, which he had trained to eat fruit.[19]

Mounira was not put off by these previous failures. She agreed with Farah Antun that she could use his script, and she hired Kamel al-

Khulai, a serious composer who was also the author of a well-regarded scholarly book on Arabic music, for the daunting task of setting the libretto. Mounira had chosen the musician well, and unlike others before him, he proved to be up to the task of making an Arabic score. By early 1917, Mounira's troupe was ready to start performances of the opera. In March, she began an unprecedented marketing campaign across Cairo. Posters were stuck up on walls, in cafés, and in bars, and advertising space was taken out in local newspapers. Nobody had ever seen anything quite like the poster that Mounira's troupe produced. In the middle was a crest emblazoned with the name of the play *Carmen* in Arabic and Latin script. At the top, two lines proclaimed: "For the first time, Mounira al-Mahdiyya appears in a female role." The poster told the public that she would be appearing as Carmen and "dancing a Spanish dance" and also that the cast of the play would include an impressive 50 actors and 40 actresses. It went on to say that 180 tunes had been composed, and 100 Egyptian pounds had been spent on the costumes. People started talking about it as the first Arabic opera ever produced, meaning that Mounira had not only moved successfully to the theatre, she had introduced a new genre.[20]

At the first performance, on 22 March 1917 in the Kursaal Theatre—a few steps away from the Printania where Mounira had first started her acting career—it was clear that her promotional efforts had worked. The crowd was enormous, and pandemonium went on outside the venue. There were middle-class lawyers, doctors, writers, and poets, as well as ordinary working Egyptians. Some people brandishing tickets in their hands were being refused entry because the theatre had run out of space inside. One reviewer described the scene: "The place was heaving with waves of people. There was chaos and crowds everywhere. Some were throwing insults, others punches. Eventually, the police had to come in to keep order."[21]

Once the turmoil in the theatre had subsided, Mounira began her performance as the seductive Gypsy smuggler, Carmen. The first night was counted as a great success. Mounira's singing met her own high standards, and Kamel al-Khulai's Arabic compositions, some songs in a purely Arabic style and others attempting to produce a blend of European opera and Egyptian musical traditions, went down very well. All the audience members, whether well versed in high culture or not, could follow the story, said one critic, because it dwelled on the universal themes of love, passion, exile, and revenge. Mounira, he added, was universally loved.

But there were some dissenting voices. A frequent complaint was that Mounira's extravagant publicity had not delivered all that it promised. Only a fraction of the actors and songs advertised ever materialised onstage. Only by the most generous means of calculation was it possible to reach the figure of 180 songs. What's more, al-Khulai had composed many of the songs in the *taqtuqa* style, which was felt more suited to a nightclub singer than to the exalted genre of opera. One spectator worried that, without a little more practice, Egyptians simply were not ready to take on the difficult task of staging a well-respected opera. Exuding a common feeling of inferiority bred by many years of colonial control, he wrote a letter to a newspaper saying, "Operas like this are the peak of what Westerners have accomplished; it wouldn't be right for us to use their pinnacle as our beginning."[22]

Another outraged spectator railed, in an article in the local press, against the indecent themes onstage. The opera was, after all, a story about a woman who seduces men and toys with their emotions. Carmen's opening song announces to the audience that "love is a Bohemian child, it has never known the law." Conservative men, who were already worried by the women's movement growing in Egypt and abroad, must have seen the liberated central character as a terrible vision of things to come. "This play corrupts the morals," he exclaimed, "it is full of hugging and kissing, upping and downing," saying that other performances had been censored for much less. He was not writing in for his own sake, he said, but for others who might be duped into attending.

Mounira al-Mahdiyya in stage costume

Most of all, he felt pity for the women who went thinking that they were going to see a respectable opera called *Carmen* and not filth, depravity, and corruption.[23]

Mounira and her fellow female performers would have been used to censorious comments like this. Ever since this modern entertainment business had begun in the late nineteenth century, people had feared that it was corrupting public morals, particularly sexual ones. More often than not, the targets of these complaints were women. The critics appealed to abstract ideas of propriety and good education, as well as conservative religious ideas. It was seldom that people suggested women should not be acting or singing at all; instead, they sought to control and police the content of their specific performances. In the end, though, these protests usually proved counterproductive as any scandal surrounding a play only made it more intriguing to the Cairene public.

In the case of *Carmen*, the opera survived any criticisms in the press to become a massive hit. This may have been due to Mounira's magnificent voice, which almost all the reviewers praised, or the skilful marketing techniques that she used to promote her new opera (accusations of overtly sexual content may even have helped). One particularly successful tactic was a careful rationing of the number of performances to make sure that the house was always full and tickets were in high demand. After the huge success of the opening night on 22 March, Mounira waited several weeks to stage it again on 12 April. Of course, that April performance created a whole new round of excitement; but she still kept audiences waiting, using the time in between to tour with her old repertoire in the countryside. It was not until 20 July that she performed it in Cairo for a third time. The fourth performance in the city came on 9 August, almost five months after the first. This careful control of the launch of *Carmen* turned it into a must-see—and it soon went from a must-see to a classic. Pleased with the success of this Arabic opera, Mounira quickly prepared two more: *Thais*, composed by

Jules Massenet and set in Egypt, and Rossini's harem drama *Adina*. She was soon performing these works regularly.

By 1917, Mounira's career had moved from one side of Ezbekiyya Gardens to the other—from the old-fashioned music halls in the east to the modern theatres and cabarets of Emad al-Din Street in the west. Early in 1918, Mounira's troupe reached the pinnacle of mainstream acceptance by mounting a special performance of *Carmen* in the elite opera house built by the Khedive Ismail almost fifty years before. To mark the occasion, the troupe commissioned a song in praise of Egypt and its ruler. They had the lyrics printed and circulated among the audience. It was a conventional ode of praise and struck a patriotic note, celebrating the progress that was sweeping the nation:

> *Art is honoured and knowledge is upheld*
> *Justice has been established and peace endures*
> *Egypt is happy and so are her children.*[24]

The reference to peace may have been a little premature, but it could be justified: by that time the British had already taken Jerusalem, and Ottoman control of the Arab world was coming to an end. Mounira's troupe could see new times on the horizon. Cairo's nightlife had totally changed in the past five years. It had moved on from the theatrical troupes performing Arabic versions of French neoclassical plays and the singers in dingy music halls to the Franco-Arab revue, farces, chorus girls, and Arabic opera. The city was on the verge of the roaring '20s. Before it got there, one last event of the 1910s would have its own powerful effects on the city's nightlife: a revolution.

Chapter 3

"COME ON SISTERS, LET'S GO HAND IN HAND TO DEMAND OUR FREEDOM"

As Mounira's theatrical career blossomed and the revue theatre was born during the First World War, the presence of British soldiers in Egypt was a constant reminder of the country's subservience to a foreign power. Their carousing around the bars and brothels of Ezbekiyya must have felt like a walking metaphor for colonialism. Egyptians who saw these soldiers drinking and fighting their way through the city with apparent impunity cannot have had any doubt about who had status in their country. Long after the war, stories of the soldiers' revels lived in Egyptian popular memory. Australians were singled out as the most loutish (though they likely were no worse than any others). When Naguib Mahfouz published his novel *Palace Walk* (1956), which was partly set in World War I Egypt, he particularly criticised the Australian soldiers, who spread across Ezbekiyya "like locusts, wreaking destruction on the land." In the novel the family's patriarch, al-Sayyid Ahmed, described how "they openly robbed people of their possessions and took pleasure in pouring all kinds of abuse and insult on to them, without fear of retribution."[1]

One incident was vividly remembered in the memoirs of most

people involved. It showed the attitude often displayed to the local Egyptians by the soldiers. This event took place in early 1919—a few months after the end of the war, but when many of the soldiers were still in Cairo and Egypt was still under British control. Madame Langlois, the fiery-haired French owner of the Casino de Paris cabaret on Emad al-Din Street, wanted to explore the financial possibilities of Arabic-speaking entertainment. She decided to commission another comic character, one modelled on Naguib al-Rihani's comic creation Kish-Kish Bey, to add to the theatrical landscape.

With promises of hefty profits, she approached the top Arabic director in Cairo, Aziz Eid, and asked him to form a new company that could rival the other revue troupes of Cairo. He assembled a group of actors that included many rising stars of the time, as well as the young hopeful, Youssef Wahbi, in his first big acting role. Aziz Eid's new version of Kish-Kish Bey was a donkey driver named Hangal Boubou, who was accompanied onstage by a real-life donkey. The play's exact plot has not survived, but it was similar in style to the Kish-Kish Bey farces that had become so popular during the war. It may have been loosely based on the French farce *Une Nuit des Noces* (A wedding night), by Henri Keroul and Albert Barré. The story involved a newly married man who accidentally spends his wedding night in his mistress's flat. The characters included an Egyptian woman, a foreign woman, and a local village mayor. Madame Langlois provided the dancers. To Youssef Wahbi's shock, she had managed to smuggle the cocaine-addicted Greek dancer, Beba, back into Egypt (she and Wahbi once had a brief romantic affair). The musician Kamil Shambir, originally from Aleppo, was hired to write musical comic monologues for the play.

When the curtain came up on opening night, the new troupe looked out into the audience expecting to see a crowd of Egyptians, but instead found themselves gazing at a sea of British soldiers. "There was not one tarboush in the whole room," remembered the actress Rose al-Youssef, who was playing one of the main parts. She was referring to the red brimless hat (sometimes called a fez) that was the uniform of modern young Egyptians.[2] Although the war was over, the soldiers had not gone home, so they were in the theatre and in high spirits. They paid little attention to the play, which was in a language they did not understand; they just kept getting drunk and shouting.

The new troupe performed the act for a few more nights, always with the same result. By the fifth night they were used to having the soldiers ignore them, but they did not expect what happened next. The soldiers had come armed with projectiles. On cue, the soldiers unleashed a volley of rotten eggs and tomatoes at the stage. Some of the soldiers had even brought bouquets of clover to throw at Hangal Boubou's donkey.

After that debacle, the Egyptian actors decided not to play to this crowd again. Aziz Eid went back to the theatre the next morning to pick up the costumes and tell Marcelle Langlois that they were through. When he asked her for some of the money that had been promised, she tore up the contract, threw it away, and told him to get out. When Aziz told her she was cheap, she replied, "Tell me something I haven't heard before!"[3]

On the British side, though, many were reluctant to blame the soldiers for anything that happened as they revelled in Cairo's nightlife. An army chaplain serving with the New Zealand Expeditionary Force defended the soldiers. He called the reports of bad behaviour "exaggerated," said that "in every large body of men there will be a proportion of 'rotters' and 'wasters,'" and asserted that the majority behaved respectfully.

The chaplain was quick to point his finger at the local Egyptians. In response to accusations that the soldiers spent most of their time in brothels or looking for women, he said the Egyptians had been serving them spiked drinks that totally altered their behaviour. He claimed, a little unconvincingly, that "I have time and again seen men walk into a liquor bar as sober as men could be, and after one or two [spiked] drinks behave like sexual maniacs." Among the other "evils of Cairo" that awaited his men, he was sure to mention the Egyptian touts whose job was to lure soldiers into bars, brothels, and can-cans, "where sensuous dances are performed by either nude or very partially clad women." Some touts were armed with pornographic photos, others only with their ability to persuade; they walked the streets, looking for customers.[4]

European visitors and British officials did not agree that the soldiers were ruining Ezbekiyya. Instead, they thought Ezbekiyya was corrupting the soldiers with its fallen women, its suspect alcohol, and "sights worse than we read about in ancient Babylon."[5]

One person who particularly outraged Europeans—and, judging from the time they spent talking about him, intrigued them too—was Ibrahim al-Gharbi, a Nubian brothel owner said to control a large part of the city's sex trade. Having arrived in Cairo in the 1890s, he first ran a music hall but then set up a network of brothels in Ezbekiyya. Although his business worried both European visitors and British officials, his lifestyle drew just as much comment. He went through the streets of Cairo dressed as a woman, wearing a white veil on his head, makeup on his face, and jewellery on his head, arms, neck, and fingers. An observer counted fourteen golden bracelets on just one of his arms. He embodied everything the British feared (and usually invented) about "the East." With his "exotic" looks and unabashed sexuality, his entire being challenged their notions of gender. Unlike the performers who cross-dressed onstage but whose gender offstage was not in question, Ibrahim al-Gharbi's identity seemed impossible to pin down.

Western visitors who first saw al-Gharbi declared themselves almost universally disgusted. His race was seldom passed by without comment—he was compared to a shining black statue or called a negress—but his sexuality and gender fluidity concerned the visitors most. One journalist claimed, giving no further details, that al-Gharbi came from a "degenerate tribe" in Nubia, where "all the boys . . . are brought up as girls and wear female clothing." Harvey Pasha, the Cairo police chief in 1916, called him a "disgusting patchouli-scented sodomite." The Australian journalist and politician William Willis, who spent much of the 1910s documenting the global sex trade, warned his readers of the "painted, perfumed, and bejewelled pervert." People were also shocked by the respect that he commanded in Ezbekiyya. They were taken aback to see him every evening on a bench outside one of his brothels, holding out his hand for admirers to kiss: this "king among the lost souls of the Wazza Bazaar." But everyone wanted to catch a glimpse of him. Willis, who misspells al-Gharbi's name, remembers how "in the season, guides made nearly as much money from showing globetrotters the infamous Ibrim Gharhi [*sic*] as they do from showing the Pyramids and other Egyptian sights."[6]

Without being able to hear directly from al-Gharbi, it is hard to know how he thought of himself—or what gendered pronouns we should even use. It might be hard to fit him into current conceptions of transgender identity or current ideas of gender more generally. However, Ezbekiyya at that time certainly included transgender people, and the concept was not unknown. In April 1930, officers brought a woman called Hamida into the Ezbekiyya police station. She had been found wandering the streets and was arrested for vagrancy. The police were uneasy about her: Hamida had been born a man, and, although she insisted she was a woman, the officers would not accept her word. When she said her name was Hamida, an officer slapped her face; she then told them that she was born Abbas Hassan Ibrahim. Since being transgender was not a crime in Egypt, the police did not know what to do. They could not arrest her, nor did they want to let her go. They kept her at the police station until they had no option but to release her. When asked about her life on the streets, Hamida said cryptically, "It is my fate. . . . We women are always rootless and dependent."[7]

Ibrahim al-Gharbi was eventually arrested for illegal trafficking in women and sentenced to five years of hard labour in 1925. He died in 1926 while still serving his sentence. But imprisonment had not dented his profits. At the end of his life, he reputedly owned 54 houses around Cairo, more than 100 golden bracelets studded with emeralds and diamonds, a crown worth 3,000 Egyptian pounds, a ceremonial robe worth 500 Egyptian pounds, and too much cash to count.[8]

Among the British stories of pimps, rowdy Australian soldiers, and moral decay, the women who worked in Cairo's red-light district usually only appear as faceless victims or temptresses. Only the campaigners against prostitution and "white slavery," who were active throughout the world in the 1910s and 1920s, treat these women as more than just extras in the drama. The most prominent of these campaigns were the International Bureau for the Suppression of Traffic in Women and Children, and the Association for Moral and Social Hygiene. These societies, primarily led by British women, worked closely with the Anglican churches in Egypt. Besides lobbying the government to criminalise the sex trade and writing books condemning this menace, the societies' work resembled that of religious missionaries, going out to save the people of the world.

The main targets of these activists were Ezbekiyya's brothels. The women working there came from all over the world, often lured by deception or smuggled against their will, and the Bureau for the Suppression of Traffic in Women and Children sought them out. In the 1920s members of the society interviewed an eighteen-year-old Frenchwoman who said she had been smuggled to Alexandria from Marseilles at gunpoint by a pimp called "Fat Louis." They found another woman, this one nineteen years old, who had met a man in a Marseilles restaurant and was invited to come to Egypt and help him run a dance hall. But when she arrived in Alexandria, after being smuggled onto a boat and given fake papers, she was soon sent to Cairo to work in a brothel.

In 1920, the Bureau for the Suppression of Traffic in Women and Children set up a refuge to provide a safe place for women in need to stay for a few months and help them find better lives. The society also kept brief records of many of its cases. The bureau focused primarily on the safety of foreign women travelling through the country and less so on the local Egyptian population. Still, the stories offer a rare—even if biased—glimpse into the lives of women on the margins of early twentieth-century Cairo.

Some cases involved domestic violence, some abduction, and others were the result of simple poverty. The society often gave much-needed help to women escaping abusive relatives. One fourteen-year-old girl whose parents, an Irish mother and an Egyptian father, had divorced turned up at the hostel saying that her father had been maltreating her (likely a euphemism). One young Frenchwoman called Nellie Plumier was swindled by a man who said he would give her work in his milliner's shop and marry her. When she arrived in Cairo, after being smuggled on a ship from Marseilles without a passport, Plumier was forced into prostitution. She ran away and stayed at the bureau's refuge before returning to France with the French consul's help.

Two Armenian cousins, who were barmaids at the Devonshire Bar in Ezbekiyya, stayed at the refuge in 1924. Neither of them was involved in organised prostitution, but they needed somewhere to stay while looking for better-paying and more "respectable" jobs, and the women at the refuge were happy to help. In another unusual case, a Syrian-Jewish dancer appealed to the refuge to look for her daughter, who had run off with a Muslim man who was wanted by the police. The daughter was eventually found, living on a houseboat with her Muslim lover, along with several other women and their lovers (or, as her file at the bureau called them, clients).[9]

It is sometimes hard to evaluate the work done by these societies. Like missionaries, their proximity to the colonial authorities, coupled with their strict Victorian morality and frequently open disdain for local Egyptians, does not endear them to a modern reader. In some cases, such as the mixed Jewish-Muslim couple on the houseboat, it is hard to know whether the societies were helping a woman in need or simply condemning a relationship they viewed as immoral or dangerous; both are possible. Yet, the case reports make clear that Ezbekiyya had an unpleasant underbelly whose red-light district thrived on exploiting vulnerable women. For many of these women, international societies like these provided vital aid.

When the war finally ended, a bad hangover was on its way. Outside Ezbekiyya, the country had been suffering; the British military administration had imposed stringent measures that served their wartime interests but were punishing for the Egyptian population. Food and goods were requisitioned to support the army, and tens of thousands of camels were needed to carry supplies through the Sinai Desert. Local Egyptian men were taken, too, many of them forced into either the Egyptian Labour Corps to do heavy manual work or the Camel Transport Corps to make those dangerous trips across the desert. The countryside, rather than the city, suffered most from the British war economy. The army got most of its workers from the country, often by inducing powerful village heads to give them men without asking questions about the methods used to enlist them. The Egyptian academic Alia Mosallam has recently uncovered a history of protests in the Egyptian countryside that go back to as early as 1917. In Cairo those demonstrations were described simply as criminal activities.

After the 1918 armistice, political tension reached a boiling point in Egypt as the British struggled to justify continued control of the country. In Cairo a political nationalist movement had been growing, in the face of increased British imperial dominance, since long before the war. In the late nineteenth century, a young lawyer called Mustafa Kamel (no connection to Ataturk) started agitating against British occupation. He and his supporters officially formed the National Party of Egypt in

1907, shortly before his death in February 1908. When war came, the British power became more formally entrenched, and promises that their presence was only temporary sounded increasingly hollow. The nationalist movement found new energy with a group of politicians whose figurehead was another popular and charismatic lawyer, Saad Zaghloul. Unlike many other public figures at the time, he had not come from a large, influential family. He had worked his way to the top, serving as Minister of Education, then Minister of Justice before the war, and marrying into an aristocratic family. He was an eloquent speaker and an intelligent politician who, in his early years, managed to win the admiration of many influential people both British and Egyptian.

The country was primed for upheaval, and all it needed was a spark. It came when the Great Powers of Europe announced a conference at Versailles to decide the fate of the post-war world. Perceiving the shock that the old colonial world order had received during the war, Zaghloul and his anti-imperialist allies saw their chance to refashion geopolitics in their favour. They petitioned the British to allow them to go to Paris and present the case for Egypt's independence to the international community. He wrote in early 1919: "Egypt believed that the hour of imminent justice had arrived for her as well as for other countries, when the victory was won, and that she could hope for the end of a slavery imposed solely by force, and that she, too, could enter into the worldwide brotherhood of nations."[10]

The British, however, did not see things the same way. Not only did they prevent any Egyptian delegation from going to Paris, they arrested Saad Zaghloul along with three other prominent nationalists and, on 8 March 1919, exiled them to Malta. This arrest and the public outcry it sparked brought on a chain of events that took the British completely by surprise. Protests began in Cairo the next day; the British tried to quash them by arresting three hundred people, but they could not keep a lid on the anger. Events turned violent as rioters attacked trams and smashed windows; within a week, the British were regularly opening fire on people in the street. On 15 March the high commissioner in Egypt, Sir Milne Cheetham, telegrammed the British foreign secretary, Lord Curzon, telling him that "an armoured car on patrol was compelled to use machine gun and some looters were summarily shot."[11] Before long, the demonstrations had spiralled out of control and were engulfing the country. Strikes were called, and Egypt came to a standstill.

The British and Egyptians seemingly observed the events of 1919 from parallel universes. The British, more often than not, saw the protests as a violent and unruly example of Egyptian irrationality, even fanaticism. "Anyone who understands the Orient knows how inflammable the crowd is," said one British police officer in his memoirs, "and how mass hysteria can seize upon it within a few minutes." Foreign journalists displayed their prejudices about Egyptians more readily: "It is to be remembered how easily the patient peasant of Egypt, the simple, long-suffering, ever despised fellah turns to savage violence. Murder and destruction are . . . the first methods he adopts," said a report in the *Washington Post*. The demonstrations were explained away as manifestations of deep-rooted religious fanaticism—or worse, as the British high commissioner suspected, a "Bolshevik tendency" ignited by the 1917 revolution in Russia.[12]

People found their prejudices confirmed in some particularly violent incidents during the first months of protest. One bloody incident was especially prominent in the British version of events: A small group of British soldiers (from seven to nine men, depending on the source) were pulled off a train from Luxor to Cairo and brutally killed by a crowd of Egyptians. Civilian deaths too, including those of twenty-nine Armenians, were frequently mentioned in British reports on the uprising.

British accounts of the events of 1919 reveal noticeable gaps. They do not include the stories of soldiers opening fire on protestors, villages being burned to the ground, and the looting or sexual assault committed by soldiers who said they were trying to bring the country under control. Whatever the physical threat to the British, Egyptians had undoubtedly suffered more. British General Edmund Allenby calculated that by 24 July 1919, the death toll was 800 Egyptians, 31 European nationals, and 29 British soldiers. The Egyptian historian Abd al-Rahman al-Rafi, writing later, put the figure of Egyptian deaths much higher—at around 3,000.

From an Egyptian perspective, the events of 1919 look totally different. For them, this was a great moment of awakening and liberation. It was dubbed the Revolution of 1919, and in Egyptian popular memory, it remains an example of unprecedented national unity. Barriers of class, religion, and gender dissolved. "Religion is for God, the country is for all," was an enduring slogan of that period. The cross and the crescent were united on the banners of protestors. In one demonstration a rabbi, carrying an Egyptian flag emblazoned with the Star of David, delivered speeches to a rapturous crowd. In another, a Christian priest and a Jewish woman both addressed the crowds at al-Azhar mosque, the centre of the country's Muslim establishment. The mixing of religions that so concerned secret police officer Mohammed Said Shimi, who sent reports to the khedive about nightlife in 1890s Cairo, had spilled from the bars of Ezbekiyya out into the streets.

There was a carnival-like atmosphere as the crowds sang comic anti-British songs to keep up their spirits. A song addressed to Reginald Wingate, the British consul general, reminded him of everything the British had requisitioned during the war:

> *Excuse us, O Wingate,*
> *Our country is conquered*
> *You took off the barley*
> *And camels and donkeys*
> *And a lot of wheat too*
> *Now leave us alone.*[13]

Another song, translated by a British police officer who had heard it sung, was more to the point:

The British lion is a-dead (or is a-dying)
Praise God he won't be missed
We've wiped our b___s in his beard
And in his blood we've p___d[14]

The revolution spawned many eccentric stories of resistance: In a small town called Zifta, in the Nile Delta, local nationalists declared their own republic, independent of Britain, and established its head-quarters in the local café. They lowered the old flag from the town hall and raised their own, put unemployed men to work on public improve-ments, and started their own Arabic newspaper, called *al-Jumhour* (The Public). Eventually some Australian soldiers were sent to stop the experiment, but when they tried to identify the members of the revolu-tionary council, nobody gave them up.

The part women played in the uprising had huge symbolic importance and is now considered a watershed moment not only in the 1919 rev-olution, but in the history of the Egyptian women's movement. The prominent feminist activist Hoda Shaarawi organised two important women's demonstrations and became a female Saad Zaghloul, the fig-urehead for women who went into the streets to protest. Hoda Shaarawi was born in 1879 and had led a typical life for a woman of Egypt's late nineteenth-century elite class. Raised in the family's harem, she had married her cousin Ali Shaarawi Pasha when she was thirteen and he was in his forties. But Hoda was not satisfied with the domestic life of an upper-class woman in Egypt. Within moderate bounds, she became active in organising lectures by women, promoting female education, and making philanthropic gestures to support women and children. But when the protests of 1919 started and the spirit of emancipation was in the air, Hoda Shaarawi threw herself into politics.

Her first step was simple: Along with a few hundred women from Cairo's most influential families, she signed a letter of protest to foreign consulates, denouncing the violence suffered by the Egyptian people after merely demanding their freedom. The women planned to hand-deliver the letter to various embassies in Cairo and urge the foreign representatives to complain to their governments about British violence. The sight of hundreds of women in the streets, carrying banners and chanting protests as they delivered their message around town, was sure to make a powerful statement.

On the morning of 16 March, the women set out from Hoda Shaarawi's house to distribute their letter, carrying placards denouncing violence and calling for Egyptian independence. The British police forces watched the situation closely, realising that attacking this group of elite women would not be wise. Also, somewhat condescendingly, the police were afraid that the demonstration could be infiltrated by people intent on causing trouble. As a show of support for the exiled leader Saad Zaghloul, the demonstrators decided to march towards his house near the quiet residential area of Garden City. But soon the demonstrators were surrounded by British soldiers. The protest reached its peak when Hoda Shaarawi approached one of the armed British men and told him to shoot her on the spot. She shouted, "Let me die so Egypt can have an Edith Cavell!" Her cry was a reference to the British nurse who was executed by the Germans in 1915 and quickly became a national hero. Embarrassed by this confrontation, the soldier backed down, and the women's anger fizzled out along with the protest.[15]

After that somewhat disappointing first attempt, the women went out to demonstrate again a few days later, on 20 March. Getting into cars or carriages, carrying placards and banners, they again made their way to Saad Zaghloul's house. Once there, they found themselves encircled by policemen. In the account of events given by Britain's police chief, Thomas Russell, he reported approaching the women to inform them that they needed permission from the British military authorities to hold a march. He then said that he would go to the British headquarters at the Continental Hotel and try to smooth over this bureaucratic wrinkle. He did, in fact, go to the Continental Hotel, but he made no attempt to ask about the group's permission to march. He spent an hour or so doing some unrelated paperwork, leaving the protestors standing in the full heat of the sun. When he thought they would be fed up with standing around, Russell returned. This is where the demonstration came to an end. In his version of the story, Russell said that he "found the poor dears in a sorry condition" and that when he ordered a fleet of taxis, the women gratefully got in them and went home.[16]

Although their numbers were small, the symbolism of these women's demonstrations was huge. They were quickly seized upon as an example of the heroic participation of women in the independence movement. One of Egypt's most famous poets, Hafez Ibrahim, wrote a short ode to the protestors. A few years later, the socialist writer Niqula Haddad published a novel inspired by these events—*The Zaghloulesses of Egypt*, in which she imagined what happened in the lives of these women when their protests had ended. After the huge impact of her actions in 1919, Hoda Shaarawi went on to devote herself more fully to public feminist causes, including setting up the Egyptian Feminist Union in 1923, starting the French-language women's journal *L'Egyptienne*, and attending women's conferences across the world. By the end of 1923, she had successfully campaigned to change the marriage age in Egypt so that no girl under sixteen (or boy under eighteen) was legally allowed to be married.

During the 1919 revolution, the men and women of Cairo's theatres and cabarets were not going to be outdone; they organised a series of protests of their own—carnivalesque affairs in which people dressed in outfits raided from their troupes' costume stores and sang nationalist and anti-British songs. One day at the height of the protests, a motley group of people from Cairo's theatrical world assembled in Emad al-Din Street, wearing the costumes. The actor and director Aziz Eid dressed as Napoleon, and other actors dressed as Othello, the Caliph Harun al-Rashid, and assorted Arab sheikhs. This eclectic group passed through Opera Square and headed in the symbolic direction of Saad Zaghloul's house.

In a carriage at the front of the parade, waving an Egyptian flag, was the rising young star Rose al-Youssef; beside her was the less well-known actress Mary Ibrahim. After going through Opera Square and passing the huge equestrian statue of Ibrahim Pasha, the parade entered one of the streets branching off the square. There, they suddenly came face-to-face with two British soldiers whose rifles were lifted. Rose, whose first child had been born only a few months earlier, was petrified. She knew that the British considered any form of protest illegal and had frequently opened fire on demonstrators. Before the soldiers could do anything, a bullet fired from the gun of a hidden Egyptian protestor sped past them. While the soldiers searched for the source of the bullet, the actors quickly turned the march around, heading back towards the Printania Theatre just off Emad al-Din Street. Years later, Rose still talked about the part she had played in Egypt's great uprising.

On 7 April, after about a month of violence and demonstrations, the main period of protests came to an end. The British relented, releasing Saad Zaghloul and his fellow exiles. The country was still under

British control, but it was a significant victory. People celebrated in the streets. The *Washington Post* journalist who had written at length about the fanaticism of Egyptians now wrote about their jubilation and the women who danced in the streets like they did in the nightclubs of Ezbekiyya. "The words they shouted were the same all over the city," he said: "'Yahia el Watan!' 'Long Live the Nation!' The cry became a refrain chanted in unison. . . . Scores of women mounted carts and with castanets on their fingers did the muscle dances which are tabooed by the police of American cities."[17]

In the celebrations following the events of spring 1919, the stages of Emad al-Din echoed with a new optimism. The troupes rode the wave of public jubilation, performing songs and plays that celebrated the people's victory. Most of the songs that have come to define the revolutionary spirit of the era first appeared in the revue shows on Emad al-Din soon after the uprising. The popular anthem "Stand Up, Egyptians" first appeared in *Tell Him*, Naguib al-Rihani's 1919 play (written by Badie Khayri), and is still considered one of the most powerful statements of Egyptian patriotism. It was sung in Tahrir Square during the Arab Spring and is even sampled in modern hip-hop songs. The song quickly became a hit in its own right; the lyrics told Egyptians to have pride in their country and unite with their fellow citizens. One line explicitly called for the religious unity that had been on display in the streets of Cairo a few months before.

> *Why are you talking about Muslim, Christian, or Jewish?*
> *They all mean the same thing: one family back to our*
> *grandfathers.*[18]

Ali al-Kassar's troupe performed a song, again written by the lyricist Badie Khayri and inspired by the growing women's movement, that had been powerfully evoked during Hoda Shaarawi's protests.

Called "The Ladies of Egypt," the song began with the words "Egyptians, take joy and salute today's women's renaissance." It continued with these lines:

> *Who said Egyptian women were worth less than Western women?*
> *Whether it be in love of their country or in raising their children*
> *The women of the Nile have no equals.*

The female chorus onstage called for their fellow women to throw off their veils and walk around in the latest fashions. In another verse, they sang:

> *We are fed up with the boasting of Parisian girls*
> *We know chemistry and embroidery*
> *We could work as lawyers or judges.*

It is hard to know what effect the writer intended these lyrics to have. They could have been meant as a joke, not necessarily to be taken literally—how would the song go over, for instance, if a troupe of men in drag were to sing it? Nonetheless, there were the singers, onstage demanding the rights and independence of women, just months after the country had done exactly the same. They sang, "Men, we are fed up. Why have you forgotten our rights and put your masculinity above us?" Then, the chorus continued:

> *Come on sisters, let's go hand in hand to demand our freedom.*
> *Long live the Egyptian woman.*[19]

Mounira al-Mahdiyya, now a star of Arabic opera, joined the celebrations too, lending her voice to the anti-colonial carnival. She produced a trilogy of musical plays celebrating the spirit of the 1919 revolution. Sayyid

Darwish wrote the music for *It All Took Two Days*, an allegorical tale about the exploitation of Egyptians in their own country. In it, Mounira plays a wealthy woman swindled out of her money by a foreign pharmacist called Marco and his daughter Mary. Left destitute, she is forced to sell butter in the market. Kamel al-Khulai, her collaborator on the opera *Carmen*, wrote the music for the other two plays: *Between You and Me*, about a group of young Egyptian women exploited in a foreign clothes factory, and *Third Time Lucky*. The script of this third play, performed at the beginning of 1921, does not survive, but some of the patriotic songs still do, including one ending with these lines:

> *Wake up, Egyptians, we have slept enough*
> *Know that the world is a stage and this is a play*
> *You are its hero and the end is coming soon*
> *Go, show Europe some of that Arab gallantry.*[20]

In addition to this series of nationalist plays, Mounira also released a hit song celebrating Saad Zaghloul, the symbolic leader of the revolution. The song made a pun on his name, which can also mean "dove," and was full of nods and winks to the Egyptian audience. The message of the first lines cannot have been lost on anyone: "A dove took off and then it came back, between Egypt and Sudan. My heart yearns for this young dove [Zaghloul]." Also around that time, she recorded a version of her hit "The Fortune Teller," adding extra lines: "I am Mounira al-Mahdyya," she sang, "and for me love of my nation is a passion. . . . For freedom and for my country I would sacrifice my life."[21]

So, Mounira, the star of the nightclub stages, became a prominent voice expressing the grievances and aspirations of the Egyptian people. She might not have known it, but Saad Zaghloul had gone to one of her shows a few years earlier. In his diaries, published after his death, he described a night he had spent at the theatre in 1917 watching a performance of *Carmen*. He was in illustrious company: three fellow politicians, all of whom went on to serve as prime ministers of Egypt—Adly Yakan, Ismail Sidqi, and Abd al-Khaleq Tharwat. But that evening Saad Zaghloul was not entirely complimentary about the show. He was unimpressed with the low class of the audience. He thought they did not know how to behave at the theatre—they clapped when they should have been quiet, were quiet when they should have clapped, and laughed when they were supposed to cry. He ended up leaving the performance early.

His view of Mounira herself was conflicted. In his diaries he said that she had "a lively soul and a beautiful voice," but he also worried about her reputation. Saad Zaghloul suspected that Ismail Sidqi and Abd al-Khaleq Tharwat had been planning to go to a party at Mounira's house after the show, and this, he thought, was going a bit too far. What would it do for their reputations to mix with a crowd like that (he had heard rumours of what they got up to)? He was nervous about his powerful friends associating with an actress—not that it stopped them.[22]

Politically, the 1919 revolution did not bear fruit for a number of years. The scope and intensity of the Egyptians' dissatisfaction had worried the British. Resorting to a standard tactic, they commissioned a report. Lord Alfred Milner, who had been a finance minister in Egypt in the late nineteenth century, took on the difficult job of assessing the situation. Saad Zaghloul's Wafd Party refused to cooperate with Lord Milner, suspecting that the project was merely an exercise in maintaining British control in the country. When the Milner Report was finally published in 1921, it downplayed the Egyptian complaints but still urged that something had to be done. The Egyptians, Milner believed, would not be satisfied with anything short of independence. Following the advice of the report, on 28 February 1922, the British government declared Egypt an independent sovereign state. On 15 March the new king (formerly sultan) Fouad I released a message to his subjects saying he hoped this day would be the beginning of a new happy age, one that would allow Egypt to remember its glorious past again.

Despite their promises of independence, the British maintained significant control in Egypt. They identified four interests they would not entrust to the Egyptians, and decreed that their administration would be "absolutely reserved to the discretion" of the British government:

a) The security of the communications of the British Empire in Egypt;
b) The defence of Egypt against all foreign aggression or interference, direct or indirect;
c) The protection of foreign interests in Egypt and the protection of minorities;
d) The Soudan.[23]

This slightly vague list left room for considerable British involvement; for decades to come, Egypt's independence from British rule seemed to exist more on paper than in practice. A few months before issuing this decree, the British had sent a message that demonstrated their continuing will to curb Egyptian nationalist aspirations. They arrested Saad Zaghloul yet again and sent him into exile, first in the Seychelles and then in Gibraltar, until 1923.

On 17 September 1923, Saad Zaghloul returned to Egypt, landing at the port of Alexandria. On the morning of 18 September, he took the train to Cairo, where he was greeted by supporters lining the route from the train station all the way to his house. Footage of the day from Ezbekiyya shows Opera Square crowded with cheering people, some of them climbing the base of the famous equestrian statue of Ibrahim Pasha. Zaghloul's car, with his followers perched on the bonnet, drove behind a troupe of cyclists appointed to keep order. So great was the city's jubilation that, according to the *Manchester Guardian*, "Cairo pickpockets had decided to abstain from exercising their vocation for three days and called on all 'unaffiliated members' to follow their example." A new era was on the horizon.[24]

Chapter 4

DANCE OF FREEDOM

"EGYPT IS A COUNTRY where the Egyptians reign, English rule, and everybody does as he pleases." So two African American residents of Ezbekiyya wrote in a letter of December 1923, published in the American newspaper *The Chicago Defender*. The pair were Billy Brooks and George Duncan, two international jazz musicians who were thriving in Cairo's 1920s nightlife. The city was coming into its golden age, part of the great international roaring twenties. After the First World War many people, fleeing a destroyed Europe, wound up looking for opportunity in Cairo. And many of them found their way to Ezbekiyya.[1]

The dance halls swelled with women fleeing the economic collapse and political repression in Eastern Europe. Many who found work in cabarets were Hungarian; so much so that the cliché of Hungarian chorus girls became a fixture of interwar Cairo, even if many of them were not from Hungary. Life was often difficult for these women. It was hard enough being an average local Egyptian dancer, but new arrivals did not know the city or how it worked. Living in bedsits or boardinghouses, many women struggled in their new lives. In 1932, one dancer took a large quantity of drugs and fell—or, as many assumed, jumped—from her balcony. Only a few managed find a comfortable place for themselves in Cairo. The most famous was Dinah Lyska, an Eastern European dancer and singer who won celebrity by dancing and singing in the Franco-Arab revues of the early 1920s. She eventually left the stage behind and opened the Bar Lyska on Emad al-Din Street.

In December 1922, the world's press announced the discovery of Tutankhamen's tomb and a flurry of excitement soon followed. By spring 1923, women in Paris were wearing Tutankhamen hats. Two film companies, one in Los Angeles and the other in Prague, had announced they were working on a Tutankhamen film. In London's West End, designers modelled their new dresses on discoveries from the tomb, and in America a handbag company had already applied to trademark the name Tut-Ankh-Amen. Egypt was all over the front pages, and Cairo's residents must have felt they were living at the centre of the world.

Billy Brooks and George Duncan had taken a circuitous route to end up in Cairo. Born in the American South in the days of slavery, the men had left the United States from New York Harbour in early August 1878. They went with sixty other African Americans to perform with Jarrett and Palmer's *Uncle Tom's Cabin* minstrel show, and they never looked back. This touring dramatic version of Harriet Beecher Stowe's novel, featuring song-and-dance numbers by a "host of genuine freed slaves," opened in London in September and then travelled across Europe. Instead of returning home with the troupe, Brooks and Duncan decided to cash in their return tickets and try their luck on their own.[2]

Over the next few decades, the pair became part of a burgeoning global African American performance scene in Europe, meeting with both success and danger as well as predictable racism (in Belgium they were given twenty dollars to play music on bones and tambourines in a cage with five fully grown lions. They left after the first night, happy to escape with their lives). Eventually, in 1914 they wound up in Egypt and decided to settle down. In the early '20s, by then veteran performers, they set up a small group called the Devil's Jazz Band. At first, they recruited four Greek musicians to play alongside them. From the start, though, the band's line-up was flexible, and in its varying forms it demonstrated the variety of people working on Emad al-Din Street after the First World War. At different times the group included a Russian-Jewish pianist, who played the piano so lightly that "if you did not look his way at times you would not know that he was touching the keys"; an Egyptian-born Polish-Jewish banjo player who "doesn't thump the 'jo badly"; a well-trained Greek trombonist; and a Russian woman on the drums, who made her own "thunder and lightning effects" at the back of the stage. In their letters Brooks and Duncan commented, archly, that "she certainly makes the big drum sweat." They once hired a local Egyptian drummer who had been to the Cairo branch of London's famous Ciro's club, where the American drummer Seth Jones, another of many travelling jazz musicians of the 1920s, led the band. Brooks and Duncan rather liked their Egyptian percussionist, who they said "caught onto the jazz stuff pretty well."[3]

After nearly a decade in Cairo, Brooks and Duncan were not even at the top of the local jazz scene. Besides the many Europeans and few Egyptians playing in the country, at least ten African American or West Indian jazz musicians were working between Cairo and Alexandria. The most successful performer in the early 1920s was Billy Farrell, another African American, whose career began in the late nineteenth century with a minstrel show and who was now making good money playing jazz for foreign tourists in expensive hotels. Brooks and Duncan were not on the hotel circuit. They played in dance halls and what they called music palaces. These haunts were frequented by local Egyptians, not wealthy travellers, from the reasonably upmarket Kursaal on Emad al-Din Street down to Ezbekiyya's less salubrious venues where the dancing could continue until dawn.

By their account, Cairo in the '20s was a great place for a couple of African American musicians. They were relieved to have escaped the racial segregation of turn-of-the-century America—as well as the dangerous "circus" acts of Europe—and they were going to enjoy themselves in Cairo while they could. The pair sent letters to the *Chicago Defender* telling readers about the fun and freedom they had found. In particular, they loved recounting their occasional meetings with white American tourists, particularly those who asked why they didn't want to return to America:

> It seems to be a wheeze which they have learned by heart to say: "I know the reason why you don't go back is because you are having a good time over here."
>
> We generally answer: "Why should I not have a good time here, in a black man's country? You have a good time in America, which you call a white man's country. Here we are on the same plank as you. If anything happens and we have to say "Good Morning Judge," we have a square deal at the cards when it is our turn to deal."[4]

In the midst of Cairo's growing cosmopolitanism, Egypt was going through an uncertain political period in the aftermath of a revolution. It was exciting and potentially liberating but also tense and dangerous. The country now had nominal independence; the sultanate had been abolished and replaced with a king. The previous monarch, Hussein Kamel, had died and been replaced with yet another of Khedive Ismail's sons, Fouad. Parliamentary politics, which had existed before, had new power and meaning in the new country.

At the beginning of 1924, the people awaited the first election results. Saad Zaghloul, the hero of the 1919 revolution, won in an expected landslide; his Wafd Party had taken almost 90 percent of the seats. At the end of January, he was named prime minister and declared his continuing commitment to Egypt's total independence. In just a few years, Zaghloul had gone through imprisonment and exile to become the popular leader of a rising nation.

For Egyptian women, the victory was bittersweet—they were left out of the new political process, denied the right to stand for election or even to vote. When a list of invitees for the new parliament's opening ceremony was released and no Egyptian women were included, it was the final straw. Two weeks before the event, Mounira Thabet, a young woman just out of high school, wrote an open letter to Egypt's main Arabic newspaper, *al-Ahram*. She would later get a law degree in France and become one of Egypt's most prominent feminist voices, but in her letter she identified herself simply as a "woman demanding the right to vote." She told the paper's readership, "Women had no less a role in the struggle than men did so it is her right—rightfully, morally, and legally—to be a part of the opening ceremony of the parliament which is the fruit of this shared struggle. You have deprived us of our right to become elected members of this parliament, will we not even get to take part in the opening ceremony in compensation for this treachery?"[5]

On 15 March, the day of the opening ceremony, a group of female students stood outside the parliament's gate holding protest signs. Half the signs made general political demands, such as the withdrawal of the British army, the right to free association, and the unity of Egypt and Sudan. The other half made appeals to specifically feminist concerns: the right of women to vote, equality of the sexes in education, and a limit to the number of wives a man could have. Public statements stressed how betrayed the women felt after sacrificing so much in the fight for independence and then had not seen the benefits they expected. The Wafdist Women's Central Committee, chaired by Hoda Shaarawi—heroine of the women's march in 1919—sent a telegram to the president and the local press. It was a reminder that women, "as half of the nation, . . . took part in the struggles and sacrifices that led to the independence of their country," and that excluding all women from the opening ceremony was "an undignified act." The newspapers supported the women, but their demands were not realised.[6]

In the exclusively male world of Egyptian politics, the 1920s and 1930s were full of intrigue and political fights: new parties were formed, others split, and power struggles were waged. Saad Zaghloul and his Wafd Party, unsatisfied with the litany of qualifications the British had put on Egypt's sovereignty, continued the campaign for genuine independence. Several other parties competed for power against Zaghloul's. The main competitor was the Liberal-Constitutional Party, which had emerged partly to call attention to Saad Zaghloul's dominance of the Wafd Party. Liberal-Constitutionalists promoted a gradualist approach towards complete independence that focused on peaceful negotiations with the British. Besides these two major political groups, the Union Party rose up, largely to support the king and the policies of the palace. Meanwhile, prime ministers came and went; very few of them lasted a year. In the early 1930s an entirely new constitution was written, only to be abandoned a few years later.

On paper, the Egyptians were no longer ruled by Britain. But the British had certainly not gone away: They were keen to maintain their interests in Sudan and around the Suez Canal and kept a significant military presence in the country as well as control in state institutions like the police force, where many senior figures remained British. Egyptians could be forgiven for wondering why their former occupier still exerted so much control in the country.

The political landscape in the interwar period was enormously complex. It is usually explained as a competition between three poles: Parliament, the king, and the British, each working to build its own power both publicly and behind the scenes. Parliament relied on its popular legitimacy, the king used his wide constitutional powers (like appointing the prime minster), and the British applied a mix of force and subterfuge. But these three also had to contend with shifting allegiances, personal feuds, and outside actors. Egypt's new "liberal age" was a convoluted mixture of ideologies, influences, and interests.

It was also a violent time. A network of secret societies with ominous names like the Black Hand or the Revenge Society organised violent attacks and assassinations, usually against British targets. The spate of bombings and shootings reached its peak in 1924 when the British governor-general of Sudan, Lee Stack, was assassinated in Cairo. This incident had far-reaching consequences: The culprits were arrested and executed, but the British, demanding further retribution, used the incident as a way to reassert power. They thought Saad Zaghloul and his Wafd Party, with their strident anti-British views, bore some responsibility for the crime. An internal telegram between British officials claimed that the "spirit of indiscipline and hatred which Egyptian Government have incited by public speeches and through activities of their Wafd cannot but be regarded as contributory to the crime."[7] On 24 November, just five days after Stack's assassination, the crisis was so severe that Saad Zaghloul resigned as prime minister and would never again hold the office. He died in August 1927, suffering the effects of a separate assassination attempt directed at him in the summer of 1924.

It is hard to know exactly how much people would have followed every step of Egypt's political turmoil. When looking at the entertainment scene, however, it is at least important to keep in mind the larger picture of a newly instituted democracy accompanied by power wrangling, rising nationalism, and continuing anti-colonial struggle.

Meanwhile, in Ezbekiyya, the stars of the 1920s were busy creating their own models for a new Egypt along with everyone else. Emad al-Din Street was booming, and grand new cabarets, cinemas, and theatres were opening in unprecedented numbers. As theatres like the Majestic and the New Printania continued to offer Franco-Arab revues, other places like the Ramses and the Semiramis opened to provide more conventional evenings of drama and a succession of melodramatic plays.

Before long, several Arabic-speaking cabarets had opened in hopes of appealing to local audiences. On their stages a new style of song called the monologue (*munulug* in Egyptian Arabic) began to spread alongside the already-popular *taqtuqa*. These solo (usually comic or light-hearted) songs were said to have roots in songs from plays of the early twentieth century. They also had a lot in common with European music hall comic monologues, combining comedy, social critique, and risqué sexual references. During the '20s and '30s, every cabaret and revue theatre had at least one monologist on the bill, often several. Badia Masabni, one cabaret owner and a popular monologist, performed fun numbers like "Honk Your Horn, Mister Driver," "I Don't Want to Forget You," and "Bring a Candle and Light It for Me." Soon major record companies got in on the craze, releasing records by the best-known monologists of the interwar period. "Everyone from the old man leaning on his stick, to the baby crawling on the floor is singing them," wrote one journalist in the 1920s.[8]

The Arabic-speaking clubs of Emad al-Din Street acquired a reputation for rowdiness and sometimes danger. In 1927, when a journalist went to the Bijou Palace to see one of his favourite singers perform, all around him he saw "a great number of our youth spending their night in high spirits and ecstasy, drinking and making a racket." Later in the night, a fight broke out and the whole place was wrecked—people hit each other with chairs, drinks were spilled all over the floor, and finally, someone pulled out a gun and shot another man in the arm. "We came to find pleasure in the sounds of music but we ended up terrified by the sounds of shooting," the journalist wrote.[9]

Alongside this kind of entertainment, European-style cabarets offered approximations of Parisian music halls. One French-language

Egyptian magazine published a fictionalised account of a night in one of these nightclubs: A "place of perdition," where "revellers, bon-viveurs, and drinkers pass their sleepless nights." There, "until dawn, jazz music hums . . . dancers perform thousands of acrobatic, fan-tastic, cabbalistic feats, amid constant uproar and constant streams of drinks." The clientele was diverse—"Germans, Poles, Bulgarians, Czechoslovakians, Italians, Greeks, Japanese, Egyptians, Argentines, and English"—with a mix of demi-mondaines, high capitalists, and everything in between.[10]

The famous Casino de Paris, owned and run by Marcelle Lan-glois, continued to thrive, offering late-night shows featuring singers, musicians, acrobats, conjurors, and more. In the 1920s she capitalised on the growing popularity of Emad al-Din Street, and her acts could be unusual; one star of the Casino de Paris 1923 season, for instance, was a dancer called Mlle. Mignon-Hett (a play on the name of the famous early twentieth-century French singer Mistinguett) and known as the "eccentric of eccentrics." Although Egyptian newspa-pers did not carry a detailed description of her act, there are clues as to what it might have been in later accounts of someone performing under the name of Mignon-Hett (either the same woman or an imi-tator of her offbeat style): One night in Paris, a newspaper reported, Mignon-Hett started by singing "a song in praise of asparagus" and followed this by "a series of two or three of the dirtiest stories ever heard on a public stage."[11]

Bars and cafés sprang up on Emad-al-Din Street to serve the large theatre audiences, quickly becoming places for people to talk, smoke, and drink coffee or zabib until early in the morning. A place that is still a part of Cairo's literary lore was *Qahwat al-Fann* (Café d'Art), which sat next to the Ramses Theatre. It played host to a new gen-eration of Egyptian writers, who often came to discuss their latest work, but there were countless other establishments too. There was the Byron, which stood at the top of Emad al-Din Street towards the train station and was known as the place where young men went in the hope of meeting an actress or a singer from the theatre. Old directories of Cairo's businesses give many more names, including Moderne, Regina, Byzance, Australia, and *Istiqlal* (Independence), named in response to current political events in Egypt. These venues played host to literary salons, provided captive audiences for itinerant sellers and street entertainers, served as late-night hangouts for theatre troupes that had finished a show, or just gave curious fans a chance to go celebrity spotting.

People could also find less conventional forms of entertainment. An unusual group of performers found their way to Emad al-Din in the '20s: a wave of mystics, palm readers, and psychics. There was Dr. Salomon, an Italian mind reader born to a Syrian mother; Khorshid, an Indian palm reader; and Dr. Dahesh Bey, an Iraqi-Palestinian hypnotist and mystic. In the '30s Dr. Dahesh was expelled from Egypt, allegedly after having an affair with a woman in the royal palace. From Egypt he went to Beirut, where a complex series of events led to him setting up his own religion that became known as Daheshism.

On Alfi Bey Street, which intersected Emad al-Din Street, was a hugely popular venue that played host to the Basque sport of pelota. In the building that originally housed the Printania Theatre (it moved to Emad al-Din Street in 1923), Basque athletes, a red team against a blue team, competed with each other while Egyptian spectators placed bets on the outcome. One devotee of Cairo's nightlife, who wrote a column for a local French-language newspaper, said the venue was "a general meeting place for everyone . . . : poets and dancers of the fox-trot, politicians and workers, women of the world and ladies of the night, the clever and the stupid, gigolos and serious men." It was one of the few indoor entertainment venues that stayed busy in Cairo's hot summers, thanks partly to a ventilation system that kept the air flowing. One pelota fan wrote to *al-Ahram* newspaper in 1929 to say that "in the past few years the Egyptian people have been exposed to many different sports, which are loved across the world. However, the one that has been most enduring, most enjoyable, and most passionately received has been Basque pelota." He put this down to its "combination of strength and beauty, skill and elegance, accuracy and speed," though the gambling must have been a big draw too.[12]

More illicit pleasures also prospered. As always in Ezbekiyya, side streets hid concealed gambling houses, brothels, and hashish dens. The Café Carillon on Emad al-Din Street was well known as a hangout for French pimps, who went by nicknames like "Paul le Petit," "Louis the Australian," and "Louis the Algerian." Doctors set up offices that offered cures for venereal diseases. Cocaine and heroin use were rife at the time, and some entertainers even turned to smuggling. In 1931, Egyptian police busted the famous "Fanny" case, so named because several young dancers were arrested after trying to hide 2.5 kilogrammes of heroin in their modified garters. Drugs like these would head, among other places, to the bars of Ezbekiyya, where some waiters were known to sell them under the table. In 1930, Giorgios Kourouzou, barman at La Lune in Mouksy, an area at the far eastern end of Ezbekiyya, was found with 21 five-gram packets of heroin and quickly deported to Cyprus.[13]

It is no surprise that a hidden criminal underworld like this existed in the demi-monde of Ezbekiyya to take advantage of what they could. Gangs led by local strongmen (*futuwwa* in Arabic) were common in working-class areas in Egypt. These groups acted like a cross between a mafia, a police force, and a small militia, controlling and (allegedly) defending their neighbourhoods. Most of these gangs were led by powerful men, but some were controlled by women. In the 1930s, the neighbourhood of Ataba al-Khadra, just next to Ezbekiyya, was run by a woman called Zakiyya. One journalist who had interviewed her said she was "a woman of great power and strength, with a wicked tongue and a harsh temper." He added, "No man had the power—no matter how strong he was—to stand in her way or disobey her orders."[14]

This underworld of drugs, gangs, and gambling made many in the conservative establishment regard Emad al-Din Street as a magnet for sin and deep moral corruption. A pushback began, just as it had in the 1890s against the old music halls of Ezbekiyya. Newspapers and magazines started to publish articles condemning the pernicious influence of the cabarets, dance halls, and vaudeville theatre, where performers openly talked about sex, drugs, and social change. In 1923, a man who had attended a performance described it to the readers of a newspaper: "It was a play of that type that is full of obscene expressions, stuffed with immoral blemishes and all based on dirty jokes and scandalous plot twists. In other words, it is the type of play known as vaudeville." One particularly anguished member of the public called on the government to "ban these night spots, bring back the beauty of good morals, and cleanse the capital of this filthy evil and corruption so it can become the centre of proper behaviour and the mantle of virtue as it has been for all its history."[15]

When the theatre business first began in Egypt in the late nineteenth century, it was justified by the intellectual class because it aimed at being educational as well as entertaining. Theatre, many at the time argued, would improve the country's morals by giving them good examples to follow or by showing the kind of bad behaviour to avoid. Now, censorious observers worried that the entertainment industry was seriously harming their society. One writer in an Arabic-language Egyptian newspaper gave a damning assessment:

> Egyptian theatre is devoid of both moral and artistic merit. Some
> of those who claim the title artists are totally illiterate, incapable
> of either reading or writing, prepared only for rags and starva-

tion. Some are only recently out of jobs working as servants in cheap hotels. Troupes are full of hundreds of lay-abouts and corrupters of morals . . . they are the kind of people who would give you anything you need in return for a shilling, a glass of whiskey or a sniff of cocaine.[16]

For years the British had told Egypt's rising bourgeoisie that their country was undeveloped; its people were not ready to rule themselves, and European occupation was for their own good. When Egypt's respectable middle class looked at Emad al-Din Street, the British assessment hit home. Egyptian theatres seemed corrupt and decadent, not like the well-organised, modern country they wanted to portray. This nightlife was not going to help their struggle for national liberation. Class prejudice also helped to provoke a lot of criticism. One of the most frequent complaints was that nightclubs and dance halls like those on Emad al-Din were filled with the wrong sort of people.

In the press, critics sarcastically renamed the street, calling it Fasad al-Din ("corruption of religion") rather than Emad al-Din ("pillar of religion," the name of a Sufi sheikh buried at one end of it). But most criticisms were not voiced on specifically religious grounds. Although a number of religious leaders did raise objections to Cairo's nightlife or entertainment industry, their complaints were rarely taken seriously. In 1925 a sheikh from the most prestigious religious institution in Egypt and the Islamic world, al-Azhar in Cairo, issued a fatwa saying that Muslim women who appeared unveiled onstage were guilty of heresy. Despite the apparent gravity of the sheikh's declaration, very few female performers heeded his ruling. The *New York Herald* even featured Mounira al-Mahdiyya in an article, claiming that "if the Moslem authorities . . . compel her to respect [the fatwa] she will become a Christian." In the end, she just kept on as if nothing had happened; the whole controversy soon disappeared. Later declarations from al-

Azhar were met with similarly dismissive reactions by the entertainment industry. In the early 1930s, after scholars from the mosque and university complained about a sheikh who was heard in a film reciting the Quran with a Turkish accent, a theatrical correspondent in the Egyptian press attacked their censorious attitude and accused them of thinking they alone spoke for Islam. He advised the sheikhs at al-Azhar to remember that "silence is golden."[17]

As usual, the women of Emad al-Din were the most common targets of moral criticism. Faultfinders said a common sign that the country was on its way to societal decline was the prevalence of women singing vulgar songs. The *taqtuqas* that were popular in the 1910s had evolved into something more daring and bawdier. The song lyrics were getting more graphic, more direct, and naughtier than popular songs had ever been before:

> *Pull down the curtain that's beside us*
> *So the neighbour cannot see us*
>
> *. . .*
>
> *No-one above and no-one below*
> *Knows when I come and go*[18]

One famous *taqtuqa* at the time, sung by a popular music hall proprietor of the 1920s, explicitly described the fun that could be had in bringing men to the Nile barrages on the edge of town for a drink and an illicit affair:

Opposite: Naima al-Misriyya (from the collection of Heba Farid)

Come on baby let's go to the barrages
Swear that you'll please me and don't disappoint me
Bring a bottle, sit down and play with me[19]

Naima al-Misriyya, the woman who sang this song, ran the Alhambra Casino on Bab al-Bahri Street near Emad al-Din through most of the 1920s. Mounira al-Mahdiyya had sung there in the early 1910s, and the outer walls of the club are still intact (although the interior has been transformed into a shop for electronics and mechanical parts). French Prime Minister Georges Clemenceau is said to have visited the club in 1923 and been so impressed with Naima that he bought her a bottle of champagne. However, unlike many other singers of the 1920s, she did not manage—or did not want—to manipulate the celebrity culture of the press to her advantage and has subsequently been largely forgotten.

By the mid '20s, *taqtuqas* had gone even further, and the lyrics were infused with the spirit of Emad al-Din's cabarets. No longer just songs of love and flirtation, they included references to drugs, gambling, and even more explicit sex, often poking fun at the wealthy Egyptian nightclub clients who came to hear them. One, aimed at a young man who has just inherited a lot of land and is blowing the money on Emad al-Din Street, gently teases him for his louche existence:

Here comes a new one
There's not a night that he's here sober
. . .
His mind has been seized by the Foxtrot
And the Tango drives him crazy
He does what he feels. Who'll tell him no?
Dancing is his life and his religion.[20]

Some songs gave voice to the power Cairo's "new women" were starting to exercise; others lamented their new freedom, seeing uncouth, uncontrolled, and lustful women everywhere. One *taqtuqa*, sung from the perspective of a woman being courted by a wealthy man, laid down her conditions for marriage. Besides wanting a healthy allowance (50 pounds a month and an account at the glamorous department store Au Bon Marché), winters spent in Luxor, and summers in Paris, the singer told the audience that she needed her freedom too:

> *I get to do what I want and make my own decisions*
> *I don't need a jealous lover getting in my way*
> *I'll go out and have fun all night*
> *I'm still free, don't try to change me.*[21]

Many saw the suggestive lyrics sung by female stars as clear evidence of a debased culture. The songs, it was claimed, were setting a bad example for a new Egypt and they—as much as the overall atmosphere that prevailed in Ezbekiyya—were the target of attacks by several magazines and newspapers at the time. One person writing to a magazine in 1927 complained about them: during the 1919 revolution, he claimed, the *taqtuqa*'s simple form and lyrics embodied the people's struggle, but lately had lost their way:

> Since the national movement has cooled and its fire has been extinguished, these little songs have made a long journey into shamelessness and vulgarity. First, they became prevalent in entertainment spots, having a terrible influence on the audiences, and then their poison reached our houses and contaminated Egypt's air.

This stern critic ended by calling on the government to enforce its censorship of these songs just as they did with novels, plays, and other publications. "We should," he concluded, "bring Egypt back to what it was before this fever came which has almost totally destroyed our morals."[22]

The critics were also horrified by the dances in both the cabarets and the revue theatres of Emad al-Din, where groups of women from all over the world performed nightly in revealing clothing. In the minds of conservative observers, behaviour like this was little different from prostitution. Many troupes capitalised on the outcry, playing up the bawdiness of their shows to attract customers. In one night of performances in 1925, a theatre advertised a group of Turkish women who were going to perform a "thrilling dance: The dance of freedom, the dance of love, the dance of wantonness."[23]

Unlike singers, female dancers faced condemnation beyond the anguished stories in the press; they could be subject to legal action. The reason stems from one of the most interesting pieces of cultural exchange of the nineteenth and twentieth centuries. Western travellers had long been fascinated by traditional Arabic dance, which they called *danse du ventre* (belly dance) and had written long accounts of it. So, when a troupe of Egyptian dancers performed at the Chicago Universal Columbian Exposition in 1893, they were an instant but controversial sensation. American police were not sure how to deal with this dance form that seemed worryingly sexualised and certainly not family-friendly. When the dancers from the Chicago Exposition toured America, many of them were arrested. In New York, police raided a show at the Grand Central Palace and arrested three dancers, who were eventually fined $50 each because their act was deemed "offensive to good morals." Following this commotion, imitators set up their own belly dancing shows all across America. For the next decade, these so-called hootchie-kootchie shows filled county fairs, cabarets, and Coney Island music halls. Even fifteen years later, in 1907, an Indianapolis police chief raided the city's Empire dance hall after hearing about one of these shows. He warned the proprietors, "Away with all cooch stuff . . . the lid is on."[24]

Back in 1893, when Egyptians heard about the dancers at the Chicago Exposition and the agitation they had caused, many were upset at how their culture was being portrayed. One Egyptian newspaper, *al-Muayyad*, suggested (probably correctly) that many dancers at the American show were only claiming to be Egyptians. However, the author sadly admitted that shows like this did exist across Egypt and that the government should take the lead in shutting them down. He worried (in large part correctly) that people were using this erotic dance to paint Egypt as backwards, oversexualised, and dissolute. For those who wanted to bring their country into the modern world, the *danse du ventre* represented decadence, not progress. In 1916 the Egyptian police announced that they would prohibit this kind of dance, which "did not accord with Eastern morals and customs."[25]

In the mid-1920s, this ban on belly dancing—in Arabic, literally "Raqs al-Batn," a phrase that had barely existed before—was enshrined in the new nation's law. Places where the dance was performed risked being fined or even shut down. In 1927 the manager of the Bijou Palace on Emad al-Din Street was charged after one of his dancers did a performance in which "she sat down and, by extreme movements of her stomach, gave an immoral display and strayed into obscenity and debauchery." The owner was given a small fine of 100 piastres, and his venue was shut down for a week.[26]

However, because belly dancing was in some ways an American and European invention, it was hard to pin down exactly what it was. It did not encompass every dance that was performed onstage, and there was probably some leeway in its precise definition. Joseph McPherson, the same British policeman who had scared his guests by organising a raid as they watched the cross-dressing dancer Hussein Fouad, told the story of one officer who entered a nightclub where a dancer was performing a *danse du ventre*. She had been warned of McPherson's approach by a young boy employed by the club and had turned her back on the audience to perform what McPherson euphemistically called the *danse du lune* ("moon dance"). Unable to stop her, the police were forced to let her continue.[27]

Despite the criticism and opposition, there was no doubt that, in the 1920s, women were becoming more prominent both onstage and in the audience. When Billy Brooks and George Duncan had started performing back in 1914, many theatres still had harem boxes where women could watch the action from behind a screen, shielded from the view of men. Those without screens strung mosquito nets across the boxes to create makeshift female areas. By 1922, the two musicians noticed that "now you cannot find half a dozen theatres in Egypt with harem boxes or anything stretched across the boxes. Women now go to all places of amusement unattended and mingle with the men. We have Egyptian women come in the dancing palace. They have not gone in for fox-trotting yet. No doubt this will come in time."[28] True, most theatres scheduled some women-only matinees or still offered female-only areas, but the women in the audience were no longer quite so hidden.

After the war, women might have been excluded from parliamentary politics, but they were entering the public sphere in other ways, both for work and pleasure. In 1926, one journalist commented on this new reality: "Doesn't it feel like Egypt is at the doors of a revolution in everything? Women are demanding an end to their seclusion and an escape from the bounds of the Harem." Another wrote soon afterwards that "there is a women's renaissance in this country and every day there is more evidence of this: from dancing with their hands round men's waists, driving cars and appearing, unveiled, in public places to leaving the house and crowding cafés like Groppi and Sault along with the men."[29]

Since the late nineteenth century, when schools for girls first opened, women had attained increasingly advanced levels of schooling—although it still took until 1928 for the American University in Cairo to admit its first woman, and until 1929 for Cairo University to do the same. Education had given women more qualifications and nurtured their ambition to compete with men. The foundation of the Egyptian Feminist Union in 1923 was another significant landmark for women's participation in public life. However, much of the impetus for these changes was less quantifiable. The increasing urbanisation of Egypt and the anonymity offered by a city like Cairo may have given space for women to push boundaries. Perhaps too, the sense of liberation offered by the events of the 1919 revolution encouraged women to claim rights of their own. No doubt a combination of all these things, as well as the growing international women's movement, led to the creation of the "new woman" in Egypt.

Writers and cartoonists continued to mock the new social developments, often in a way that betrayed some nervousness. They imagined a near future in which women had taken the place of men, doing hard manual labour, playing sports, and taking four husbands (Islamic law allowed men four wives but women only one husband). The increasing presence of women outside their homes and in the public sphere was often interpreted as attempts to usurp male positions.

The same people looked on in worry as women began to experiment with more masculine clothing fashions. In the 1910s, Mounira al-Mahdiyya had caused a stir by appearing in the leading male role in all of her early performances. By the 1920s, many actresses were dressing as men for roles on the stage. Fatima Rushdi, one of the great actresses of the 1920s, also made a name for herself by playing male roles including Mark Antony in *Julius Caesar* and the role that Sarah Bernhardt had made famous, Napoleon II in Edmond Rostand's *L'Aiglon*.

Actresses as well as other women now posed in countless photos dressed as men for both public and private audiences. But Mounira al-Mahdiyya still remained Cairo's preeminent cross-dresser. She arranged photo shoots and sent the results to the press, which reproduced them dutifully, sometimes asking readers if they could guess who the man in the photo was and revealing the answer in the next issue. She even appeared on a magazine cover in a suit and tie; the caption identified her with the male title Mounira al-Mahdiyya *Bey*. A journalist who saw these photos of Mounira said, "She has lived her life up to today as a woman and what is stopping her living the rest of her days as a man?"[30]

There were many different interpretations of this phenomenon. When she was young, the singer Oum Kalthoum was dressed in boy's clothes by her father as a way to curb her youthful femininity and pretend that she was a boy. On reflection, she thought it was all really about her father trying to hide the shame of his daughter becoming a singer. Many journalists saw this as a global trend and identified the flappers of Europe and America as instigators of what was happening in Egypt. In 1926 one newspaper traced the new fashion back to the French author Victor Margueritte's novel *La Garçonne* (1922), about a woman who decides to live as a man. Although few people put it this way at the time, cross-dressing could easily be understood as part of the growing rejection of traditional gender roles that characterised this new decade. Tempting as it might be to see this practice as evidence of a queer subculture in Cairo at the time, I have found no direct evidence to support it. But, of course, queer history from this period is not often preserved in conventional or mainstream sources. There is certainly evidence of same-sex romantic relationships in Cairo generally, and Ezbekiyya specifically, from the 1890s onwards, but confirming the existence of a significant gay "scene" would require either fresh sources or creative readings of the material already available.[31]

Although some Egyptians viewed these liberated women who were making their way into the entertainment industry at that time as corrupters of the country's morals, many others idolised them. Fans avidly followed the rise and fall of their favourite's career; every famous singer and actress had her own *balat,* or "court." This was the group of men who formed the inner circle of fans. They would sit in the front row at her shows, cheer loudly for her, and sing her praises in letters to the press. In return they expected to go to parties at her house, meet her in a café, or attend her salons. The members of these courts had a strange relationship with their idols—it fell somewhere between lover and fan, not as close as the former but more than the latter. Sometimes they were rather sensitive about their own treatment. In the early 1930s, when she was one of Egypt's biggest stars, Oum Kalthoum was on a tour of Iraq. During her travels, she wrote a letter to one member of her court but neglected to write to another, and the spurned fan was so upset that he threatened to join a rival singer's court.

Attention like this made the women of Emad al-Din Street hot property in the press. Newspapers and journals clamoured for interviews to feed the public appetite for minute details about their lives: what their houses were like, what they had for breakfast, or what they thought of their rivals. The questions were sometimes pedestrian, sometimes intrusive, and sometimes presumptuous. But the stars' answers offered their own perspective—sometimes quite a radical one. Female stars in previous decades had usually been seen only through the eyes of their male admirers. In the '20s, famous women began telling their own stories in their own voices and answering some of the long-standing charges made against them.

So, in the mid-'20s, when an article in a weekly newspaper attacked the morals of female actresses along with those of any men who encouraged them to go onstage, the author was forced to defend himself. There was nothing special about the article. It was the kind of thing that men had written before, decrying the immorality of the theatre, particularly focusing on its women. The concerned author warned readers that "when a woman acts scenes of love and passion, especially when she starts to do it as a profession, she soon becomes a passionate lover herself." He went on to impugn the whole generation, saying that people nowadays saw concepts such as "the *haram*," "the forbidden," and "the shameful" as mere "obstacles standing in the way of their lust." At the end of his tirade, he wrote: "Anyone who supports the profession of acting is doing nothing other than supporting . . ." He left out the last word, unable bring himself even to write the word *prostitution*, which was what he meant.[32]

Had this article been published ten years earlier, that would have been the end of the matter. People would have read it, agreed or disagreed, and forgotten about it. But in the 1920s, a young actress reading the article felt a duty to answer it. She saw no need to leap to the defence of actors—"the men can defend themselves"—but she felt that a woman had to respond on behalf of her gender: "We women know that we are the ones who have to defend our own honour and dignity. . . . After all the damage that has been done to the Eastern Woman and despite everything that has been done to kill her talents, we have been able to become a powerful force in human society. We have been able to work as actresses, succeeding in an art form whose greatness has laid low many male stars." The actress went on to ask the critic why he wanted to curb women's ambitions. "We take comfort in acting and in other things like it . . . do you want to ban us doing everything, even having a little comfort?"[33]

She was particularly annoyed that this man was attacking women who had worked hard to improve the quality of art in Egypt—a service to the whole nation. She compared the plight of Egyptian actresses to the ancient architect Cenmar (or Sinimmar). In the fifth century CE he had designed the palace of Khawarnak in Mesopotamia for the Arab king al-Numan. When the palace was finished, it was so magnificent that the king wanted to make sure nobody ever had a palace so grand. So, he sentenced Cenmar to be thrown from the top of the palace to prevent him from designing anything like it again. Egypt's actresses, this anonymous woman declared, were just like that architect. They had struggled to create a great theatrical tradition, and now they were being sacrificed for their efforts.

Her defence did not change the critic's mind. In fact, he replied a few weeks later by saying that most actresses were prostitutes and giving a series of nodding and winking anecdotes about actresses being caught in compromising positions or in cars full of men on their way to the pyramids. So even though the actress's words had little effect on the writer himself, she had at least made her point.

Elsewhere in the press, responses of actresses and singers were even more strident. They did more than defend themselves—they went on the attack against criticisms they felt were holding them back. In 1928, one of the many entertainment magazines that had appeared in Cairo in the 1920s ran an article made up of interviews with famous actresses on the subject of love and marriage. The cynicism and disdain the women expressed shocked the interviewer. "Love is all empty talk. There's no such thing; it's all nonsense," said Ratiba Rushdi, a singer, actress, and nightclub impresaria. The interviewer went on to ask Ratiba what she thought about marriage: "And where can I find a true husband?" she replied, doubting the faithfulness of the entire male gender. "Men all have roving eyes. That's the thing that annoys us women the most." At that point the interviewer seemed to struggle for a positive conclusion and asked a mild, but rather banal, question: "So, which do you prefer: Acting, Love or Marriage?" Rushdi laughed at him uproariously and said, "None of them! . . . I'm only out for myself."[34]

The same journalist later met two more actresses, Mary Mansour and Salha Kasin, in a café. They responded to his interview questions with even more derision. Mary Mansour had little to no trust in marriage and a distinctly negative opinion of love. The man couldn't quite believe what he was hearing. "Do you really have no hope at all for marriage?" She took a drag of her cigarette, he wrote, and watched the smoke rise in front of her face. "Well, since the disaster of my first husband, I've come to hate any talk about love and marriage. I have a son and a daughter who have never done anything wrong and it pains me that now they will not get to experience their father's love."[35]

At that point, Salha Kasin interrupted Mansour and launched into a diatribe of her own. Salha was a veteran of the Egyptian stage, an Egyptian-Jewish actress who had started her career at the beginning of the twentieth century when most actresses were Christian or Jewish. Since then she had been a member of almost every theatrical troupe in the country. She was well known for her wicked sense of humour, never missing a chance to make fun of people around her, and for her fiery character. She herself had once claimed in an interview that all actresses had a "holy flame" inside them that distinguished them from other people and often made them behave in ways that others thought strange or unusual. It was this flame, she said, that made actresses change their lovers as often as twice a week.[36]

In the interview, Salha Kasin did not entirely agree with Mary Mansour. She vigorously agreed with her on marriage, exclaiming that there was no hope at all for the institution. However, she thought that love could still be amazing. As the actress got more heated, other customers in the café began to notice her, which only encouraged her more. She started chanting, "Down with marriage! Long live love!" The journalist, who was a little worried about what she had said, asked her if she knew that he was going to print it all. "Yes!" she replied. "Print everything I am saying to you. Don't leave out a single letter! L-O-V-E!"[37]

Act II

THE LEADING
LADIES

Chapter 5

"IF I WERE NOT A WOMAN, I'D WANT TO BE ONE"

ONE EVENING IN AUGUST 1925, one of Cairo's many young stars, Rose al-Youssef, was sitting in a café just off Emad al-Din Street in central Cairo. It was here, in the 1920s, at the centre of the city's nightlife, that cabarets and music halls competed for customers with theatres and cinemas. Rose's theatrical troupe was taking a break that month, and she was enjoying a period of rest: no rehearsals, no lines to learn, and no shows.

Rose al-Youssef was, at the time, one of the most famous actresses in Egypt, part of a generation of women who pushed Cairo's nightlife into the new age. She is the first of seven women whose intertwined stories make up the second part of this book and without whom 1920s and 1930s Cairo would not have been half as exciting. In the summer of 1925, Rose was best known as a gifted vaudeville star who had played the main roles in a series of melodramas for Egypt's newest theatrical troupe, winning even more admirers. One entertainment magazine said, "Whoever has seen her, knows from that first moment that she is made for acting" and went on to claim that "she is one of the

leaders in the world of Arabic acting—if there really are any leaders besides her."[1]

When an itinerant salesman passed by the café with a bundle of newspapers and magazines, Rose decided to buy one. She turned to the arts section and, as she recalled in her memoirs, was dismayed to see that these so-called theatre journalists dealt in nothing but gossip, lies, and personal attacks. Among all the articles about her and others like her, there was no serious criticism or even anything resembling it.

Rose al-Youssef complained to her friends in the café about this state of affairs, asking them where actors and actresses were supposed to go to reply to the critics' abuse and wishing that she could do something about the quality of magazines like these. Then she had an idea. Why didn't they start a publication of their own to give their side of the story? At first the others thought she was joking, but as soon as they realised that she was serious, they were intrigued, wondering what such a magazine might look like.

A few other people sat at the table that evening. Rose was with her second husband, Zaki Tolaymat—a fellow actor who had married Rose a few years earlier and had recently become the father of her second child, a daughter called Amal. Also there were two of the actors' friends, young intellectuals who frequented the cafés around Emad al-Din Street: the writer Mahmud Izzi and the journalist Ibrahim Khalil, who was then working for the popular daily newspaper *al-Balagh*. All of them offered their opinion about the new project.

Zaki Tolaymat, who had an elevated view of art, started to voice his big ideas about refined culture. "The people are hungry for 'high literature,'" he claimed, saying that the Egyptian people were so eager to see serious intellectual material that they would camp out on the street in front of the printer waiting for the next issue of any magazine that covered it. The others couldn't help teasing Zaki a little—"High

Opposite: Rose al-Youssef

literature . . . How many floors high?" they asked. Still, they all agreed that there was a place in the market for a journal that took artistic, literary, and theatrical criticism seriously.[2]

Almost instantly, their new magazine started to take shape; but they still had to come up with a name. Tolaymat, somewhat predictably, put forward "High Literature." Others suggested that they should call it *al-Amal* (which means "hope"), or maybe name it after some great Egyptian historical monument or natural wonder. In Rose's mind there was only one thing it could be called—*Rose al-Youssef,* after its founder, herself. When the rest of the group dissented, she paid no attention; it was her idea, she was the star, and she was going to call it what she wanted. So it was that a new magazine for Egypt's growing entertainment press was conceived, and it would have one of Cairo's newest female celebrities at its helm. It soon became one of the most important cultural-political journals in interwar Cairo, and it continues to this day under the same name, albeit in a very different form. In the 1920s and 1930s, *Rose al-Youssef* (*Ruz al-Yusuf*) magazine was one of the key chroniclers of Cairo's nightlife.

The story of Rose al-Youssef, the woman, and how she became one of Egypt's most famous actresses is a strange one. It is full of struggle, mystery, hard work, determination, and more than a little mythologising. Her rise to prominence gives us the first close-up look at the world of the Egyptian stage, of the doors that the new entertainment industry opened for women in Egypt, and of how a life in the theatre during the early twentieth century enabled young women with little education to find their place in society. In going from comic actress to magazine magnate, Rose was in many ways exceptional; but she was part of a new generation of women in Egypt who were coming of age and were determined to make their voices heard.

Writing in 1925, Rose remembered the event that started her career in acting. It was back in 1912, when she was around fourteen years old, and Cairo's entertainment scene had not yet reached the heights of the 1920s and 1930s. She was living in Faggala, an area near the centre of the city, making a little money working backstage or as an extra in one of Cairo's biggest theatres. While looking through the theatre's wardrobe one day, Rose found a beautiful black velvet dress embroidered with gold and silver threads and studded with sequins. It was the costume worn for the role of Mary Tudor, daughter of Henry VIII, in a play focused on European history. She fell in love with the gown and secretly took it back to her house. In her bedroom, she tried the dress on, put on makeup, and let her hair down around her shoulders. Then, dressed as the English queen, she walked triumphantly through the streets of Cairo and back to the theatre with the train of the gown trailing behind her. Rose described how intoxicating it felt to be walking through the city, as the centre of attention. Her reaction convinced her that she was destined for a life on the stage.

Typical of almost all female stars of this period, Rose's early life before she became famous is obscure and largely undocumented. She never talked publicly about her early years, and most of what we know comes from later accounts of family and friends. She was born in the late nineteenth century (probably in 1898, but other dates have been suggested) in Tripoli in what is now Lebanon. Her mother had died during Rose's birth; her father, a Muslim Turkish merchant who had little interest in raising his daughter, left the infant Rose in the care of a local Christian family. From that point, all we really know is that sometime in the first decade of the twentieth century, she mysteriously appeared, alone, in the Egyptian port city of Alexandria. There are many different accounts of how she got there. Most of them agree that the family that raised her emigrated to South America, and she did not travel with them. We can only guess about how they were separated: she may have run away, her family may have given her away to be married, or they may have sold her into domestic service.

When she turned up in Alexandria, so the story told by friends and family goes, Rose was still very young; she had no job, no money, and no companions. It is hard not to suspect that she was running away from *something*. Tired and hungry, she first tried to sleep in the gardens of a large villa. The gardener, taking pity on this forlorn intruder, gave her enough money to get the train to Cairo and stay a few nights there in a cheap hotel. When the girl got off the train at the city's main station, she would almost immediately have been thrown into the world of Ezbekiyya, already home to most of Cairo's nightclubs, theatres, and dance halls.

To survive in a place like that, Rose had to become tough, capable, and independent. Many potential dangers awaited her there; teenage prostitution was common in Ezbekiyya in the 1910s, and it was one of the few ways a young woman with no family or resources could get by. Yet she spoke very little about what it had been like. Rose's reticence about her early life and the vague stories others told about her may well have hidden something—either from her childhood in Tripoli or her first arrival in Cairo—that she did not want to confront or reveal.

How she landed her backstage job at the theatre, we do not know. But soon after making her dramatic entrance into Egypt's theatre scene dressed as an English queen, Rose was discovered and then mentored by the legendary actor and director Aziz Eid. So, she started her career under the wing of one of the most important and influential men in the rapidly changing world of 1910s Ezbekiyya. This was the age of the revue theatre and vaudeville, which had grown in popularity following the British wartime legislation that led to the closure of Cairo's nightclubs.

Rose's new guide through Cairo's entertainment industry, Aziz Eid, was an almost mythical figure among early twentieth-century Egyptian actors and actresses, famed for his artistic vision and his highly constructed Bohemian persona. In the role of penniless artist, this short, bald man haunted the hash dens of Ezbekiyya, theorising about theatre over his water pipe. He cared little for money and, as a fellow actor recalled, was happy to sleep two in a bed with a friend if it meant he could save enough cash to buy his bedtime hash joint. Playing a martyr to his dramatic ideals, Aziz frequently turned down high-paying jobs if they did not meet his stringent aesthetic criteria.

Rose al-Youssef idolised Aziz Eid. To her, he was a free spirit, "an artist right down to the tips of his fingers," as she later called him. In her view, no one in Egypt had sacrificed as much for his art as Aziz had. He, in turn, took it upon himself to train Rose al-Youssef in the fundamentals of acting: diction, how to hold herself onstage, and how to interact with other characters. He gave Rose her first major role, as the grandmother in an Arabic version of the French play *Martyre!* by Adolphe d'Ennery and Edmond Tarbé. Rose remembered that, although just a teenager, she took the part of the grandmother because none of the other actresses wanted to play an old woman.[3]

After Rose's debut, her career gained momentum in Cairo's wartime theatre scene. In 1915 she began collaborating with Aziz on a new project: introducing contemporary French vaudeville comedy to Egypt. Here, she would get her first taste of fame and everything that came with it, especially for women. This new theatrical experiment took shape just as Cairo's theatre scene teetered on the verge of a huge shake-up: the Franco-Arab revue was about to be born, and Mounira al-Mahdiyya was about to form her new troupe. Aziz decided that it was time to leave behind the tired old classics of European drama and start presenting French vaudeville. For this early attempt, he had selected the work of Georges Feydeau, whose intricately plotted bedroom farces—a sensation on Parisian stages—offered something that few people among the Arabic-speaking public of Cairo had seen.

The first play Aziz chose was *Take Care of Amelie* (*Occupe-toi d'Amelie*). It was a light farce about a sexually liberated young woman, Amelie, and an unusual love rectangle involving her lover Etienne, his friend Marcel, and a Russian prince; much of the action was pre-

sided over by Amelie's snobbish but hapless father. Like the jokes of
this period, the plots of most farces are destroyed by trying to explain
them. Suffice it to say that numerous layers of scheming, subterfuge,
and revenge result in a marriage (which is genuine, though most of the
characters believe it is fake) accompanied by many charges of adultery.

Once the play had been translated into Arabic, Aziz chose Rose al-
Youssef for the starring role. It was a chance for Rose prove her worth
onstage. For their performance venue, Aziz chose an unused open-air
skating rink near the train station that had lots of space and something resembling a stage at one end. With a little creativity, it could
be turned into a theatre—albeit an unorthodox one. For the curtains
and decorations, Aziz bought a large bundle of cheap fabric. Instead of
buying chairs, he let potential audience members know that all those
who did not want to stand for the performance should bring their own.
After christening his makeshift outdoor theatre the Champs Elysées,
Aziz opened it for performances.

Although the first play was not a runaway success, it did well
enough to convince Aziz that putting on more vaudeville in Arabic was
worth the effort. As they entered 1916, the troupe began to push the
boundaries of Egyptian taste. The next Feydeau play that Aziz chose
for translation was *Don't Walk Around Stark Naked* (*Mais n'te promène
donc pas toute nue!*), which had premiered in Paris in 1911. It was a
short, simple farce about an image-obsessed politician whose wife is
constantly embarrassing him in front of journalists and other politicians. With faux naiveté she walks around in her nightgown, stroking
her husband's colleagues on the knee, claiming to be feeling the fabric
of their clothes. At one point she even begs a rival politician to suck a
wasp sting on her arse. As the play goes on, the husband becomes more
and more exasperated. By the end he is convinced that his wife's bad
behaviour has ended his political career.

The action of the play was no more scandalous than other works
by Feydeau, but the title, translated into Egyptian Arabic as *Ya Sitti,*

Ma Tamshish Kida Aryana (Don't walk around naked like that, lady), caused a stir and catapulted Rose al-Youssef to fame. It is easy to suspect that, for all his high-minded ideals, Aziz was inviting controversy with that title, which many took as a literal description of the action. When protests inevitably ran in the press, people got the impression that Rose, the female lead, appeared onstage naked or at least semi-naked, and she became the prime target of attacks. It was her first experience of the kind of hysterical and misdirected criticism that Cairo's new female stars would soon get to know well.

One anonymous woman wrote to the press alleging that Rose appeared onstage in a costume that was more revealing than anything worn by music·hall dancers (who, she added, were also prostitutes). "The French and Egyptians are different," she said, "we have our customs and morals here and they have different ones over there." Some people were so incensed that they called for a boycott of the whole new genre of vaudeville. Rose, for her part, tried to reassure her detractors that she wore a nightgown for the whole performance and was never actually naked or even scantily clad. The people who accused her of appearing in indecent attire had most likely never seen the play.[4]

Still, the outrage was not universal, and a few critics appeared to defend both Rose and this new genre of theatre, arguing that audiences are not damaged by seeing naughty scenes onstage; in fact, one writer reasoned that seeing a scandalous event onstage, and thus being able to identify impropriety, might even do people some good. Vaudeville had, after all, been about in France for almost fifty years, and the French seemed largely unharmed.

Amid the furore, one journalist gave Rose al-Youssef the chance to speak for herself about the play. It was the first time the young actress, still only in her late teens, had spoken directly to the press. She had agreed to the interview because she wanted to "stand up to this onslaught that is trying to sweep away my life." With wounded sarcasm, Rose wondered why she had ever bothered to try to entertain the Egyptian public at all. Piling on the irony, she added that her experience would "serve as a warning to naïve women not to try to bring joy to their audiences." Her critics, she told her interviewer, were not making constructive comments; they were just attacking her. "No one has given me a single comforting word, something to soothe the spirit that lies wounded in my body. I found so little sincere criticism, nor any advice from wise teachers or knowledgeable advisors. Quite the opposite. I have, with few exceptions, found only people exaggerating the play's defects and ignoring its positives." With theatrical disdain, she concluded that they must be "either jealous, spiteful, or bitter."[5]

In the end, the most tangible effect of the controversy—which might have been Aziz's plan all along—was an increase in ticket sales. Rose al-Youssef, for her part in the play, became an overnight celebrity. She even got her own nickname: "the Beautiful Vaudevillian." It had been a heated debate, but she had come through it victorious on many counts and was well on her way to becoming a star.

The next few years saw Rose moving between various troupes, picking up whatever jobs she could. One company she joined was led by the ambitious Okasha brothers, who were famous for both flamboyance and theatrical success if not always for acting. In her memoirs, Rose described the brothers' eccentricity, recalling that they did not believe in rehearsals, so the actors just learned their lines before the performance and hoped for the best. The company's star actress, Victoria Musa, had a problem with her throat that kept her from laughing with any volume. So, Rose claimed, another actress would stand behind the curtain and make laughing noises in the appropriate places.

While part of that theatre company, she faced another attack—not from the audience this time, but from the troupe's main source of funding. Again, the attack involved the clothes she wore—or didn't wear—

and again, she emerged with her dignity intact. In her memoirs, written in the 1950s, Rose looked back on the event triumphantly: One summer day, she remembered, they were in Alexandria doing a series of performances, and the troupe members were taking a break down by the sea. But when Rose got into her swimming costume and went down to where the Nile met the Mediterranean, she was in for a surprise. She did not know that the troupe's main financier, the conservative, nationalist politician and banker Talaat Harb, was also there by the water. A prominent figure in early twentieth-century Egyptian politics and a supporter of the high arts, he is commemorated with a statue that still stands at the centre of one of central Cairo's busiest roundabouts. A financial backer whom no theatrical company wanted to lose, Talaat Harb was also a leading opponent of women's participation in the public sphere. So, when he saw a female member of "his" troupe exposing herself in a bathing suit in front of everyone, he demanded that she immediately cover up or be sacked and sent back to Cairo.

A few of Rose's friends in the troupe tried to mediate. If she just apologised, they told her, they could smooth it over. Rose, undaunted, said that she would not apologise. She had already faced criticism for (allegedly) wearing revealing clothing onstage, and she was not going to back down now. She said that she would rather leave the troupe on the spot so that she could spend the whole day on the beach. And she did exactly that, while the prudish banker looked on. In fact, after leaving the troupe, Rose stayed on a few extra days and sat on the beach in her swimming costume just to annoy him.

In 1923, after over five years as a jobbing actress, Rose got what turned out to be the most important gig of her acting career and also the last—with a newly created troupe called Ramses. Widely touted as a revolutionary new experiment in Egyptian theatre, Ramses was the brainchild of Youssef Wahbi, the ambitious young actor from a wealthy family who had spent his teens avidly exploring Cairo's night-life, boasting of his affairs with the Armenian actress Ihsan Kamel and a succession of Greek chorus girls. Worn down by disapproval of his conservative family, he had left Egypt for Milan in 1919. In the early 1920s he was happily enjoying Italy, studying at the Società Umani-taria, Milan's famous institute for the education and improvement of the dispossessed. He was also finding his way in the Italian theatre, where his colleagues had given him the stage name Ramses, after the ancient Egyptian pharaoh.

This young Egyptian actor might have stayed in Milan indefinitely. He had married Louise Lund, an opera singer from California who was working in the city. He had no pressing reason to return until 1922, when his father, Abdallah Wahbi, died. The elder Wahbi had been a successful engineer and government irrigation inspector in a country whose economy was still largely based on agriculture, and he willed part of his large fortune to Youssef. News travelled quickly among the-atrical circles in Egypt that the ambitious teenager they had known in wartime Cairo had inherited a significant amount of money, and a few enterprising actors hoped he would use it to finance a theatre in newly independent Egypt. Aziz Eid was always on the lookout for some cash to fund his artistic ventures, and he went to Europe to plead the case for theatre. It took a trip to Paris, several long conversations in cafés, and a string of letters sent from Egypt, but he eventually persuaded Youssef to fund the creation of a new venue in Cairo to be called the Ramses Theatre. This would become the most important theatrical event in early-1920s Egypt.

Aziz returned to Cairo while Youssef, by then full of enthusiasm for the venture, stopped off in Italy to buy some costumes before going on to Cairo. In Egypt, Youssef began to prepare his return to the stage. His first task was to find a suitable place for the new theatre. In that search, his family connections helped him out. His brother had recently bought Cairo's distinguished club Ciro's, one of the city's elite dining and dancing venues and an outpost of a famous European restaurant-nightclub chain. Soon after arriving in Cairo, Youssef and his new wife were invited to a costume ball at Ciro's. They took that opportunity to try out the costumes he had brought from Italy; Youssef went as a maharajah and his wife as Aida.

That evening Youssef happened to meet Joseph Adda, a young businessman from another wealthy Egyptian family. Joseph chanced to mention that his father, Abram Adda, owner of the Cinema Radium on Emad al-Din Street, was having a dispute with the current tenants and wanted to find someone else to move in. Youssef lost no time; within a few days, he had agreed to rent not only the cinema but also two large adjoining rooms that could serve as smoking lounges.

Quickly, work began on the new Ramses Theatre. With Youssef's newly inherited wealth, he could make this a state-of-the-art theatre, doing everything possible to distinguish it from the other venues. He even set up a kind of magic lantern device that projected bright images of the cast members on the wall outside the building. At some point, Youssef was so committed to developing the theatre that he installed a revolving stage. Adamant that this new project would help to elevate Egyptian theatrical culture, he set himself the task of reversing the trend of rowdy vaudeville and revue theatre that had dominated most of the past decade. It would involve putting on more respectable plays as well as remoulding the habits of Egyptian audiences. To curb the talking or heckling common during these comedies, Youssef enforced a rule of silence. To keep the theatre clean and tidy, he also prohibited smoking tobacco and eating sunflower and pumpkin seeds—popular snacks in Cairo.

Once the venue had been secured, he collaborated with Aziz Eid to assemble a cast of actors and musicians, as well as create a repertoire of plays. Altogether they recruited seven actresses and fifteen actors. Youssef instituted a strict rehearsal schedule and harshly punished anyone who disobeyed his instructions. He bought a loud bell that could be heard across Emad al-Din Street, and he rang it when rehearsals started so the actors would not waste time sitting in cafés and then claim not to know they were wanted in the theatre. Out of the seven actresses, the undisputed lead was Rose al-Youssef, whose years of moving between different troupes had finally led to a central role in Cairo's most talked-about theatrical company.

In the days leading up to the opening production, Youssef took out adverts in the newspapers to promote "the renaissance of Egyptian Theatre."[6] He made sure to proudly mention that he had trained in Italy with the distinguished actor Amedeo Chiantoni, a star of the Italian stage and father of the film actor Renato Chiantoni. In Cairo, the ability to claim a prominent European mentor gave Youssef a certain kind of credibility. But various Egyptian actors and journalists speculated that his claims were either invented or severely exaggerated. Some people who had never heard of an Italian actor called Chiantoni thought he might be a figment of Youssef's imagination. Many suspected that he had taken self-mythologising a step too far and was claiming unearned prestige.

After all these preparations, Ramses Theatre opened on 10 March 1923 with a play called *The Madman*, written by Youssef himself and starring Youssef and Rose in the central roles. It was a story of insanity, love, and murder, inspired by the gory horror shows Youssef had seen at the Grand Guignol theatre in Paris. The main protagonist, Doctor Rudolf (played by Youssef), escapes from a mental hospital, running off into the stormy night to search for his old lover, Madeleine (played by Rose). Her new husband has gone out to a nightclub and she has been left at home (a plot device to ensure that Rudolf finds her alone, but also an excuse to feature a scene at a Montmartre cabaret). When Doctor Rudolf appears at her house, he sees that Madeleine is petrified; but when he hears the sound of the baby and realises that Madeleine is married to someone else, he relents. He sits down and plays a mournful song on the piano. When Madeleine's husband returns from the cabaret to find Doctor Rudolf in the house, he pulls out a gun and shoots the doctor on the spot. The curtain goes down on this tragic end.

The opening play of the Ramses Theatre's first season was generally well received. Rose al-Youssef's acting won particularly high praise in newspapers and magazines. Critics were happy to see the Beautiful Vaudevillian back in a starring role on the stage after a few years of relative quiet. Many reviewers commented more generally that they did not appreciate the exaggerated, melodramatic style of the play. The slasher-horror aesthetic and the zany storyline were not what people expected from the refinement that Youssef Wahbi had promised; as one observed, "*The Madman* is about as close to artistic theatre as the novel *Tarzan* is to the works of Charles Darwin."[7] But no one questioned the quality of Rose's performance, and most agreed that her moving depiction of Madeleine's hysteria was particularly effective. For the first time since her 1916 appearance in *Don't Walk Around Stark Naked*, Rose's name was all over the press. For a change, it was full of effusive praise; and this was only the beginning.

For the rest of that first season, the Ramses troupe performed eight different plays. Like most Egyptian companies at the time, they did not offer extended runs of a single play but performed all of them in frequent rotation. For Rose, the season was primarily defined not by her portrayal of Madeleine in *The Madman* but by her performance as Marguerite, a successful courtesan who was the main character in a new Arabic translation of Alexandre Dumas's *La Dame aux Camélias*. The play is the tragic story of a prostitute who falls in love with her client, the wealthy Armand, whose condescending father finds out about the relationship and compels her to leave him. The play ends as

Marguerite dies from tuberculosis in Armand's arms, but not before she has told him what his father made her do and insisted that she did it out of love.

Critics and audiences loved Rose al-Youssef's performance. "Her love for Armand was above money, above business, above any crude or shameful materialism," wrote one reviewer. "In the final scene, all the spectators—men or women—got out their handkerchiefs to wash the tears from their eyes," commented another. They particularly admired the way she so accurately replicated the consumptive cough of Marguerite's last days. The Beautiful Vaudevillian had proved that she had the gravitas to act in serious roles too.[8]

What made the critics warm so much to this prostitute from nineteenth-century Paris when they had been so scandalised by Rose's earlier performance in Feydeau's vaudeville? Perhaps it was the respectable veneer of serious drama that made the character acceptable. Youssef Wahbi's new troupe's promise of "artistic" theatre may have polished the rougher edges of this sympathetic demi-mondaine, but other factors may also have helped: Not long before Rose got the part, Sarah Bernhardt—regarded in Egypt at that time as the world's finest actress—had played Marguerite. This gave Rose's portrayal a seal of approval. Moreover, Giuseppe Verdi had adapted the play into the opera *La traviata* (Ramses Theatre had actually bought the play's sets from an Egyptian production of this opera), which may have helped, too. Maybe it was Marguerite's tragic end that allowed the critics and audience to feel sorry for her instead of being threatened by her sexuality. Whatever the reason, Rose al-Youssef's humanising performance of an active courtesan touched the Egyptian public and, along with the other plays of this successful season, helped her shoot back to fame.

Rose herself embraced the character of Marguerite and made it one of her signature roles. Some of the power in her acting may have come from the echoes she saw of her own life. Only a few years before, she had been in a similar situation. In 1917 she had married the comic actor Mohammed Abd al-Quddus, by all accounts a loveable eccentric with an appealing sense of humour and love of acting who never took himself too seriously. "He has some ideas that he is totally convinced of," one article reported. "He insists that there are stars inside the earth and water in the sky. He also has some peculiar theories . . . he says that people on this earth should be like donkeys; anyone who tries to be clever will only get worn out."[9]

However, the relationship did not last long. As other family members recalled, it fell apart because Mohammed's conservative family opposed his marrying an actress—they considered a life onstage a disreputable profession that was not much different from prostitution. By late 1918 the pair divorced while Rose was pregnant. She gave birth on 1 January 1919 to a son, Ihsan Abd al-Quddus. She was a single mother in a world where a steady job or any stability was hard to find, so the young Ihsan was brought up in her husband's family. Although mother and son later became close, and she eventually made him editor of the magazine *Rose al-Youssef,* their early years were largely spent apart.

Despite the tremendous initial success of the Ramses troupe, it did not take long for cracks to appear. Rose, in particular, quickly began to feel the tensions grow. They were partly caused by Youssef Wahbi, whose demeanour and management style did not win him many friends. His personality—and huge ego—could be grating. He swanned around town, acting the young playboy, pretentiously wearing a monocle wherever he went and insisting that people address him by the aristocratic title *bey,* which he could use because his father had been a pasha. He used his family money to buy an expensive new car (he was probably the first Egyptian actor to own a car) that he drove around the city after rehearsals. The rest of the company members, who walked home or took the tram, were resentful.

Youssef may have insisted on a strict regime of discipline during rehearsals and tyrannical control over the company, but Rose started to question his work ethic and felt that he made little effort to learn his own parts. Predictably enough, the pair also argued about money. Members of the troupe accused Youssef of exaggerating how much he had personally spent on the theatre; he wanted to present himself as a martyr to his art but had actually played down the amount of money brought in by ticket sales, it was said. Rose remembered that the actors were asked to make financial sacrifices without receiving much gratitude. She was forced to buy some of the costumes for their production of *La Dame aux Camélias* out of her own pocket and was never reimbursed. For his part, Youssef began to worry that the other actors saw him as a rich dilettante, using "daddy's money" to indulge his hobby— and he may have been right to be concerned.

The second season of the Ramses troupe would be Rose al-Youssef's last. To open the programme, Youssef Wahbi had written a play based on the life of Rasputin. He was inspired, as he asserted in his memoirs, by a chance meeting in 1924 with Prince Felix Yusupov, who claimed to be the Mad Monk's assassin. The encounter took place at an unusual country house party outside London. Youssef was in England to accompany his wife, Louise Lund, who was making her operatic debut on the London stage in Verdi's *Il trovatore*. When he found himself staying under the same roof as Yusupov, he took advantage of the situation. One night, after the prince had drunk several glasses of whisky, Youssef—an actor particularly fond of playing over-the-top villains— mentioned that he had always wanted to play the part of Rasputin and needed some advice for the role. In Youssef's memoirs, which do have a tendency to exaggerate, he said that Yusupov obliged and gave a detailed description of Rasputin's mannerisms and character. Youssef used all this material to produce a graphic version of the story: in one scene, he used a shadow sequence to depict a scene in which Rasputin bathes with a coterie of young women. Even if the scene did push at the boundaries of taste, the public loved it.

There were some other big successes in this season, including a theatrical adaptation of *David Copperfield* and an Arabic translation of Victorien Sardou's *Fedora*, another play made famous by Sarah Bernhardt. Rose, however, was increasingly convinced that the project was losing its way. In her eyes, Youssef was becoming lazy; he was starting to produce plays in colloquial Arabic because those in high classical Arabic required more training and rehearsals. He was pandering to the tastes of the audience rather than leading them, she claimed.

The distrust was mutual. Youssef Wahbi later had his own things to say about Rose al-Youssef: she wanted to control the troupe, she asked for unreasonable pay increases, and she was jealous of him and the other members of the troupe. Some of the players more or less confirmed this claim, saying that Rose always wanted the best roles in every play and got angry if Youssef did not give them to her. In his version of the Ramses troupe's second season, Rose comes across as emotionally unstable and difficult to handle. He recalled one time in Alexandria when an ambulance turned up at the theatre 5 minutes before the curtain call with Rose al-Youssef inside. She had apparently fallen from the corniche and was found lying on the ground in a bad state. After gathering her strength, Rose still managed to perform the lead role in *La Dame aux Camélias* that night. Her speedy recovery suggests that the incident was not as serious as Youssef made out, but he still used it as proof that she had problems with her mental health and hinted that it may have been a suicide attempt. Although neither Youssef nor Rose mention it in their memories of her last season with Ramses, she gave birth to her daughter Amal (the young "hope" who almost gave her name to Rose's magazine) during that time. After her divorce in 1919, she soon married her second husband, Zaki Tolaymat. She continued acting in roles while visibly pregnant with his child.

Rose al-Youssef (photo courtesy of Lucie Ryzova)

In the summer break between theatrical seasons, Rose gave herself a way out of the Ramses troupe by launching *Rose al-Youssef* magazine. In part, the toxic atmosphere building in the company may have pushed her to announce, before the third season had started, that she was leaving the theatre and entering the world of journalism. She began to assemble a team, and the magazine took shape.

The magazine called *Rose al-Youssef* was launched in a crowded market in the mid-1920s. Despite Rose's complaints about the terrible state of dramatic criticism, newspapers were starting to hire theatrical correspondents and run stories about the arts more prominently. In fact, several arts publications had already appeared and disappeared—including a cinematic magazine called *The Weekly Moving Image* and a theatre magazine called *al-Tiyatru*—before Rose started her new magazine. Shortly after her project was launched, many more magazines came along; they included *al-Masrah* (The Theatre) and *al-Mumathil* (The Actor), which, like their earlier rivals, only lasted a few years. The mid-1920s saw a huge boom in these publications full of news, gossip, and photos of celebrities; but starting a magazine like this was no guarantee of success. In many ways, keeping a magazine afloat was similar to running a dramatic troupe—a constant struggle to find an audience, funding, and support.

Rose was working hard even before the first copy of her magazine was in production. Her experience of theatrical publicity served her well: She had posters made to advertise the imminent release of *Rose al-Youssef* and got a group of her colleagues to walk around town attaching them to walls and shop windows. She walked around downtown knocking on doors and trying to solicit subscriptions. Some people were sceptical, concerned that subscribing to the magazine might associate them with the shady world of Emad al-Din Street's theatres and cabarets. When Rose tried to convince a respectable doctor to subscribe, he expressed interest but refused, saying he was nervous about having a "theatrical magazine" delivered to his own house.

Still, Rose was determined that hers would be a serious magazine. For the first issue, she had solicited contributions from some of Egypt's biggest names. The poet, novelist, and literary critic Ibrahim al-Mazini, a rising star in a new generation of Egyptian writers, wrote a short article; the young romantic poet Ahmed Rami, lately returned from studying Persian in Paris, contributed four poems. As theatrical correspondent, Rose recruited a journalist called Mohammed al-Tabai from Egypt's biggest newspaper, *al-Ahram*.

In October 1925, the first issue of *Rose al-Youssef* was finally released. On the cover was a reproduction of Titian's painting *Flora*, accompanied by these words: "In the name of art and good work, here is a new effort." This phrasing may well have been a play on "in the name of God," which is the traditional way to start an Arabic book— in other words, Rose was saying the protector of this new venture was not God, but Art. "Finally, my wish has been realised," Rose wrote to her readers. The magazine included poems, a short story, a theatrical section, and a women's section. She had not followed her husband's suggestion to feature only "high literature." Rose did insist that her writers use a sophisticated literary style and treat her magazine as a serious creative endeavour, not just as a place for gossip and scandal. She had also planned several pieces demonstrating the literary renaissance taking place in the Arab world. She wanted to show that a magazine run by an actress could be important and well respected.[10]

The theatre had given Rose an extraordinary path to acclaim and success. It is hard to imagine that a young girl who had turned up alone in Alexandria at the beginning of the twentieth century could possibly have started her own literary journal in Egypt if she had not found her way into the world of arts and become one of Egypt's biggest stars. But her celebrity did not necessarily come with respect. The doctor who refused his subscription was not the only person to be nervous about being seen in public reading a magazine run by and named after a former vaudeville star. When she was on the tram, Rose saw embarrassed riders hiding her magazine inside other publications so people could not see the cover and would not know they were reading its potentially unseemly content.

At that time, Egyptian women led much more public lives than they ever had before. Helped by Hoda Shaarawi's protests and activism, the country's feminist movement was gaining support, and the work of actresses like Rose herself had created a number of female stars. But very few women had made it into prominent positions in either the country's literary or political world. Rose ended up using her celebrity in the battle for greater female participation in the public sphere. In her memoirs she recalled an atmosphere where a woman "did not have the right to enter public life. Society only accepted her as a second-class citizen, with a veil covering her face." As she was running the magazine, or going to interview leading politicians and public figures, she said she had to fight with men who "considered women as only for pleasure or enjoyment." Rose recalled the day she had approached Abbas al-Aqqad (a prolific poet, writer, and political analyst) about contributing to the magazine; he immediately responded, "I am not working for a newspaper named after a woman" (though she did eventually persuade him).[11]

Rose al-Youssef turned out to be a huge success, but soon the publication that had started in October 1925 as a serious arts, literature, and drama magazine started to expand its scope. Perhaps sensing that readers really wanted to hear the salacious stories of Egyptian society, despite Rose's original noble intentions, the magazine soon started to feature a gossip section. It was dedicated to "publishing both news that is true and news whose truth has not been confirmed, covering important events and trivial events."[12] Gradually the magazine started to write about politics and current affairs too, and included satirical cartoons, both on the cover and inside, that ridiculed leading politicians. Among the varied artists the magazine hired, the most famous was the Armenian cartoonist Alexander Saroukhan, who had trained in Europe and come to Cairo in the mid-1920s. With Rose, he created a little mascot for the magazine called *al-Misri Effendi* (The Egyptian effendi), an everyman character who mocked the absurdity of contemporary political events.

Whether *Rose al-Youssef* was a consistently feminist magazine is not an easy question to answer. In her professional life, Rose certainly did show some commitment to helping her fellow women. In the 1930s she came up with a new kind of distribution plan for the magazine, one that would give women the opportunity for a decent job. She hired fifty female Egyptian distributors to sell *Rose al-Youssef* in streets around the country. She hoped this plan would give work to poor women who were otherwise in domestic service or simply begged on the streets, picking up cigarette butts and gathering the tobacco to roll a new cigarette. She may have been too optimistic: despite her worthy aspirations, the scheme did not succeed. After the women were harassed on the street by young men, Rose had to put an end to the plan. Still, when she looked back on this time through the lens of the 1950s, Rose was able to think positively about it as a small step to advancing women's employment. When female lottery ticket sellers started to appear on the streets of Egypt, she thought her own small venture may have helped a bit to encourage women to work outside the home.

In the offices of *Rose al-Youssef*, however, the staff were always overwhelmingly male. Rose was used to being surrounded with men and always projected a tough exterior. When women did occasionally come through the office, she warned them not to show too much emotion or the men would not take them seriously. When one young woman who was new at *Rose al-Youssef* started crying after some particularly harsh criticism, Rose took her aside and warned her:

> This is the last time I want to see you cry in front of those men. If you do, they will all try to calm you down, hold your hand or put their hand on your shoulder. They will see you as just an ordinary girl not a strong woman, with personality and courage, who is no less than any of them.[13]

Some people thought that adapting herself to this male environment had made Rose manly, but she vehemently disagreed. In 1956, when the journalist Kamil al-Shinawi wrote an article for *Rose al-Youssef* stating that she was more like a man than a woman, she responded angrily: "No, I am not a man nor do I wish to be. I am a woman who is proud to be a woman and the problem with our press is that there are too many men in it." When her own son, Ihsan, told her that he thought a woman's place was in the home, she asked him if he thought *her* place was in the home. He laughed and said, "Mum, you're a man." No, she retorted, adding, "If I were not a woman, I'd want to be one."[14]

The magazine's content only raises further complications. In its early days, *Rose al-Youssef* promoted a staunchly feminist agenda. In the women's section, one of the earliest articles called for female participation in the workplace: "Why don't you work as your European sister has been doing for a long time and as your Turkish *abla* ["older sister"] has just started doing? The doors of employment lie open before you." One of Rose's own editorials called on the government to support and train actresses as it had been doing with their male counterparts for years. "Theatre cannot thrive with only one wing," she concluded, referring to the disparity of support given to one gender over the other.[15]

But as the years passed, some of these messages were diluted, even contradicted, perhaps because Rose was taking a less active role in the day-to-day running of the magazine; for example, in 1926 Rose went to Paris for a few years to stay with her husband Zaki Tolaymat, who was training at the Comédie Française. Because of Rose's apparent unwillingness to talk about her private life and partners in her memoirs, she left behind little record of her life in that period. We do know that she kept in touch with the editors through long weekly letters, but they might not have been enough to exert her influence. Or perhaps she had begun to accommodate her message to the views of conservative readers. Either way, the content gradually became less progressive, at times even attacking or undermining the idea of female power.

Throughout Egypt, people were unsure how to deal with a new generation of increasingly liberated women. The cartoonists employed by *Rose al-Youssef* often took to mockery and misrepresentation. Caricatures appeared showing Egypt's "new woman" scantily clad, out of control, and devoted to pleasure. One cover of *Rose al-Youssef* from the late 1920s satirically depicted the "three principles of the women's revolution: Liberty, Equality and Brotherhood." Above the word *brotherhood* (we should perhaps say "sisterhood"), two women were shown fighting; above *equality*, a woman pulled a man on a leash; above *liberty*, a woman in a short skirt was dancing and smoking. Another, depicting the perceived new sexual mores of the age, showed couples kissing and canoodling in front of the pyramids; one woman holds a bunch of grapes as a man fondles her naked breasts from behind. The caption below it says, sarcastically, "forty centuries look down on you from the pyramids."[16] These covers might seem to be supporting a permissive society, but they were intended as warnings about a dystopian future of women out of control.

Written contributions in a similar vein sometimes appeared inside the magazine as well. One issue included an extended letter from a reader praising the Nizam of Hyderabad for forbidding Muslim women from appearing on the stage—hardly in step with Rose's earlier editorial in support of actresses. Having a woman at the head of the magazine did not mean that the content was always feminist.

Over time, the magazine developed in other ways. Before leaving for Paris, Rose had told her fellow journalists that the magazine ought to become more involved in Egypt's political life. In her absence the publication began to take some bold stances that often got it into trouble, facing censorship and even official raids on its offices. Egyptian politics in the 1920s were unstable, full of scandal, and fraught with power struggles. In 1928 King Fouad stepped in to dissolve the parliament and appoint a new prime minister. The editors at *Rose al-Youssef* were incensed by what they saw as an attempt to frustrate the country's democracy. So, they quickly arranged for a cartoon showing the new leader of parliament, Mohammed Mahmoud, treading on the constitution as he ascended the throne (symbolising power rather than an explicit attack on the monarchy). The authorities felt the magazine had gone too far; they had the police raid the printer's office and confiscate 20,000 copies as well as the printing block of the cartoon itself.

After a while, the staff at *Rose al-Youssef* became used to events of this kind. Rose calculated that between October 1927 and October 1929, of the 104 issues that should have appeared, 62 were banned and 42 published (this accounting was affected in part by a government order to suspend publication for four months). After returning from Paris, Rose often stood trial alongside her editors. During the 1920s and 1930s, in an attempt to avoid scrutiny, she even set up magazines with different names but similar content. In 1936, after a particularly rough search of the magazine's offices, Rose al-Youssef protested that the authorities were abusing their power. In response, the police claimed that she was obstructing their search; they took her into the station and then ordered her to spend a night in a women's prison, surrounded by what she took to be murderers, thieves, and drug dealers.

Even when the magazine was becoming more and more politicised, it did not forget its theatrical past, and Rose claimed she still wanted to promote the advancement of Egyptian theatre. In 1931 she got a chance to prove it. The previous year a group of veteran actors, including Zaki Tolaymat, had set up a theatrical institute in Egypt. They had hired some of the most prestigious scholars in the country to teach there, including the dean of arts at Cairo University, Taha Hussein, who had a PhD from the Sorbonne. To teach "rhythmic dance," they had hired a woman named Mounira Sabry, a staunch proponent of the Girl Guide Movement who had studied at the Chelsea College of Physical Education in England. The choice of teachers demonstrated the school's mission—it was to be an elite training academy, endorsed by the country's most respected intellectuals, mostly with European training.

Yet around the end of the institute's first year, complaints began to flood in. The objections were explicitly religious. The head sheikh of al-Azhar, Egypt's oldest and most respected Islamic institution, had complained about the mixing between men and women. In particular, the rhythmic dance classes seemed to him like a step too far. Egypt's education minister at the time, Hilmi Isa, bowed to pressure and closed the academy. Rose al-Youssef, through *al-Sarkha*, one of the magazines she had set up to dodge censorship, confronted the minister. She declared the decision to close the place down ridiculous and launched a personal campaign against Hilmi Isa himself, sarcastically dubbing him "the Minister for Morals."[17] In the end, her *al-Sarkha* tirade was not enough to save the institute; but Rose had not forgotten the theatrical world that she had come from and supported the battles still being fought.

By the 1940s Rose felt that her time as an editor had run its course. Her son from her first marriage, Ihsan Abd al-Quddus, was an aspiring writer himself. In 1945 she commissioned him to write an article for the magazine, in which he sharply criticised the British ambassador to Egypt, Miles Lampson. Shortly after the article was published, Ihsan was briefly jailed and the issue was banned. After Ihsan's experience, one so familiar to Rose, she finally deemed him ready to continue her mission. As soon as he got out of jail, Rose appointed him editor in chief at *Rose al-Youssef* and retired after twenty years in charge and some thirty years of fame. In a letter explaining his new role, she gave him some pieces of advice:

> However big and famous you get, don't give way to conceit. Conceit is deadly.
> However much you advance in years, don't let old age obscure your thinking . . . always be young in thought, heart, and affection.
> Fight oppression, wherever it is, and always be on the side of the weak against the powerful. Never ask the cost.

Finally, she told him:

> Now let your mother rest . . . a little.[18]

Rose al-Youssef had arrived in Cairo, penniless and alone, in the early twentieth century. She went from a vaudeville actress to the editor of a major political magazine still published in Egypt today. She made her name in the theatre and then managed to carve out space for herself amid the difficult politics of interwar Egypt. After stepping back from the helm of her magazine in 1945, she began work on her memoirs, which were published in 1953.

A friend remembered one of the last times he saw Rose—it was in the Ezbekiyya Gardens theatre, where she often went in the weeks before her death. She sat next to him for a while before suddenly saying, "I saw death for the first time in this theatre." She went on to explain that, many years before when she had still been an actress, she had heard the man who pulled up the curtain for the show let out a strange cry. Her theatrical company had all rushed over to him, and someone reported that he had died. Rose had not been able to believe it: "How can someone who lives with us, talks to us, walks about in front of us . . . just die?"[19]

One day in April 1958, Rose al-Youssef went out to see a film. During the showing she had a heart attack, but she did not complain, nor did she rush to the hospital. She calmly stood up, said she wanted to leave the cinema, and hailed a taxi to take her back home. There, she climbed the stairs, put on her nightclothes, climbed into bed, and died that night.[20]

Chapter 6

SARAH BERNHARDT
OF THE EAST

A T THE TURN OF the twentieth century, the French actress Sarah
Bernhardt was probably the biggest star in the world. Her eccentric behaviour—which included sleeping in a coffin, kissing skeletons when journalists came to interview her, and keeping a menagerie of exotic animals including lions, tigers, and snakes—won her many admirers. Oscar Wilde wrote the play *Salome* with her in mind; Marcel Proust based the character of La Berma in *À la recherche du temps perdu* (*In Search of Lost Time*) on her; when she was acting the role of Hamlet, Victor Hugo gave her a real human skull, inscribed with some lines of verse. She kept the skull on prominent display in her house, and it is now held at the Victoria and Albert Museum in London. Her acting skill, combined with a gift for self-presentation, made her "the godmother of modern celebrity culture."[1] Many female stars of the twentieth century followed, whether consciously or not, a model created by Bernhardt.

Bernhardt mania spread through Egypt, just as it did across the world, and the public there idolised her as much as anyone else. But Cairo's devoted "Bernhardtisans" had just two chances to see her perform live. The first was in the winter of 1888–1889 when, after arriving in late December from Istanbul, she performed a series of her signature plays at the Cairo Opera House, which had been built by the Khedive Ismail a couple of decades earlier. When the actor George Abyad was training in Paris on a scholarship from the Egyptian government in 1904, he managed to meet Sarah Bernhardt in her dressing room and tell her that Egyptians were still talking about her performances that winter season fifteen years earlier.

Bernhardt's second appearance in Cairo, in November 1908, had even more effect on the world of Egyptian theatre. Although she was suffering from a leg injury sustained in 1906, her performance was ecstatically received. (The injured right leg troubled her until she finally had it amputated in 1915, claiming her surgery was an example to the men in the trenches.) On that second trip, Bernhardt told the newspapers in Egypt that she was struck by how much more enthusiastic the Egyptian public were now than they had been twenty years earlier. Her shows were all sell-outs; an extra night was added to cope with demand, and soldiers were brought in to manage the crowds. A few Egyptian actors, who could not afford the tickets, managed to get in by working as extras in her company. Among these enterprising fans was a young Aziz Eid, who went on to mentor Rose al-Youssef and dominate Egyptian theatrical life in the '20s. Aziz later remembered the displays of devotion that followed Sarah Bernhardt wherever she went. After one performance, a huge crowd of her admirers thronged around the stage door, throwing flowers at her feet. Then, as she got into her carriage to go home, a team of starstruck young Egyptians detached the horse and started to pull it themselves. They dragged the carriage all the way to her room at Shepheard's, one of Cairo's grandest hotels.

The nickname of "Sarah Bernhardt of the East" was one of the biggest compliments Egypt's newspapers could bestow on an actress. In the 1910s, the sobriquet had been given to Milia Dayan, the principal actress in Sheikh Salama Higazi's troupe. In the early years of the next decade, Rose al-Youssef won the accolade after her starring performance in a Sarah Bernhardt classic: *La Dame aux Camélias*. When Rose quit acting in 1925, Youssef Wahbi's troupe got a new prima donna, and Egypt soon got a new Sarah Bernhardt: Fatima Rushdi. In the second half of the 1920s, Fatima Rushdi became the newest theatrical superstar in the generation of actors and actresses who had grown up on the stages of Cairo's post-war revue theatres and music halls. After a short and successful spell as the leading actress in Youssef Wahbi's Ramses troupe, Fatima left to form and run a theatrical troupe of her own. Within a year, she was already challenging her old troupe for dominance of Cairo's nightlife; by the early 1930s she was one of the most famous actresses in the entire Arab world and the permanent holder of the title Sarah Bernhardt of the East.

Fatima's route to stardom was not easy. The youngest of four sisters, she was born in Alexandria in 1908 to an Egyptian mother and a father who died when she was just a child—that much is fairly certain. Beyond that, however, things become less clear. In one version of her life story (in the ten years between 1961 and 1971, four different versions of her memoirs appeared), she says that her father had been an Ottoman army officer from the Balkans; he had been forced to flee to Egypt in the early twentieth century because of his links to the revolutionary Young Turk movement and close relationship to its leaders Enver Pasha, Niyazi Bey, and Mustafa Kemal Ataturk. In Alexandria, Fatima's father set up a successful confectionary business, importing sweets from Istanbul. Her mother's side was equally grand. Her grandmother had been lady-in-waiting to one of the Khedive Ismail's wives and had developed a love of high culture in the palace when accompanying her mistress to theatrical performances at the Opera House.

When her father suddenly died, Fatima's comfortable life was disrupted forever. The family lost whatever money they had, and Fatima's mother and her four daughters were left to survive in 1910s Alexandria with nothing. Life for a poor, all-female family at that time would have been hard. Instead of menial labour, crime, and prostitution, which were some of the main ways to make ends meet, the Rushdi sisters—in descending order of age, Aziza, Ratiba, Insaf, and Fatima—chose the life of the stage. Insaf was the first to find a job—as a singer in Alexandria, playing cafés and theatres around the city. Fatima, at the age of nine, followed her sister, who could only have been in her early teens at most, into the business.

Around 1920, as Fatima and Insaf were performing in the cafés and theatres of Alexandria, they were spotted by Sayyid Darwish, one of Egypt's most celebrated musicians. He had already composed the tunes to some of Egypt's most popular songs of the twentieth century, including one that eventually became the country's national anthem. In the aftermath of the 1919 revolution, he had captured the anticolonial spirit in songs like "Stand Up Egyptians" and "Long Live Justice." Besides his song writing, Sayyid was also infamous for his unorthodox working habits—according to Rose al-Youssef's memoirs, he could compose music only after taking a cocktail of several drugs. She remembered that Aziz Eid once spent twenty days following Sayyid through the cafés and bars of Cairo with a large supply of hashish and opium, taking notes as the illustrious composer came up with hit new tunes in a narcotic haze.

On that night in Alexandria, when Sayyid Darwish saw Fatima and her sister perform, he was impressed. As luck would have it, he had just formed a theatrical troupe of his own in Cairo and needed some singers. He told their mother that if the family came to Cairo, he would have a place for the girls. To prove that he was serious, he advanced them 10 Egyptian pounds. With that money, the family took a train to Cairo and checked into a hotel on Clot Bey Street, among the brothels of Ezbekiyya's red-light district. But just days after the family arrived, Sayyid Darwish's vaunted troupe folded and their only

source of income vanished. Sayyid's own star did not shine much longer, either—his lifestyle quickly caught up with him, and he died of
a heart attack in 1923 at only thirty-one years of age. Rumours still
abound regarding what caused his death: some say, with good reason, that it was the result of a cocaine overdose; others allege that the
British, threatened by his popularity and his politics, poisoned him;
in 1927, an article published in the Egyptian press suggested that he
may have committed suicide. Sayyid Darwish's songs and persona are
still so iconic that in 2017, an Egyptian lawyer requested that his body
be exhumed and tested to determine the cause of death. As yet, this
request has not been granted.

For the Rushdi sisters, the early years of the 1920s were difficult.
After the demise of Sayyid Darwish's troupe, they spent a few months
in Naguib al-Rihani's Franco-Arab revue, which was riding high on
the success of his character Kish-Kish Bey—the fast-living village
mayor. But that job, too, soon vanished. Naguib al-Rihani helped the
sisters by putting them in touch with a troupe in Port Said, on the Suez
Canal, that was looking for performers; the unknown young singers
had little choice but to join. However, once they had arrived in the
city, the sisters discovered that the troupe Naguib al-Rihani had found
for them was not a theatrical or a musical company; it was a circus.
On the first night, Fatima and Insaf went out together into the ring,
only to find themselves surrounded by a rabble of audience members.
It was a terrible setup for any sort of musical performance. No matter
which way the two girls turned, part of the audience was behind them
complaining that they could not hear the songs. The girls tried to spin
around as they sang; but that only made them dizzy. They collapsed
on the floor, succumbing to a fit of giggles (by then they were barely
into their teens). Seeing his two singers lying there on the floor, the
ringmaster sent out a burly young wrestler who walked into the circus
sands, picked up one sister in each arm, and threw them to the side of
the ring. Their experiment in the circus came to an ignominious end

and, immediately after the show, their mother used up the last of their fee to take a late-night train back to Cairo.

For the next few years, the sisters kept their family afloat by performing in various cabarets about town. Fatima worked as a singer, specialising in monologues and *taqtuqas*. She started in the Monte Carlo dance hall in the suburban entertainment district of Rod al-Farag, a smaller and less prestigious version of Ezbekiyya. The area was popular with many Egyptians but lacked some of the glamour of the nightlife district in the heart of Cairo. Fatima next graduated to the famous Bosphore Casino, past the end of Emad al-Din Street near the train station—a step up, as the casino was starting to attract the stars of Egyptian popular music. Fatima's three older sisters were also making their way in Ezbekiyya's nightlife as dancers, singers, and actors. All four women were working the city's stages, and the performing Rushdi family was treated as a fascinating curiosity in the entertainment press. Strangely, Fatima's memoirs barely mention her sisters, focusing instead almost exclusively on her own career and rise to fame.

Throughout her early career, Fatima recalled, her real goal was to move from singing in nightclubs to acting on the stage or in the cinema. She used to come up with ideas for film scripts in her head and dreamed of giving herself the starring role. But, with little education to speak of, she could neither read nor write. So she went to the cafés and bars of Ezbekiyya, trying to find people who could write out her scripts. At one of these places in the early '20s, she first met Aziz Eid, the bohemian actor and director who had recently taken it upon himself to train Rose al-Youssef.

Aziz, then in his late thirties, immediately found a new protégée in this young teenager who came in and out of the cafés of Ezbekiyya.

Their relationship quickly became a Pygmalion story (with all the problems inherent in that tale): He taught Fatima to read and write, even sending her to lessons with a sheikh to learn the Quran and perfect her classical Arabic grammar and pronunciation. He also helped her enter the world of respectable drama, giving her a small part in a play he was putting on: *The Red Village*, a morality tale about the greedy, venal *omda* of a small rural village who tyrannised and exploited its residents, enriching himself from their suffering. Aziz took the part of the *omda* and asked Fatima to play a young girl from the village—one of the targets of his lust.

Fatima's first appearance in a play was a nerve-wracking experience, and her mother waited in the wings for support. When Fatima's moment came, Aziz Eid, playing the lecherous village mayor, started to bear down on her. His performance was too believable, and Fatima forgot that it was all just a drama; ignoring the audience, she cried out in terror and ran offstage into her mother's arms. The curtain was quickly lowered as Fatima's furious mother shouted at Aziz, calling him crazy and accusing him of scaring her daughter. Aziz tried to explain that it was all just acting, but this did nothing to calm her anger.

In her memoirs, Fatima told this story as an almost comic debacle; but it is hard to escape the feeling that something darker lay beneath and that her mother's suspicions may have been more correct than she knew. After Fatima's calamitous debut, Aziz continued to act as her patron in earnest, working to educate her and shape her acting talent. He took her out to see different shows that played around Cairo: touring European plays, performances by Arabic troupes, and Cairo's most popular nightclub singers. Then in 1923, when Aziz joined Youssef Wahbi's newly formed Ramses troupe featuring Rose al-Youssef as its prima donna, he brought the teenage Fatima with him to play a series of minor roles in the opening season and continued moulding her into his vision of a leading lady.

For two seasons, Fatima developed her craft. She improved her classical Arabic, which was the language of most of the plays, and watched performances around Cairo, always picking up tips. She also turned to Hollywood for inspiration, modelling her style on the famous American actress Pearl White—perhaps the best-known silent movie actress of the early twentieth century—who had starred in the popular silent film serials *The Perils of Pauline* and *The Exploits of Elaine*. As she sat in the cinemas of Ezbekiyya, Fatima especially admired the American star for the courage and strength she showed on-screen and tried to emulate those traits in the small roles she was being given in the Ramses troupe.

If anyone had suspicions about Aziz Eid's long-lived interest in mentoring teenage girls, their suspicions would have been confirmed when, in February 1924, he announced that he had converted to Islam from Christianity and would marry Fatima (under traditional Islamic law, Muslim women cannot marry non-Muslim men). She had recently turned sixteen; Aziz was forty. Within a year Fatima had given birth to their daughter Aziza and, in March 1925, she returned to the stage. She starred in an Arabic adaptation of Henri Bataille's *La Possession* (a romantic melodrama about a high-living woman who goes through a series of relationships with predatory men while managing to support her lavish lifestyle, but eventually drives her true love to suicide). Gossip about Fatima and Aziz's marriage filled the press; even the imam who conducted the ceremony was rather put off by the age difference. Few journalists gave much thought to Fatima's wishes in the affair. One newspaper article saw the whole thing as just another sign of the depravity of the theatrical scene—and of actresses in particular, whom the writer implied were dangerously seductive. Aziz Eid, in the writer's view, had cheapened both the words and spirit of Islam by converting simply out of lust for his young pupil.

Fatima's mother was nervous. Not only was Aziz Eid so much older, but he had basically no money to his name and didn't seem to care about making any. When Fatima confronted Aziz with her mother's accusation that he was poor and idle, he was defensive and perhaps a little conceited. "I am not an ordinary person," he told her. "Normal people divide their thoughts between lots of things: their work, their house, their future, their income and expenses. I only think about one thing: the theatre." Fatima was apparently satisfied with that response, though her mother continued to oppose the match even after their marriage.[2]

The unequal balance of power in this relationship is striking. Although Fatima's own memories of Aziz Eid, even after his death, were always positive, simply reading between the lines of the story of their marriage suggests a more disturbing version of events: an influential man promises career advancement to a much younger and aspiring actress in return for sex, possibly coercing her in a variety of ways.

Fatima was explicit about the predatory behaviour of other men at the time. The reality for young female performers in Cairo in the 1920s was typically full of what may euphemistically be called unwanted sexual advances, but could as easily be described as rape. Growing up as a performer on the stages of Rod al-Farag and Ezbekiyya, Fatima had been a sexual target from a very young age. In her memoirs, she recalled one night when she was walking home on Emad al-Din Street after a performance. She was alone on the street when two men came up to her and tried to abduct her in their car. Fortunately, she was saved when one of her fellow actors saw what was going on and came over to protect her. When Fatima was only fourteen, the aristocratic dandy Ali Fahmy, claiming to be in love with her, is said to have approached her mother. He offered a dowry of 4,000 Egyptian pounds and asked for Fatima's hand in marriage, which Fatima's mother refused. A few years later, Fahmy married the French socialite-courtesan and former lover of Edward VIII, Marguerite Alibert (it was not a happy marriage; Marguerite shot Ali Fahmy dead in a room at the Savoy Hotel in the summer of 1923, creating one of Egypt's biggest scandals of the decade).

In the summer of 1925, Fatima's career took a huge turn. The two-year-old Ramses troupe faced a crisis when its main star, Rose al-Youssef, left to start her new magazine. With no obvious lead actresses in the troupe, the women took turns in the starring roles during the 1925–1926 season. For the first time, the young Fatima was given the lead female part in a play: as Panthasilea, the love interest in an Arabic translation of *The Tyrant*, by Rafael Sabatini (a relatively obscure work first published in Britain in 1925 and based on a story from the life of Cesare Borgia). In Cairo the play became famous for a scene in which Fatima shared a long onstage kiss with Youssef Wahbi, who played Cesare Borgia. That scene was such a hit with the audience that Youssef made a short film of the kiss; unnervingly, he would play it on a large screen during the intervals at his shows.

For the next two seasons, Fatima cemented her position as one of Egypt's most dynamic new actresses. One woman's principled departure became another woman's opportunity. Fatima played the lead roles in plays made famous by Sarah Bernhardt: Marguerite in *La Dame aux Camélias*, or Napoleon II in an Arabic version of *L'Aiglon*. She took the title Sarah Bernhardt of the East away from Rose, who had held it for several years. A new star of Egyptian theatre had arrived.

Nobody was quite sure what to make of this apparently confident and self-assured young girl, who was now being thrown into the limelight, playing roles normally reserved for more experienced actresses. She had little time for the strictures and niceties of Egyptian society, and one contemporary remembered her as "a creature of fire and flame."[3] Some said she was flirtatious, saying that she told everyone she loved them and called her favourites by the affectionate diminutive "Toutou." Others said she was wild and unruly. Once, when she happened to meet a critic who had given her a bad review, she took off her shoe and threw it at him across the crowded street. The papers told stories of her staying at elite hotels and confusing the European waiters by asking them to bring her some fatty, low-class Egyptian food that they had never heard of, like *mumbar*, a spiced sausage served in cow's intestines. Growing up poor in Alexandria and then on the cabaret stages of Cairo, Fatima had quickly shed any affectations; many habitués of Ezbekiyya were taken aback by her bluntness and apparent fearlessness.

Some observers interpreted all this as evidence of a vulgar and coarse nature, accusing her of being dangerously masculine. For them, Fatima was the figurehead of a new generation of women that had given up on traditional femininity. One journalist lamented that "men have become women and women have become men," justifying his statement with a pointed barb at Fatima: "How can I deny it when I see Fatima Rushdi acting so manly?" Some people were so committed to this judgement that they even claimed her depiction of Napoleon II in *L'Aiglon* was "excessively manly" (bizarrely, as the character *was* a man).[4]

The comments were not always criticisms of the way she played particular roles; sometimes they were about Fatima's private life. When she attended the funeral of a prompter in the Ramses troupe, instead of weeping and mourning with the women, she insisted on following behind the bier and then going to drink coffee in the funeral tent with the men. A confused journalist commented, "How strange Fatima is, always doing something odd. What a real man!" In one interview, when Fatima had invited a reporter into her house to talk about her career, he bluntly said to her: "They say that you behave like a man . . . though you are a woman you may actually be tougher than a man. . . . They say that you don't have any emotions, you don't have the feelings of a woman, feminine delicacy or gentleness. . . . What do you think about that?" She just laughed—Fatima was not afraid to answer these kinds of questions. "I don't have time for stupid things like this. I do absolutely everything that a woman should do. . . . My mind is constantly working, my body is heavy and worn out. My ambitions are greater than my mind and stronger than my body. I don't have time to do all I need and at the same time flaunt my femininity. What do they want from me? . . . What do they even mean by femininity? How do they want a woman to live?"[5]

From 1925 until 1927 Fatima spent two lucrative seasons with Youssef Wahbi's Ramses troupe. During that period, she and her husband Aziz had made enough money to move into Youssef Wahbi's old villa on what is now Champollion Street, in walking distance of Emad al-Din Street. But nothing in the Egyptian dramatic world was certain, especially not at the Ramses Theatre. As Rose al-Youssef had before her, Fatima soon became disenchanted with the company. Arguments between actors about roles heated up, and at a 1927 performance of *L'Aiglon* at the Kursaal music hall, Fatima finally broke. During the emotional final death scene, she heard her fellow actors in the wings chatting and laughing while she was performing. As soon as the play ended, the magazine *Rose al-Youssef* reported, Fatima rushed backstage and told everyone that if anyone "old or young, man or woman" laughed when she was onstage, she would punch them. Then she stormed into Youssef Wahbi's dressing room and, if his story is to be believed, called him a "son of a whore," then tried to punch him too.[6]

That summer, Fatima decided it was time to leave the troupe. Taking Aziz with her, she set up her own theatrical company to compete with Ramses. Her company was to be known, simply, as Fatima Rushdi's troupe; it would put on the plays she chose, in the way she decided, and give her the roles she wanted. With Aziz as artistic director, the two of them hired the actors and actresses, including the charismatic veteran Salha Kasin, whom Fatima convinced to join the troupe by paying a visit to her house at 2:00 a.m. In the final years of the 1920s, Cairo's theatre would be dominated by the battle between Fatima's new troupe and the Ramses troupe that she had left behind.

Before her company could put on any plays, Fatima had to face the battle of raising the money needed to set up a new company (paying actors, hiring theatres, buying costumes, etc.). Aziz was from a middle-class family—not poor, but not wealthy either—and thanks to his life-style had no savings and little disposable cash. To raise the money for their first production, Fatima and Aziz pawned their villa's elegant furniture. Fatima, no doubt intent on cementing her reputation as Egypt's Sarah Bernhardt, decided to herald the debut of her troupe with an Arabic version of another play made famous by the French superstar: *Adrienne Lecouvreur*, a heavily fictionalised tragedy about a real, historical eighteenth-century French actress and her love affair with the count of Saxony.

Without a permanent artistic home, the couple was forced to put on a series of stand-alone performances across several different venues in Cairo and Alexandria. In the theatres and music halls that were not burdened with Youssef Wahbi's strict rules of decorum, audiences were unafraid to air their opinions about the plays. In the Majestic Theatre on Emad al-Din Street, usually home to Ali al-Kassar's comic revue, Fatima's troupe staged a chaste dramatic interpretation of *L'Aiglon* in high classical Arabic. When the audience turned up, they did not expect to see such an earnest performance. People shouted from their seats, "We don't understand what you're saying," then called, "We want singing" and "We want dancing." Aziz Eid was so irritated by the hecklers that he came onstage to tell them off. "What do you want then? A circus? You want acrobats? . . . This is refined theatre. If you don't like it you can leave." But the audience members continued to protest until the police had to escort Fatima's troupe out of the theatre.[7]

Money troubles were chronic, and rumours that the troupe was on the verge of bankruptcy appeared in newspapers as early as July, just months after the company had formed. But their luck changed one day in August 1927, when Fatima went out for dinner at an elite Cairo club with some visiting friends from Alexandria. At the club, Fatima's friends noticed the wealthy cotton trader Elie Edrei sitting at a nearby table. Elie and his brother Clement owned one of the largest private cotton plants in the Nile Delta, consisting of 64 gins and two hydraulic presses. He had another brother, Max Edrei, a famous architect who had designed many iconic buildings around Egypt. Max had also recently been part of the team that designed the French memorial for the fallen at the Battle of Verdun in World War I, the strikingly phallic Douaumont Ossuary. Elie was known all over Cairo for his extravagant spending and love of the theatre (particularly the women who worked in it). Fatima's friends, who had been hearing all about her money problems, also happened to know him and spotted an opportunity. They called him over to their table and started chatting, hoping that he might be persuaded to spend a little money on Fatima's new venture.

Their plan was more successful than they could have imagined. He sat down next to Fatima, ordered her a fruit salad (she had rejected a glass of wine), and listened to her talk about the struggles of starting a dramatic troupe. Impressed by her ambition, her hard work, and, no doubt, her looks, Elie decided that he wanted to help this energetic young actress. He suggested that she come for tea at Shepheard's Hotel at 11 o'clock the next morning. When Fatima got home that night, she was excited about the next day's plans. Then, she opened her handbag to find that he had secretly slipped into it a wad of 400 Egyptian pounds (almost £25,000 in modern terms) and was even more excited.

The next morning, Fatima went to meet Elie at Shepheard's Hotel. Over tea they discussed the theatre and her new troupe (Elie suggested including a few comedies in the repertoire because audiences liked them). After the tea, he took her to Madame Rita's boutique, the most fashionable dress shop in Cairo, where he bought her a new handbag and several dresses. Next they went to the bank, where Elie opened an account in her name and deposited a large sum of money, telling her to use it to make her art. In her memoirs Fatima said he gave the troupe 10,000 Egyptian pounds, but a report in *Rose al-Youssef* from 1927 put it rather lower at 4,000 pounds (still close to £250,000 in today's money).

With this unexpected windfall, Fatima and Aziz suddenly had enough money to put on an impressive theatrical season and truly compete with Youssef Wahbi's Ramses troupe. Fatima brought in nine actresses and twenty-one actors to be part of the troupe. The company could pay for the best venues, best costumes, best decor, and best new translations. The troupe's adverts announced that they had imported over five thousand costumes from a tailor's shop in Milan. Aziz Eid, who had a reputation for lavish scene staging, went wild with this new-found money. In one desert-themed play, he filled the stage with real sand; in another play, set in ancient Egypt, he constructed an entire mudbrick fort.

The rivalry between Fatima's troupe and Youssef Wahbi's Ramses troupe dominated the Cairo theatre scene. Their companies were sometimes known to compete for audiences directly by offering the same plays on the same night. The repertoires of both troupes included European classics, as Egyptian theatre had for decades—Fatima, for instance, did versions of two Sarah Bernhardt plays, *La Dame aux Camélias* and *L'Aiglon*, and Youssef did Shakespeare's *Julius Caesar* and Alexandre Dumas' *Princess of Baghdad*. In the late 1920s, demand grew for new plays with more Middle Eastern themes to reflect Egypt's newly independent spirit. Both theatre troupes put on original plays, as well as reworkings of old stories, to appeal to the public's desires— Fatima collaborated with the Turkish writer and filmmaker Vedad Urfy (Vedat Örfi) to put on a series of historical plays, one about the Ottoman Sultan Abdel Hamid, one about Mehmet the Conqueror, and one evocatively titled *Byzantium City of Blood*. Youssef's offerings had a more Egyptian focus—*Shajarat al-Durr*, a historical drama about a thirteenth-century female ruler of Egypt, and a theatrical adaptation of the Arabic epic of Antar ibn Shaddad, which had both been written by contemporary Egyptian writers. At the end of her first season, Fatima, confident that she was winning the battle, ostentatiously told Youssef that if his troupe was having problems, he was welcome to join hers. She would pay him 40 Egyptian pounds a month; but he would not be her leading man, as that position was already taken.[8]

Elie's money had saved Fatima's troupe, but it came at a price. Fatima's marriage to Aziz quickly fell apart as rumours spread that she was having an affair with her new funder. Aziz, it seems, could not bear the tension and jealousy. Fatima's later accounts of that period are often a little reticent about her relationship with Elie—not exactly saying they were more than close friends—but in one set of memoirs, published in Beirut, she more explicitly admits that their relationship was sexual. In reading between the lines of all the stories, it seems hard to believe Elie was motivated by love of theatre alone. Newspapers at the time certainly believed the two were lovers and published frequent articles about their relationship, mentioning the trips she took to his country estate, the lunches they had, and the time he spent in her dressing room after shows.

Surprisingly, after Fatima and Aziz separated (it is a little unclear when they officially divorced), their artistic relationship continued much as it had before. Personal split or not, Aziz remained the troupe's director and, according to Fatima, even became quite friendly with Elie. Aziz had lost his wife, but he had attained the artistic freedom and financial backing to make the theatre he had always dreamed of.

Fatima, in turn, lived a life of luxury beyond anything she had ever imagined. At the end of her first season, while Aziz took care of their daughter, Fatima travelled to Europe for the first time with Elie. In the summer of 1928, Fatima did a grand tour, staying on the Grand Canal in Venice and visiting Milan, Paris, and Monte Carlo. She went from a childhood of poverty in Alexandria to a life of opulence, staying in the world's best hotels, visiting Europe's famous art museums, and seeing the theatres and cabarets of Paris. Then, back in Egypt, the couple moved into an apartment on Qasr al-Nil Street, in the heart of elegant downtown Cairo. Fatima said little about the intimate details of her relationship with Elie Edrei, but the age difference between the two (estimates of his age differ, but he was almost certainly over forty) and the dynamics of power invite comparison with her earlier marriage to Aziz Eid.

When the next season began in late summer 1928, Fatima quickly confirmed her place as leader of one of the most exciting theatrical troupes in Cairo. The troupe's big show that year was an Arabic version of Shakespeare's *Julius Caesar*, in which Fatima took the part of Mark Antony. She spent almost a thousand Egyptian pounds on costumes, scenery, and extras, and Aziz went wild with the set design. He set up a stage among the theatre seats so that Caesar's body could be placed there in some scenes, surrounded by the audience. For Fatima the role of Mark Antony was a chance to play a male part, which she had always enjoyed. It also allowed her to compete directly with Youssef Wahbi, who had acted the role for the Ramses troupe in the previous season and was still performing in the play that season.

Giving such prominence to a play about the death of a beloved populist leader and the spectre of revolution was bound to be controversial. The timing of the performance did not help. In August of the previous year, that great Egyptian nationalist leader Saad Zaghloul, whose exile had prompted the Revolution of 1919 and who had been a constant thorn in the side of the British ever since, died. At his funeral a procession of four thousand official mourners marched through the streets of Cairo for over an hour, surrounded by crowds of onlookers. For well over a decade, Zaghloul had embodied the struggle of Egypt against British colonialism; since 1919, he had taken on legendary status. In life he had faced political rivals, but in death he represented

Fatima Rushdi on a balcony overlooking the Grand Canal in Venice
(photo courtesy of Lucie Ryzova)

abstract hopes of complete independence for Egypt—which the British continued to frustrate in the 1920s through an array of public and private actions.

In 1928 the government was run by a new prime minister—Oxford-educated Mohammed Mahmoud, leader of the Liberal-Constitutionalist Party. This new party had split from Saad Zaghloul's Wafd Party after accusing the nationalist hero of having dictatorial ambitions. The new party recognised the Egyptian people's ambitions for independence but tried to work within the established framework and be less openly antagonistic to the British. So, when Fatima, in the role of Antony, delivered his funeral speech over the dead body of Caesar, a beloved leader who had been wronged by treacherous former friends, the implications must have been clear. Mahmoud may well have worried that people might see echoes of him in the murderers of Caesar, Brutus, and Cassius, and even that the audience might take Antony's not very subtle incitements to mutiny seriously.

Before the first performance, the manager of her troupe phoned Fatima and told her that the Ministry of the Interior had ordered them to stop production. Fatima rushed directly to Mohammed Mahmoud's house to plead her case. She tried to allay the prime minister's fears about the revolutionary potential of the action, assuring him that she knew nothing about politics, only about art. She pointed out that Shakespeare's *Julius Caesar* was a world-renowned play that the Egyptian audience should have a chance to see. Although not entirely convinced by Fatima's argument, Mahmoud agreed to let her troupe put on the play as long as the censor could cut certain scenes.

In the next season, another Roman play by Shakespeare inspired one of Fatima's most memorable performances—again with a highly political subtext. *The Death of Cleopatra*, written by the Egyptian "Prince of Poets," Ahmed Shawqi, was a modern, nationalist reworking of *Antony and Cleopatra*. Shawqi, who had been famous since the late nineteenth century, chose Fatima's troupe as the first company to perform his new work, which would be remembered as one of the great pieces of early twentieth-century Arabic dramatic writing. The play was clearly designed to speak to contemporary Egyptians and their struggle against the British Empire. In it, Fatima took the role of Cleopatra, who is portrayed as an eloquent critic of Roman tyranny in the Mediterranean and a staunch defender of her country's sovereignty. As Cleopatra sacrifices herself for Egypt at the end, the high priest of Isis delivers a prophecy that the Roman Empire will meet its end in Egypt.

The new play was a smash hit for Fatima's troupe; she later said it was the "best play [her] troupe ever performed." When two Egyptian-born Italian futurist poets, Nelson Morpurgo and Filippo Marinetti, attended a performance, they were more concerned with its artistry than its anti-colonial message. Morpurgo complimented Fatima's strong performance, deep voice, and majestic form, comparing her to an Egyptian sculpture. "Art had crossed linguistic boundaries," he said. Marinetti, for his part, was particularly taken with her "naked, voluptuous back," which he believed to be "a true revolution of Muslim customs."[9]

By the end of the 1920s, Fatima was a huge celebrity in Egypt, and her fame was also spreading across the Arab world. Every self-respecting Egyptian theatrical company in the 1920s had started to branch out beyond Egypt. It had become more or less expected that, usually during the summer breaks between seasons, successful singers and troupes would do short tours abroad to perform their shows. The most common destination was the Levant, which offered well-established venues as well as audiences guaranteed to give them a good reception—Beirut, Aleppo, Damascus, Jaffa, and Jerusalem were all common stops. More intrepid travellers went to other countries in the Middle East and

North Africa. Some even went as far as South America to entertain the diaspora audience there. Road shows like these could be very lucrative for constantly cash-strapped acting troupes, and in the 1920s, before the Egyptian film industry had really taken off, they helped spread Egyptian entertainment across the Arabic-speaking world.

In fact, Egyptian plays became so popular that copycat acts soon started to emerge. By the mid-1920s, Naguib al-Rihani's famous and much-loved lascivious village *omda*, Kish-Kish Bey, was the target of frequent imitation—many people started to make money by claiming to be the "real Kish-Kish Bey." When Naguib first toured the Levant as Kish-Kish Bey, the audience there complained that he had stolen his iconic character from someone else. In truth they had seen an old member of his troupe, the Lebanese actor Amin Atallah, touring the Levant without telling anyone that Kish-Kish was not his own creation. Even after Naguib had exposed his ruse, Amin Atallah persisted. Around Syria, Palestine, and Lebanon, both men continued to perform Kish-Kish Bey plays, each telling the audience he was the character's true incarnation.

Even in South America, Naguib met other impersonators. When he toured Brazil in 1925, the crowd told him about another Kish-Kish who had been in the country for ages. Naguib soon discovered that this actor also had a complicated connection to Amin Atallah. Amin had married the actress Ibriz Estati, whose sister Almaz had moved to Brazil. Almaz's son (Amin Atallah's nephew) George was making a good career for himself in the family business of impersonating Kish-Kish Bey. Naguib al-Rihani took advantage of the situation and agreed to combine troupes and do four nights at a local theatre with both Kish-Kishes.

If the tours went well, the troupes could make a lot of money, enough to fund a large part of the coming year's activities. It was no surprise, then, that both Fatima Rushdi and Youssef Wahbi were keen to get in on the act. In the summer of 1929, they both set out for the

Levant in search of big audiences. Youssef's troupe performed to full houses in Beirut, Jaffa, Haifa, and Latakia. In Damascus his troupe was so popular that every night when the actors got back to their hotel, they found bunches of flowers and bowls of fruit waiting for them.

Fatima's experience in the Levant was more action packed. In Beirut her troupe got into a scrape while performing a new play about Jamal Pasha, the Ottoman governor of Greater Syria during the First World War. Fatima most likely had miscalculated how controversial the play would be. This Turkish general, known in the city as "Jamal the Bloody," had been instrumental in the execution of several important Arab nationalists and the imprisonment of many more. In Beirut he was extremely unpopular: During the play a member of the crowd pulled out his gun and fired a shot in the direction of Aziz Eid, who was acting the part of Jamal Pasha. Fortunately for Aziz, the assailant missed and the curtain was quickly lowered.

After the Levant, Fatima had her sights set on Baghdad. In those days the journey across the wide desert was risky, but the rewards that lay on the other side were great and the audiences were phenomenal. After a car trip of several days, Fatima arrived in Baghdad, where she rented the Royal Cinema for a series of performances—the plays included *Julius Caesar*, *Sultan Abd al-Hamid*, and *L'Aiglon*. As promised, the troupe performed to full houses; people were forced to sit in the aisles. A welcome party was held in Fatima's honour. One of Iraq's greatest poets, Jamil Sidqi al-Zahawi, who was by then in his sixties, stood up and recited an ode he had composed for her. "Never before have my eyes seen an actress like famous Fatima," it began and then continued for almost fifty lines of fulsome praise—"Today you are the princess of Near Eastern art," he told her. Fatima also gave a speech, thanking her hosts and praising the country that had welcomed her so fulsomely. As one of the most prominent women in Arabic theatre, she was always keen to voice her support for other women. During her speech, she was pleased to say, "I have found the Iraqi national awakening on a fast track, I have seen the Iraqi woman—her progress and her love of art—and it has made me so happy. . . . I feel like Iraq is my second country." Later, the troupe members were invited to a tea party given by King Faisal, where they ended up giving a private performance of *La Dame aux Camélias* in Arabic for the king, the Iraqi government ministers, and the British High Commissioner Gilbert Clayton.[10]

The next summer both Youssef and Fatima went on tour again. Youssef assembled a troupe of the best actors and actresses he could find and then set sail on the long trip to Brazil. At the port of Santos, they were immediately met by a crowd of hundreds of the country's Arab community, who carried signs reading "Long Live Youssef Wahbi, Long Live Egypt." The tour took them from São Paulo to Rio de Janeiro, on to Buenos Aires, and then back to Cairo. Youssef Wahbi, in his memoirs, was astounded at how successful the tour had been. He even sent back newspaper clippings to the Egyptian press, including all the glowing reviews that appeared in the Arabic-language newspapers of South America. Much to his disappointment, nobody in Egypt published them.[11]

Fatima returned to Iraq, where she had enjoyed so much success the year before. She planned to continue to Palestine, where she would do a series of performances. But she had not grasped the political situation there, particularly the growing levels of Arab–Jewish animosity. She sent a letter from Baghdad to a theatre and fine arts club in Jaffa, telling audiences to get ready for her troupe. As she often did, Fatima sent her special greetings to women—specifically "the working women of Palestine and the rising youth," whom she described as "the armour of the present and swords of the future." She arrived in Palestine to find a country full of tension. Her booking agent caused a minor controversy in Jerusalem when he booked the troupe into a Jewish theatre, apparently without thinking. One nationalist newspaper attacked the decision, saying Fatima should support Arab businesses, and she was forced to cancel her performance.[12]

Fatima was not the only one generating controversy in Palestine. Her rival, Youssef Wahbi, also had problems dealing with the country's growing sectarian tensions. If he were to put on a show in a Tel Aviv theatre, he lamented, no one would come: Jews didn't want to see any Arabic theatre, and Arabs did not want to go to the Jewish city. In an interview with the *Palestine Post* in 1933, Youssef complained that even art had become segregated. He compared the situation in Palestine unfavourably to that in Egypt, where the Palestine-based, Hebrew-speaking Habima troupe attracted large audiences and the local Jewish community had theatrical companies of its own. "I hope to see a day when Arab theatres in Palestine will be as crowded by Jews as the Jewish theatre is crowded by Arabs in Egypt." He said that it greatly affected him to see "such a neutral institution as the theatre is subjected to political and national differences." "Is not art international?" he asked the newspaper's readers.[13]

❖

By the beginning of the 1930s, when she was still only in her early twenties, Fatima had conquered Egypt's theatre scene. In about five years, she had gone from a minor actress in Youssef Wahbi's troupe to one of the biggest celebrities in the Arab world. In 1930, one journalist said, "In her present position, she can rightly be considered a heroine of Egyptian theatrical history."[14] It was a truly remarkable accomplishment, but it would not last long. In 1932, her relationship with Elie ran into trouble. She was spending all her time obsessing over the troupe, which she was still running with Aziz Eid. Whenever the theatrical season ended in Cairo, she would quickly head off on tour. Finances were also strained; in the late 1920s, Elie could throw his money liberally at Fatima's theatre; but in the worldwide economic depression of the 1930s, such reckless extravagances were no longer possible.

When Fatima told Elie in 1932 that she was planning a tour in

French North Africa, they reached an impasse. Elie said the tour was
not worth the effort and advised her not to go: the region was having
political troubles, the audiences were more used to French than Arabic,
and the theatrical infrastructure was not as sound as that in Egypt. But
Fatima insisted that she wanted to go and that he could not stop her.
He finally retorted that if she did, it would be the last time she ever saw
any of his money. She did not back down; the troupe was assembled,
and they headed to Tunisia, leaving the disgruntled Elie back in Egypt.

North Africa was the perfect place for a rebound. Shortly after
Fatima left Egypt, *Rose al-Youssef* published shots of her on a beach in
Tunisia getting friendly with a muscular young man in tight swimming
trunks. In Algeria she developed a close relationship with the head of
the French security services, who proved useful in easing her troupe's
travel across the country and getting their plays through censorship. In
her letters back to Elie, she happily told him how well everything was
going and that his pessimism had been misplaced. Her tour had earned
her 3,000 Egyptian pounds and "had solved her terrible problem; she
no longer had any need for financial support." Elie replied with letters
declaring his love and trying to save their relationship, but she told him
there was no point—it was over.[15]

When the tour ended, Fatima took some actors to a sound studio in
Paris, where she intended to complete the spoken parts for a film that
she had written and planned to both direct and star in: *The Marriage*.
In the 1920s and 1930s the Egyptian film industry was expanding at
a rapid pace, and Fatima had made a few largely unsuccessful forays
into this new business in the late 1920s. After starring in the silent film
Tragedy on Top of the Pyramid, where she played a woman whose lover
is falsely accused of killing her brother, she had tried to produce her
own film, funded by Elie Edrei, called *Under the Light of the Sun* (alter-
natively, *Under the Sky of Egypt*). Written and directed by the Turkish
author, actor, and director Vedad Urfy, the film was screened only once,

to a private audience. Fatima was so dissatisfied with the final product that she took the reel out into the desert of Heliopolis and burned it.

In 1932 Fatima decided to try again, this time putting herself in creative control. The plot of *The Marriage* revolved around the sufferings of a young woman in love with her poor but ambitious cousin. Her parents, who do not respect her wishes, force her to marry a wealthy man who does not care about her. She submits to her family's desires, but her marriage is extremely unpleasant; her husband mistreats her and is having an open affair with a nightclub dancer. The film ends when the main character, played by Fatima, is hit by a car. Her poor cousin, who is now a successful doctor, sees her but cannot save her, and she dies in his arms.

After writing her own script for the film, Fatima planned an expensive production. She may have been driven partly by competition with Youssef Wahbi, who had released Egypt's first talking feature, *Sons of the Elite*, in 1932. The locations alone reveal her ambition—it was to be shot across Egypt, France, North Africa, and Spain, where the Alhambra palace provided some impressive set pieces. In the summer of 1932, she had even entered into (unsuccessful) negotiations to collaborate with the Irish director Rex Ingram.

On 19 January 1933, *The Marriage* premiered in Cairo at the American Cosmograph cinema on Emad al-Din Street. The first Egyptian film both written and directed by a woman, it was publicised as "lifting Egypt's name up in the world of cinema." Throughout the spring and early summer, it played at cinemas across the country. The Egyptian film critic in the international magazine *Variety* briefly noted in March 1933 that it was "doing well." However, despite some level of popularity, it did not become an instant classic. Now, as with so many films of that period, no prints survive.[16]

In Fatima's own version of her story, professional success was often closely tied to romantic relationships. One of her memoirs is even called

Fatima Rushdi: Between Love and Art. This leads to an uncomfortable contradiction when telling her story. On one side, she was unquestionably a remarkable woman who managed to rise from poverty to the top of Egypt's entertainment industry by the time she reached her twentieth birthday—and remained a bold, outspoken woman as she did it. But her story, as she told it, cannot escape the pull of powerful men who dominated her life. The sense of something unpleasant below the surface of these relationships, although hard to prove, is also difficult to avoid. In 1930 *Rose al-Youssef* magazine published a set of cartoons of celebrities above the title "How to Win the Hearts of These Actresses and Singers." For some celebrities the answer was romance and poetry or money and jewels; for Fatima Rushdi it was force and compulsion. Her career serves partly as a reminder that, no matter how much more public visibility women were gaining, and no matter how much power and independence they claimed to have, this was still a world run by men.[17]

In the mid-1930s, now separated from Elie Edrei, Fatima drifted between different jobs but never truly regained the success, fame, and upward momentum she had in the 1920s. In 1933 she also stopped collaborating with Aziz Eid. By 1934 her once esteemed theatrical troupe was fading out of existence. In 1935 she briefly joined the new Egyptian National Troupe, which was inspired by the Comédie Française. But when it came time for rehearsals, she discovered the company had given her only extremely small roles with hardly any lines, and she quit in protest. In 1936 she set out to tour the Arab world once again, across the Levant and North Africa. In 1938 she found herself in Paris performing an evening called *Variétés de Fatma Rouchdi* in a theatre that stood on Rue Cadet (about 100 metres from the famous Folies Bergère). There she entertained the French audiences with selected highlights of her career, scenes from her plays, and short song-and-dance numbers.

In 1939 Fatima had the last big hit of her career when she accepted the starring role in a film called *Determination*. Led by the promising young director Kamal Selim, the film was a huge success; today it is considered one of the greatest works of early Egyptian cinema and a pioneering work of social realism. During the production, Fatima started a relationship with Selim. It soon turned into a marriage that quickly soured as Selim grew jealous of Fatima's continued close relationship with Aziz Eid. In her memoirs, Fatima remembers that the young director publicly humiliated Aziz, giving him an embarrassingly small part in his next film and poking fun at his acting style in front of the crew. She had seen enough of this posturing male rivalry. Storming off the set, she went home and packed her clothes to leave. When Kamal came back, Fatima informed him that their marriage was finished.

By the 1940s, Fatima's career had peaked. She continued making films into the 1950s, and in the 1960s, as her various memoirs were being published, she retired from the stage. She spent the next few decades of her life in obscurity until, by the 1990s, she was said to be living alone, broke and ill, in a pension in downtown Cairo. There are even stories that she had been forced to beg on the streets to stay alive. After a report published in the Wafd Party's newspaper *al-Wafd*, people learned that Fatima Rushdi was living in poverty. The veteran movie star Farid Shawqi arranged for her to move into an apartment and to receive medical treatment. Fatima spent the final years of her life giving television interviews and reliving her glory years. She died at age eighty-six in January 1996.

One Egyptian journalist recalled the last words she said to him: "Make sure the television keeps showing my films so people don't forget me: I am Fatima Rushdi who made Emad al-Din Street tremble whenever she walked on it."[18]

Chapter 7

THE SINGER, THE BABY, AND THE BEY

O NE DAY IN EARLY 1924, the young singer and actress Fatima Sirri received a phone call. This call triggered a series of events that would come to define the rest of her life. When she picked up the phone, she heard the voice of Ibrahim Heblawi Bey, an eminent lawyer and politician. He was calling on behalf of his friend Hoda Shaarawi, the hero of those legendary women's protests of the 1919 revolution. Since then she had become the main figurehead of the women's movement in Egypt, setting up the Egyptian Feminist Union in 1923. That same year, Hoda had caused a stir by publicly removing her face veil at Cairo station in a symbolic protest against the life of seclusion that was imposed on aristocratic women. Hoda Shaarawi was also the member of an important and aristocratic Egyptian family that owned a famous villa in central Cairo near the Egyptian Museum and whose male members were actively involved in the country's high politics. On the phone that day, Ibrahim Heblawi told Fatima that Hoda was throwing a party at her famous villa, and she wanted someone to sing for her guests. Heblawi mentioned that the singer would be paid a decent amount, 20 Egyptian pounds, and after a little persuading (she had to reschedule another gig), Fatima agreed to perform.

Fatima Sirri's career had so far been successful but largely unremarkable, at least by the standards of some other celebrities of the period. As usual, little is certain about her early life; it seems that she came from a middle-class family, married in her teens, had two children, and then divorced. However, during the marriage Fatima's husband, who was a music lover, hired the composer Dawoud Hosni to give her singing lessons. After the divorce, he proved to be a vital contact in the entertainment industry. Dawoud, in the early 1920s, was among the most prolific composers in Cairo's nightclub scene. After Sayyid Darwish died in 1923, Dawoud wrote music for almost every singer and musical troupe in the city. His songs and comic operas came to dominate Ezbekiyya, and Fatima had starring roles in many of them—including an operatic version of *Samson and Delilah* and the new opera *Hoda*—a fantastical love story about the daughter of the king of the jinn ("spirits") falling in love with a mortal Egyptian.

After her early success in the theatre, Fatima moved into cabarets too, singing *taqtuqas* to the rowdy audiences in the Bosphore Casino or onstage at the Santi restaurant (a Cairo institution located in Ezbekiyya Gardens). She also signed a multi-song deal with Odeon Records. When Fatima got the phone call inviting her to perform at Hoda Shaarawi's party, she may not have been the most sought-after artist in Cairo, but she was certainly in the upper echelons of the city's singers.

The night of the party, Fatima went to the Shaarawis' villa, sang her set, and left with enough time to do another gig that evening at Youssef Wahbi's Ramses Theatre. Sitting at the back of the room during her performance at the private party was a young man in his late teens—Hoda's son Mohammed Shaarawi Bey, who was apparently captivated by her. This chance encounter would lead to a love affair, a marriage, a child, and, finally, to a protracted lawsuit in which Fatima sued Mohammed for support, alleging that he had deserted her and left her to care for their daughter Layla alone. By taking him to court, the well-known performer launched a challenge not only to her ex-lover, but to a whole generation of Egyptian men. From 1925 to 1931, the entertainment industry followed the trial intently. Between December 1926 and April 1927, *al-Masrah* magazine serialised Fatima's account of the entire relationship for its readers. The story that survives today comes almost exclusively from these articles, giving us a detailed female perspective on the events of a failed marriage but only allowing us to guess at what Mohammed's side of the story might have been.

In her account of the beginnings of this relationship, Fatima recalled that, just a few days after her gig in Hoda Shaarawi's villa, she received another telephone call. This time it was one of Mohammed's friends who had also been at the Shaarawis' party. He was calling to invite her to tea with Mohammed at the Mena House, an old royal hunting lodge near the pyramids that was now a luxury hotel. Fatima said that she flatly refused. She knew what these wealthy young men were like; they would shower her with money and jewellery, but their affections soon cooled.

But Mohammed did not blink after Fatima's snub; he began to show up at almost all her gigs. One night, when Fatima was performing at the Santi restaurant, she turned around to see him sitting in the audience. Soon after that, he turned up at the Bosphore Casino to see her again. From his seat in a private box, he spent the show wildly applauding her act; at one point, she looked out into the audience and realised that he was the only person in the room clapping. Many women would have been put off by these constant appearances at her concerts; but it seems Fatima was not. Instead, in her own retelling of these events, she says his persistence wore her down, and she even began to feel sorry for him. She recalled that she even began to enjoy the attention he lavished on her and the intensity of this young love. Finally, she agreed to go for a drive in his car, and, sitting next to him, she felt an unavoidable spark of electricity. Her heart began to beat faster and she found herself falling in love, too.

Fatima's story is full of romantic clichés like this, but they are not merely sentimental asides; they served an important purpose after the affair ended. The young singer was partly responding to detractors who might claim that she had manipulated the rich, aristocratic Mohammed, playing hard to get in an attempt to lead him on and exploit him for his money. Fatima wanted to make sure these faultfinders knew that her love was genuine and that *he* had come after *her*, not the other way around. Sometimes she even addressed her critics directly:

> All you male authors who write about the female psyche, not one of you has ever been a woman, so how can you know anything about the female psyche? Write what you want about me; say that I tried to take advantage of his emotions, that I was hard hearted, or that I toyed with him. . . . Go ahead. Say those things that you always say when you are trying to explain a woman's actions. All your words and all your great philosophy cannot stop me knowing what I know and feeling what I felt.[1]

Her love affair with Mohammed moved slowly but inexorably forwards. That summer they went to Alexandria, swam at the beach, went on long drives in his car (a car was a real luxury in 1920s Egypt), and eventually shared their first passionate kiss. In looking back at that kiss, Fatima said it had sparked in her "a desire like the fires of hell, one that could only be extinguished by the mixing of two souls and the touching of two bodies." That evening, for the first time, they had dinner alone in his flat—at least, that's how Fatima, no doubt euphemistically, described the evening.[2]

Once the couple had been seen all over Alexandria together, their affair was hard to hide. It was here that their problems started. Mohammed's aristocratic friends and family disapproved of his relationship with a woman they saw as a low-class singer. Their objections seemed to affect Mohammed. The couple began to fight when Mohammed accused Fatima of wanting his money, and there were theatrical gestures on both sides: He threatened to leave her and even went as far as writing her a cheque to compensate her for the time they had spent together. She, insulted by the insinuation, ripped up the cheque in front of him, telling him that her love could not be bought or sold. She then took the first train back to Cairo.

Mohammed had to do something big to win her back. So, to prove his sincerity, he asked her to marry him. There were some strings attached: Mohammed insisted that Fatima give up her singing career. He would buy her a new apartment and support her financially, but he did not want his wife working in nightclubs. This demand would probably not have come as a surprise; in 1920s Cairo, men who married singers felt uncomfortable watching them sing to strange men all over town and often asked their new wives to give up the trade. After a little thought, Fatima told him she was happy with these conditions, and it may have been the truth—making ends meet by performing in front of rowdy, drunken crowds had its downsides. She broke off her contract with Odeon Records and retired from the stage. A few months later, an article in a theatrical magazine told its readers, "We hoped that Fatima Sirri would become the number one Egyptian comic opera star but she had decided leave the theatre and pursue a family life."[3]

On 1 September 1924 she formally accepted Mohammed's proposal, and he gave her a 500-pound dowry along with a pair of diamond earrings. These nuptials, however, were not quite official; the couple had made an agreement often referred to as a customary (or *urfi*) marriage: a privately drafted arrangement signed before witnesses but not registered with the state. It was a common but controversial practice often used by Egyptian couples to avoid the rigmarole of a wedding or get around families that disapproved of the match (or, in the eyes of some, a workaround to legitimise sex before marriage). The state could theoretically recognise an *urfi* marriage; but due to its only quasi-legal status, it would make things difficult if any problems arose.

By all accounts, the early days of the couple's marriage were blissful. After signing the papers, they holidayed again in Alexandria.

When they returned to Cairo, Fatima moved into a flat near Emad al-Din Street. On their first night in the city, the couple stayed up all night talking and making love; when the sun came up, they drove to the Mena House for breakfast. One newspaper article later described how Fatima, in a moment of romantic whimsy, had got a horn for her car that played a special tune. So, while Mohammed was studying at law school, she could drive past the classroom hooting it, and he would know that she was nearby.

The honeymoon period lasted less than a year. Looking back on those early days, Fatima regretted her naivety. "Love cannot last and a lover can never stay true to his pledge. . . . I am sorry to say that this young man was awful enough to deceive a woman with the false love, that seemed for all the world to be honest and true." There had been some clear early warning signs. Fatima found her new husband both demanding and fiercely jealous, sometimes turning up at her apartment unannounced to look for evidence of infidelity. Probably the biggest red flag of all was his attempt to keep the marriage a secret from his friends and family because he knew they would have disapproved. Mohammed was still living in his family house and had installed Fatima in her new flat by herself, so he could visit her away from other eyes. Fatima later suspected that he was particularly worried what his mother, Hoda, would think about his new wife. Hoda had already made plans for her son to marry a young woman called Mounira Assem, the elite daughter of a family friend and a suitable match for a member of the Shaarawi family.[4]

It was the following summer, when Fatima was several months pregnant with their first child, when the relationship began to look unsustainable. Mohammed had to go to Europe and then to America. The plan was for him to go off first and for her to join him later. She agreed, as long as he gave her a written statement confirming that they were married—in case she gave birth away from him and had to confirm the child's legitimacy. On 10 July 1925, she waved away Mohammed's boat from a friend's rooftop in Alexandria. Then, on 16 July she, along with one of Mohammed's servants, got on a boat to Genoa, and from Genoa, took the train to Lausanne, where she checked into the Hotel Mirabeau.

Once she was in Europe, Fatima started to feel that she had been brought there on false pretences. Mohammed was staying in the luxurious spa town of Carlsbad in western Bohemia with his family and was reluctant to leave them to visit his pregnant wife. Besides that, his habit of going away on long trips into the countryside without leaving a postal address to reach him made even the couple's correspondence sporadic. Fatima remembered finding herself in a strange town in Europe, sitting alone in her hotel room, writing letters, gazing lovingly at photographs of her husband, and missing Egypt.

Bored, restless, and only a few months from giving birth, Fatima decided to leave the stuffy Hotel Mirabeau. She travelled first to Montreux and spent a week there before moving on to Paris, where she was a little happier. Finally, her husband got in touch and agreed, a little reluctantly, to come to Paris—he would have preferred it if she had stayed in Switzerland. When they were at last reunited, Fatima recalled thinking there was something different about him. He no longer seemed like the devoted husband she had married. Worse, he was repeating those old suspicions that she was just using him for his money.

Mohammed soon left with his mother on a trip to Washington, D.C., to visit his sister and her husband, who was the Egyptian ambassador to the United States. But before departing, he asked her, as a sign of her devotion and trust, to give him back the statement he had signed to prove they were married. She lied and told him she did not have it with her (in fact she always carried it), but she would give it to him as soon as they got back to Egypt. He also warned Fatima not to register the baby with the Egyptian embassy in France because his family knew the ambassador, and he would be sure to tell them about it. He sent her, instead, to the private Loew Sanitorium in Vienna, where the artist Gustav Klimt had previously been a patient, where the philosopher Ludwig Wittgenstein had been treated for a hernia, where the composer Gustav Mahler had died, and where, on 7 September 1925, Fatima gave birth to Layla Mohammed Shaarawi.

Fatima went back to Egypt with her daughter and by then could clearly see that her relationship with Mohammed was doomed. When he returned from America and came to see his new daughter, all he could say was "I wish it had been a boy." Again, he asked Fatima to give him that written statement confirming their marriage. She shrewdly handed over a zincograph copy that she had made a few months before, passing it off to him as the original. She kept the actual one for herself, sensing that it could come in useful later. Mohammed, believing that he had freed himself from his responsibility to Fatima and her daughter, spent the night on the town and did not get back to the Shaarawi villa until four in the morning. When Fatima called to talk to him the next day, he told her what she had known for a while: it was over.[5]

Feeling betrayed, lied to, and used, she blamed Mohammed, of course, but also identified other culprits. Fatima was convinced that his mother, Hoda Shaarawi, had been instrumental in the breakdown of the relationship. She thought that the great feminist had encouraged her son Mohammed to leave the mother of his child, trading her for the embrace of his class. It is certainly possible, even if she had little direct evidence to support her claim. Hoda Shaarawi was a famous campaigner for women's rights, but she was still the product of a class that looked down on women in the entertainment business. In 1926, not long after the marriage debacle, Rose al-Youssef, early in her journalistic career, had asked Hoda Shaarawi if she might send a picture to appear in her new magazine. Hoda had apparently refused, saying, "Why do you want my photo? So you can publish it alongside photos of actresses?" Rose al-Youssef, unimpressed with this response, published an open letter to Hoda, telling her bluntly that "an actress, madame, is not worth less than you." Fatima Sirri did have some reason to be suspicious that Hoda Shaarawi would not countenance seeing her son marry a vaudeville singer.[6]

However, Fatima also had the future of her daughter Layla to think about; the child was not going to be denied her right to the Shaarawi family name and everything that went with it. She tried to reason with Mohammed, but to no avail. He returned her messages with barbs and dismissal. Late one night, after what she suspected was an evening of heavy drinking, he even rolled up to her flat to deliver a few insults personally. It was then that she decided she had no option but to get lawyers and prepare to fight him in the courts.

Before taking that drastic step, though, Fatima had one last card to play; she would appeal directly, from one woman to another, to the better feelings of Hoda Shaarawi. Surely, she reasoned, the grande dame of Egyptian feminism, who spent her life campaigning for women, could be convinced to help out a poor mother in need—even if she was just a nightclub singer. Fatima also knew she had some power of her own in this fight. The Shaarawi family would surely want to avoid the potential scandal that might come from an extended court case, particularly about such an unseemly subject. Gossip—and the fear of it—was a powerful weapon in her arsenal: if the parties settled out of court, no one would have to worry about their name being dragged through the mud.

Fatima sent a letter to Hoda Shaarawi, laying out her position. It began with compassion, telling Hoda that if she worried about her son's reputation and future being damaged by marrying an actress, then Fatima was sympathetic. But that was not the problem here, she continued. What mattered were the rights of Fatima's daughter, who, she reminded Hoda, was also *her* granddaughter. The letter then begged Hoda to convince her son to recognise both his marriage and his daughter. Otherwise (and here she bordered on threatening) she had a lawyer, as well as the statement Mohammed had signed confirming that the two were married, and was ready to see them in court. It would be a shame, Fatima concluded, to release all of this nasty business into the public; but, if pressed, she would.

A few days later Hoda Shaarawi's private secretary came to Fatima's house to talk about the letter. Over a cup of coffee, he laid out his mistress's opinion. Fatima's letter had apparently come as such a shock to her that she wasn't sure whether to believe it. At first she had doubted that her son could do something like that; but, when confronted, Mohammed had confessed everything. The secretary insisted in his version of the story that Hoda had then instructed Mohammed to marry Fatima and take care of his child, but he had refused. Mohammed had apparently retorted that he had started this, and he was the one who was going to finish it, adding that he was perfectly ready to defend himself in court if it came to that.

Hoping to defuse the rapidly escalating crisis, Hoda had authorised her secretary to make Fatima a generous offer. In an act of personal largesse, he said, Hoda would be happy to pay Fatima a monthly allowance that would allow her to raise and take care of the child. Fatima interpreted the offer as an attempt to buy her off and replied that she was not interested in charity; she wanted only what she and her daughter were due. If she wanted money, she could always go back to her lucrative singing career. She told the secretary, "Tell her that I don't need her handouts or her charity to feed and raise Mohammed Shaarawi's daughter." It was now a matter not just of principle, but of her daughter's future; the advantages and opportunities that would flow to Layla as part of the Shaarawi family were worth more than money alone.

As she refused the offer, Fatima also suspected that she was being deceived and perhaps even lied to by the greatest icon of Egyptian feminism at the time, who had dedicated her life to the women's struggle. Fatima simply did not believe that this was the first time Hoda Shaarawi had heard about this relationship. In fact, she was convinced that Hoda had a major role in convincing Mohammed to leave her. To Fatima it was a puzzling kind of hypocrisy: "When she saw a woman demanding her rights and her daughter's rights, Hoda Shaarawi stood with her hands tied before her son. But, at the same time, she was busy filling foreign and local newspapers with her own defences of the rights of women."[7]

When attempts to settle the dispute had failed, the only option left was court; in December 1925, the case began. Facing down the Shaarawi family at trial was never going to be simple, and Mohammed did not make things easy for Fatima. He had spared no expense in mounting his defence; he hired four prominent lawyers as well as private investigators who followed Fatima around, looking for anything that might incriminate her. She also began to suspect that his legal team was bribing her witnesses not to testify in court. In the first proper session of the trial, he flatly denied ever meeting her. He claimed that, like most other people in Cairo, he had heard of her—she was a famous singer, after all—but he did not know her personally.

As the case dragged on, sporadic articles in the newspapers followed its winding path through new judges, changes in the law, and a verdict in Fatima's favour that was subsequently challenged. Eventually, Fatima needed money to keep the prosecution going. In the early days of the lawsuit, she had rejected offers to perform, saying that she wanted to focus on the trial. But ultimately, beset with legal fees and the expenses of her daughter's upbringing, she returned to her former career. Rumours started to circulate that she was going to form her own theatrical troupe, but she denied them. In any case, money was better for singers, and she needed as much as she could get, so she went back to singing in the cabarets and making records with Odeon. In 1930 she spent the summer running her own cabaret in Alexandria, complete with the usual variety sets and a stream of actors, singers, and dancers. It was this independent source of income (which few women at the time had) that allowed her to continue her legal battle for as long as she did.

Through all the legal wrangling, the case lasted almost six years. Fatima began to collect newspaper clippings about the case, thinking she could give them to Layla when she was older to show her how hard her mother had fought for her. Finally, in March 1931, against all the odds, Fatima won. The court ruled that Mohammed Shaarawi had to pay maintenance to his wife and child support to his daughter for a total of 110 Egyptian pounds per month, backdated to November 1925. The payments ended up totalling around 6,000 Egyptian pounds. Layla was recognised as Mohammed's legitimate daughter, and Fatima was his legal wife.[8]

In the months after her victory, Fatima celebrated this newfound status. She printed visiting cards bearing the name Fatima Shaarawi. She gave interviews to the press, retelling her story and informing the world that she had won her due. She was Mohammed Shaarawi's wife before God and the law—she saw the verdict as His justice for a good woman. To show her gratitude, she vowed to slaughter two calves to feed the poor and to pay a sheikh to spend the night publicly reading the Quran. The press heralded the result as a class victory and a sign of changing times when the aristocracy could no longer do whatever they wanted.

When the public celebrations ended, there remained the question of what to do with Layla. When she turned eleven, her father would legally have the right to decide what he wanted for his daughter; but until then, Fatima was her guardian. After six years of legal battles, Fatima was determined to keep her daughter for as long as possible. The magazine *Rose al-Youssef* reported that she refused an offer from Hoda Shaarawi of 3,000 Egyptian pounds to hand over her daughter to the Shaarawi family immediately. Fatima made a few concessions, letting the Shaarawis decide which school Layla would attend and allowing them to visit her there. But she insisted that if Mohammed wanted to visit his daughter, it would be at her house, and all three of them would remain in the same room.[9]

For a few years, things seemed to be going well for Fatima. She bought herself a fancy car and tried, with varying degrees of success, to invest her money around town. She even considered financing a film about the whole affair with Mohammed, thinking that she would play herself, but it was never made. Before long, she had settled into a more mundane life. Eventually, Layla left her mother to live with the Shaarawi family. Fatima had fought hard for her daughter's rights, giving her a life that few people could even imagine at the time. It was a terrible irony that her success in establishing her daughter's paternity had led directly to Fatima's loss.

Once the excitement of the trial had subsided, the press was not particularly interested in Fatima's rather ordinary daily life, and the Shaarawis certainly did not want to comment about this embarrassing affair. In 1932, soon after the paternity case was settled, Mohammed was engaged to Mounira Assem—the woman his mother had always intended for him.

It is difficult to find a satisfying end to this story. Fatima spent her later life in relative comfort, living in the high-class neighbourhood of Zamalek and spending her summers at the Hotel Windsor in Alexandria. In 1933 she retired from singing, but she made one comeback in 1938: the palace hired her as one of many singers to perform in celebration of the royal wedding.

But what about Layla? What role did Fatima play in her daughter's later life? Did Layla's new family eventually accept this unsuitable woman, or did they shut her out? Did Layla keep that collection of news clippings Fatima had gathered? Did she look back on them and remember her mother's sacrifices? These questions are difficult to answer from the historical record. In 2008 Nehad Selaiha, an Egyptian theatre critic, published a short account of her attempts to piece together Fatima's later life. She went around Cairo looking for information, interviewing people close to those involved and reading old newspaper reports. Despite all this work, Selaiha came up with many contradictory stories and few conclusive answers.

The true story of Fatima, Mohammed, and Layla has no easy or uplifting conclusion. However, it re-emerged in 1947 with a more satisfying outcome with the release of the film *Fatima*, starring the great singer Oum Kalthoum. The Egyptian film industry had turned the couple's struggles into a story of reconciliation and true love. The film begins as Fatima's character—who is not a cabaret singer, but a nurse from a humble family in a poor Cairo neighbourhood—is sent on a house visit to a stubborn, unpleasant aristocrat. During the visit the patient's brother, called Fathi, sees her and falls in love. After a passionate courtship, they are married in secret because his family disapproves of the match. Just like Fatima Sirri had done, the heroine of the film makes her lover sign a statement testifying to their marriage; and the document later becomes an important part of the story. Not long after, Fathi leaves her (and their new-born child) to marry a more suitable woman of his own class. Incensed by his betrayal, Fatima and her local community go to court to fight for the rights of both mother and child.

Later in the movie, Fathi, the aristocratic cad, comes home to find his new, apparently suitable wife having an affair. In a tangle of emotions, he gets into his car and drives around the city to clear his head. But he forgets to pay attention to the road and has an accident. Coincidentally, the crash occurs just outside Fatima's house. Hearing the commotion, she rushes out into the street to find him in the car and brings him to hospital, where she helps nurse him back to health. While lying in his hospital bed, Fathi realises how badly he has treated Fatima. As soon as he is able, he rushes to the courthouse to declare the truth: Fatima really is his wife, and the child is his legitimate son. The happy couple returns to her poor neighbourhood together, and the community celebrates the positive turn of events. Unfortunately, in real life, a woman in 1920s Cairo fighting her ex-lover (and his feminist icon mother) for the rights of her child is not a tale of joyful rapprochement, but one of heavy social, financial, and emotional cost. Fatima's story ended in victory but not in triumph.

Fatima's early twentieth-century lawsuit has continued to echo in twenty-first century Egypt. In similar circumstances, the costume designer Hend al-Hinnawy launched a paternity case against the actor Ahmed al-Fishawy in 2006 following a similar *urfi* marriage and the birth of a daughter, Leena. Like Fatima, Hend went through years of legal battles but eventually won the case on appeal. She was quoted, after her victory in 2009, celebrating with words that could just as easily have been Fatima Sirri's: "I got your rights, my baby! I got your rights, my baby!"[10]

Chapter 8

STAR OF THE EAST

IN THE LAST HALF OF the 1920s, a fierce rivalry between two women dominated Cairo's singing scene. The first was the veteran Mounira al-Mahdiyya, former star of the music halls in the early 1910s, inventor of Arabic opera, and the first woman in Egypt to lead a theatrical troupe. The second was her talented and hardworking young rival from the countryside—Oum Kalthoum, star of the film based on the events of Fatima Sirri's life—who had grown up singing religious songs in her father's small band. The two singers could not have been more different. Mounira revelled in eccentricity, unconventionality, and dangerous sexuality. Oum Kalthoum, by contrast, was demure, reserved, and respectable.

But Oum Kalthoum is the singer now remembered worldwide as the most popular icon in the history of Arabic music. Her concerts, often lasting into the early morning; her virtuosic melody lines and trademark fashion sense, including her thick-rimmed sunglasses, are enduring symbols of the Egyptian national character. Still, looking at her career from the standpoint of 1920s Ezbekiyya, her later success was far from assured. With a mixture of luck, talent, and skilful shaping of her public image, Oum Kalthoum was able to rise to the top of Cairo's music industry, above Mounira and every other singer of her generation. In the early decades of her fifty years of celebrity, she laid the foundations for the future and set herself apart from her competition.

Oum Kalthoum's early years were to become an important part of her public image, and her conservative, rural upbringing in a village in the Nile Delta gave her career an enduring origin story. She was born in 1904 in a small village called Tammay al-Zahayra, which was not particularly close to anywhere. Her father was not a rich or illustrious man; except, perhaps, in his small rural world. Known to everyone simply as Sheikh Ibrahim, he took a small salary from his work at the local mosque and supplemented it with whatever else he could get. Unlike the fathers of many other stars of the period, he did not die when Oum Kalthoum was young, and he took a considerable interest in his daughter. He had insisted, apparently against his family's wishes, that she be named Oum Kalthoum, after the third daughter of the prophet Mohammed. It is sometimes said that her birth name was actually "Fatima," but through the force of her father's will, the name Oum Kalthoum stuck. Her friends, as well as those who wanted people to *think* they were her friends, just called her Souma.

When his children were young, Sheikh Ibrahim often toured religious festivals in the area, singing hymns and other songs for a small fee, to support his family. Then, as soon as Oum Kalthoum and her brother Khalid were old enough, he brought them to these little gigs to add some variety to his set—although he dressed his daughter as a boy. He was either ashamed about letting her perform onstage or trying to protect her reputation. As a reward for singing well, she later recalled, the children would get a bowl of *mahalabiyya*, a sweet Egyptian pudding, or a bottle of Spathis, an Egyptian brand of soda water.

This family band soon became something of a hit in the Egyptian countryside, graduating to the larger towns in the Delta. They travelled up and down the Nile, which they called the Long Sea, playing at religious festivals as well as weddings and private parties.[1] The family usually performed on temporary stages, accompanied by drumbeats alone or a couple of instruments and singing mostly religious songs in praise of the prophet (not the *taqtuqas* or romantic songs that were popular in Cairo) to an almost exclusively male crowd of farmers, workers, and small-town functionaries. In later accounts of Oum Kalthoum's life, her history of homespun performances like these gave her symbolic roots in a rural, "traditional" culture free from the degradation of Ezbekiyya.

Eventually, the family began touring away from their home, riding the train and staying overnight in cheap hotels. They were also invited to perform at the villas of the local elite with big-city tastes; in the absence of cabarets and dance halls, they held musical soirees in their homes. Oum Kalthoum—a rural girl who, according to a friend, did not even know how to use a knife and fork—felt out of place at these luxury parties. By around 1920, she and her family had moved on to perform at the villas of Cairo's upper crust; in a series of recollections that were probably at least partly constructed, she claimed to be even more shocked by the wonders on display. In a slightly contrived tale of her own naivety, she told how, when taken into the harem of an elite Egyptian villa to perform, she saw what she assumed was a crow, which suddenly started speaking to her. Backing away in terror, she screamed at the crowd who had come to hear her sing, "A talking crow! A talking crow!" The women had to calm her down, telling her it was a parrot and birds like it could speak. Back in her village, she told her family and friends all about this strange place called Cairo, "a city where the crows talk."[2]

The family soon won some important admirers in the city. Oum Kalthoum could count the wealthy Abd al-Raziq family among her earliest fans in Cairo. It is hard to imagine a greater contrast with village life than the concerts at the Abd al-Raziq villa, where the guest list would have included the leading lights of Egyptian politics and letters: writers, translators, religious thinkers, and government ministers.

The band's popularity with upper-class families like these soon convinced Sheikh Ibrahim to move his family to Cairo permanently. There, Oum Kalthoum could start singing in music halls and theatres, not just private houses. By the summer of 1922, she was putting on public shows in the theatres of Emad al-Din Street. One of her first performances was on 27 July, when she appeared on a bill with actors presenting a short farce, a dancing troupe, and "a young Italian girl dancing and doing tricks on a rope in an astounding and artistic fashion." She repeated similar concerts through the summer and into September.[3]

Oum Kalthoum was getting her first glimpse of the Ezbekiyya scene that had produced stars like Mounira al-Mahdiyya. This was a world of nightclubs and music halls that traded in risqué excess. The racy lyrics of the songs, which combined sexual suggestion with carefree disregard for social mores, would have been enough to shock any conservative rural Egyptian. Popular hits of the time included "After Dinner, Let's Fool Around and Have a Good Time" and the comically blunt "Who Is My Father and Who Is My Mother? I Have No Idea." They could hardly contrast more with the religious repertoire of Sheikh Ibrahim's traditional family band.

Oum Kalthoum mentioned that she and her family were rather taken aback by the raunchy musical trends. She told stories, some no doubt exaggerated, about Sheikh Ibrahim's strict parental control over her career and attempts to preserve her image. When a poster advertising a show was put up with her photo on it, he was so worried about what it might do to her reputation that he marched to the printers and forced them to make a new version without her picture. It was even said that he refused to let her sing the word *layl* ("night") because that was when people got up to no good. Considering that a huge number of Arabic songs contain the refrain *Ya Ain, Ya Layl* ("O eye, o night"), which has about as much meaning as "La, la, la" or "Oh baby," he was either very strict or extremely literally minded.[4]

During these early years in Cairo, Oum Kalthoum was constantly battling the seedier side of the entertainment business in the nightclubs of Ezbekiyya. One story from her memoirs stands out as an example of the always present threats of the cabarets and the courage Oum Kalthoum needed to face them. One night she was performing at the Bosphore Casino. The drunk and raucous crowd did not want to hear the religious songs that were part of her usual act, such as "My Lord, in Your Grace and Generosity, You Have Established Yourself as a Mercy for the People." They wanted the popular hits, the ones with raunchy lyrics that made her uncomfortable. As she sang, the audience started to jeer, shouting out requests for other songs.

Confronted with this rowdy nightclub crowd, Oum Kalthoum stood her ground; despite their protests, she kept singing her religious songs. When the crowd realised that she was not going to give in, they started shouting and whistling. She kept going. She even got angry, telling them that they knew very well who she was and what kind of songs she sang. If they wanted to hear immoral songs, she said, there were plenty of cabarets where they could do that. This did not calm them down; some of the crowd even tried to climb onto the stage and pull the curtain down in front of her. At that point, her father got up from his place in her band. He grabbed his daughter and slapped her face. Shocked, Oum Kalthoum started crying and ran off the stage.[5]

There are reasons to think that the beginning of Oum Kalthoum's career in Cairo was more complex and varied than her later accounts let on. The stories about her early life, many of them from memoirs written several decades after they took place, likely involved at least an element of myth-making. Her assertions that the family only sang religious songs, for instance, are questionable; as early as 1922, adverts in the contemporary press about her performances announced she would sing crowd-pleasing *taqtuqas*, not just the traditional songs that had made her famous. In 1924 she began collaborating with one "Doctor Sabri," who combined a day job as a dentist in the large city of Tanta with a sideline as a composer, to record some romantic songs for Odeon Records. The title of one hit they recorded in this early period was far from conservative; its title was "Flirting and Debauchery Are My Creed."[6]

While navigating Cairo's mid-1920s music scene, Oum Kalthoum also sought out one of the most well-regarded artists of the early twentieth century in Egypt—the singer and composer Sheikh Aboulela Mohammed, whose poetic religious songs were held up as outstanding examples of the genre. Oum Kalthoum had already heard his records while living in the Delta and even met him a few times at concerts; but now that she lived in the capital, she began to train with him. After his death in 1927, she described him as "one of the Arabs' greatest musicians—very knowledgeable, full of refined feelings. He completed what our forefathers began and preserved the venerable musical traditions laid down by our ancient Arab ancestors." His mentorship, brief as it was, became an important part of her self-image. She was not just any nightclub singer; she was a serious and respectable artist in a great classical tradition.[7]

It was also through Sheikh Aboulela that she met the young poet Ahmed Rami; their encounter would drastically alter her career for many years. He was among the new generation of Egyptian romantic poets who were attempting to free Arabic poetry from what they saw as the shackles of dry formality. Poetry, they said, was more than just a way to show off mastery of the Arabic language and ability to devise eloquent puns and wordplays; the new generation wanted to use verse to express their deepest feelings. Rami had been an important member of this avant-garde for several years. In his twenties, he had published two *diwans* (poetry collections)—one in 1918 and another in 1920—

to considerable acclaim. One reviewer in 1921 called the young man "one of [Egypt's] leaders to be, in thought and literature" and praised his work for being "musical without being cloying . . . passionate without being turgid."[8]

In 1925 he was one of the writers featured in the first issue of *Rose al-Youssef*, but in the early 1920s, before he had even gone to Paris to study Persian, he was a good friend of Sheikh Aboulela. The musician admired Ahmed Rami's work and asked if he could set one of his poems to music for his pupil Oum Kalthoum, who was still a relatively unknown singer. Ahmed Rami agreed and, giving little thought to the fate of the song, he went to Paris to focus on his education and work on a new Arabic translation of Omar Khayyam's *Rubaiyat*.

When he returned to Egypt in 1924, he was curious about what had happened to his poem. He went with Sheikh Aboulela to see Oum Kalthoum perform in Ezbekiyya Gardens, and that was the start of a relationship with a strange dynamic. The story goes that from the moment Ahmed saw her sing, he was captivated. After the show, he wanted to hear what Oum Kalthoum and Sheikh Aboulela had done with his poem and asked her to sing it for him. As she did, he became totally infatuated with her. A few days later he went to see her again, this time at the Bosphore Casino, and was convinced that he was in love.

The relationship that followed was intense and commercially successful, but resolutely platonic. Ahmed, so the heavily romanticised version of events goes, began putting all his feelings into poems and sending them to Oum Kalthoum. She showed no romantic interest in him at all, but did have the verses set to music (she wrote the tunes of at least two of them herself). And so their relationship went: Ahmed Rami composed painful lines of love, desire, and separation, which he gave her to sing and which quickly became integral to her repertoire. It has been hard for people to resist the conclusion that he poured his own feelings into these lyrics, imagining himself as she sang lines like:

Doubt gives life to passion, increasing its fire and flames

Or

Do you still think of me or have you forgotten me,
You who did me wrong, you who left me?[9]

This oddly chaste relationship only added to Oum Kalthoum's image of respectability. While living in Cairo, she may have been singing more love songs and fewer religious ones, but she was still careful to set herself apart from other singers. The press bought into the tale of unrequited love and started printing stories consoling Ahmed Rami. Their relationship, it was said, was sustained by the pair's mutual admiration of music and poetry alone. He introduced her to the greats of Arabic poetry and literature: Isfahani's *Book of Songs*, the Sufi poetry of Rumi and Ibn al-Farid, and many more. She proved an eager student and was soon a voracious reader of both classical and modern Arabic literature.

A singer who read books in her spare time was a dream for Egypt's new university-educated bourgeoisie, who formed part of the diverse clientele at theatres and nightclubs. They pined for a lover who could be intellectual (in a nonthreatening way) and could enter into deep discussions. A short story published in interwar Cairo by one such intellectual, Mahmoud Kamel, captured this desire neatly. It described a fictional love affair between a worker in the Cairo tram company and a virtuous nightclub singer. The young man realises that she is not just any singer when he catches her between sets in a quiet part of the cabaret reading *The Book of Eastern Music*, by Mounira al-Mahdiyya's former collaborator Kamel al-Khulai (a meticulous scholarly work on the principles of Arabic music). He promises to save the singer from her life in the cabarets by marrying her. She tells him that she has had relationships with men before who she thought loved her but never truly did. Then she sends him a letter saying that she doesn't think she is "a suitable wife for an honourable man" and leaves Cairo forever. The story ends when the young man, on a trip in the countryside, finds the nightclub singer there totally by chance. They recognise each other, and they later agree to live together happily ever after in the village, far from the cabaret stage.

Many men projected their fantasies of an intellectual and honourable cabaret singer onto Oum Kalthoum. They thought she was different from the others: deep, emotional, and literary. In early 1926, when a magazine published a story accompanied by a photo of her looking demure and expressionless, its writer launched into a flight of fancy about her inner feelings: "She is dressed in modest clothes, as if to say: 'I am a singer not an actress. And I am not like the other singers.' Her face is full of deep thought and pain. . . . There is a beauty that I cannot describe. Is it Arab? Greek? Egyptian? Is it Modern or Pharaonic? . . . She is a tender branch, heavy with flowers. But she wants to look like a fig-tree in winter, crooked and bare, lamenting every green leaf." After his long contemplation, all focused on her appearance, he concludes, "She is a weary soul in revolt but her revolution is internal. She does not betray her beating heart."[10]

Other men went wild for the elusive singer, giving free rein to their imaginations. When the poet, doctor, publisher, and pioneer of modern beekeeping, Ahmed Zaki Abu Shadi, heard one of Oum Kalthoum's records, he was so enchanted that he wrote a poem, which he then sent to a theatrical journal. It began:

Well done, my hope! accept my surrender.
You have defeated me as you made me weep.[11]

Oum Kalthoum almost certainly contributed to the construction of this image herself. In an interview with a Lebanese newspaper, given when she was an established star across the Arab world, the reporter asked what she did most days. She replied that in the mornings, she would take a walk along the Nile to be among the gardens and flowers and contemplate. "And if the weather is bad," she told the interviewer,

"I shut myself in the house and study my books of Arabic literature, both classical and modern."[12]

As Oum Kalthoum's career boomed, people began to draw comparisons between her and Mounira al-Mahdiyya—the woman who had been queen of Cairo's nightlife for over a decade. The differences between the two celebrities were stark. Oum Kalthoum was seen as reserved, sensitive, and emotional; Mounira was tough, brusque, and no-nonsense. A journalist from *Rose al-Youssef* told a story that encapsulated their opposing natures. He had visited Oum Kalthoum when she received a shipment of one of her own records. As she put one on the turntable, she began to cry, and "the muscles in her face began to contract and her eyes reflected a mix of pain, joy and ecstasy." The same journalist then went to see Mounira al-Mahdiyya and told her what he had seen at Oum Kalthoum's house. He reported her dismissive reaction: "What rubbish! Never in my life have I heard of someone crying when they heard their own voice."[13]

In 1925 a young critic called Abd al-Majid Hilmi, in a theatre review, made a much blunter comparison between the two women. Oum Kalthoum, he thought, represented everything that entertainment should be. Go to see her, he said, and you would hear "an angelic voice that rises from a sensitive heart which has a feeling for life and a heavenly tune which will send your soul the joy of hope and the strength of youth. . . . The tone of pure gold rings out in the air, in harmony with the art of nature."

Then he turned to Mounira al-Mahdiyya, whose musical theatre was still thriving in Cairo, and the comparison was unfavourable. "Mounira," he said, "has turned the theatre into a dancehall. The crowd cheer for the tune 'Shake It,' and she just laughs back at them. So, gentlemen, what now is the difference between your 'refined' theatre and

Opposite: Oum Kalthoum publicity photo

the *cafés chantants* in the dirty, 'native' areas?" He had to ask, "Isn't what Mounira is doing corrupting our morals and spreading vice?"[14]

In 1926, after four years of success in Cairo, Oum Kalthoum took another step forward. Her father, Sheikh Ibrahim, was dropped from her band, and she brought in a new line-up. Three of the best musicians in Cairo joined her new ensemble: on violin was Sami al-Shawa, the so-called prince of the violin; on the *qanun* was the veteran Mohammed al-Aqqad; on the oud was the rising star Mohammed al-Qasabji—also a noted composer who had written the melodies accompanying Ahmed Rami's lyrics. With this step, the girl from the countryside had become an urbane diva.

Around this time, Mounira al-Mahdiyya started fighting back against her new challenger. Later accounts of Oum Kalthoum's life are full of rumours about Mounira's jealousy and her attempts to sabotage Oum Kalthoum's career. Some of these stories might be based on old misogynistic clichés as much as they are on reality. Some have claimed, for instance, that Mounira used to disguise herself in a long black dress and face veil so she could sneak into Oum Kalthoum's gigs and watch her nemesis without being recognised. Others have said that Mounira secretly cast spells and curses on Oum Kalthoum to sabotage her career.

One of the most enduring and well-attested of Mounira's attempts to derail Oum Kalthoum took place in either 1926 or 1927. At that time, according to Oum Kalthoum's memoirs, a small but scandalous article about her appeared in the new journal *al-Masrah*, edited by Abd al-Majid Hilmi (the same man who had written such a complimentary review of her show the year before). Oum Kalthoum did not disclose exactly what the salacious article had said, but its revelation was apparently so incendiary that when her father saw it, he vowed to take his daughter out of Cairo for good.

More recent writers have tried to identify the article in question. Virginia Danielson, one of her biographers, suggested that Oum Kalthoum's father was offended by the succession of articles spreading gossip about her romantic affairs: first was a claim that she had married a palace functionary; a second article retracted that claim but implied they might be living together out of wedlock, as "a large number of her friends reported that every time they went to her house this 'husband' was there behaving in a way that left no doubt that he was her husband." Another biographer, Ratiba al-Hifni, has suggested that her father's indignation might have been to do with *al-Masrah* magazine's announcement that it was going to publish a police report about a sexual assault Oum Kalthoum had suffered as a child. (In the end they never published this secret report, which may well not have existed at all.)[15]

Whether Sheikh Ibrahim was incensed by a single article or a combination of many, few people doubted that the instigator of their appearance was Mounira—who was then rumoured to be having an affair with the editor, Abd al-Majid Hilmi. Oum Kalthoum herself, in her later memoirs, was sure that Mounira was to blame. Eventually, though, the scandals blew over, and a friend persuaded Sheikh Ibrahim to let Oum Kalthoum stay in Cairo by convincing him that taking her away looked like an admission of guilt.

The Egyptian press at the time needed no encouragement to print gossip about the lives of female celebrities. Throughout the '20s and '30s, they frantically searched for Oum Kalthoum's other possible suitors and were perturbed by her apparent unwillingness to marry. In one interview Oum Kalthoum, when yet another journalist asked about her love life, told him explicitly that she was not interested in marriage. "Love is just empty talk, brother," she said, claiming that she was like someone walking into the kitchen and seeing so much choice of food that she stopped feeling hungry. "I see hundreds of different kinds of men who declare their love and announce that they have set their hearts under my feet . . . and I just don't feel any pleasure in love."[16]

But people did not take her protestations seriously. They found it impossible to believe that a woman would freely stay single and speculated that she must have been recovering from a tragic love affair. In 1930, a small article in the press announced that "Oum Kalthoum has grabbed a broom and is sweeping away her male fans and admirers. From now on, she is saving her affection and friendship for her female fans." Of course, this did not stop the speculation, and people have since suggested that she was a lesbian.[17]

By the end of the 1920s, helped by a lucrative contract with the Gramophone company, Oum Kalthoum was one of the most successful singers in Egypt and almost certainly the richest. She had money in the bank, land in the Delta near her home town, and a villa in the wealthy district of Zamalek. In late 1929, *Rose al-Youssef* magazine estimated her personal wealth at 22,000 Egyptian pounds (equivalent to over £1.25 million now). These were the rewards that came to a celebrity singer who was performing in Egypt almost every night and whose records were selling from Morocco to India.[18]

Her career entered a new phase in 1931 when her father, Sheikh Ibrahim, died. Throughout the 1920s Oum Kalthoum had rejected offers to tour in the rest of the Arab world, at her father's request. No one was quite sure why he did not want her to travel outside Egypt. Some newspapers guessed that he was too nervous to let her travel on a boat, because she could not swim. Others theorised that he insisted on accompanying her if she travelled abroad and that it was he who was afraid of taking the boat. He claimed that horse or donkey were the only modes of transport he trusted—though it is not clear why his daughter couldn't travel by train or car. Nevertheless, after his death she was free to do what she wanted, and by the end of 1931 she was already performing across Lebanon, Syria, and Palestine.

In September of that year, she caused a stir in Damascus when she entered the city in a convoy of thirty cars. No one had seen anything quite like it; the once modest, restrained religious singer had become an international diva, and thousands of people thronged to her concerts. The crowds surrounding the Umayyad Hotel, where she was staying, were so large that the police had to clear a path to the door for her. Back in Egypt, *Rose al-Youssef* proudly reported her enthusiastic reception in Damascus, telling readers that she had met with the Syrian prime minister, the interior minister, and the governor of Damascus.

Across the Arab world, Oum Kalthoum had thousands of fans who loved her records and were desperate to see her perform live. When she travelled to Iraq in 1932, a crowd of dignitaries officially welcomed her, put her up in a luxurious hotel, and drove her around in a car decorated with the flags of various countries (with the Egyptian flag flying highest). At the Parisiana in Jaffa during summer 1933, her performance was completely sold out. People climbed nearby trees, peering over the walls for a glimpse of the stage; a newspaper reported that one determined spectator fell out of a tree during the show and broke his leg.[19]

Throughout the 1930s, Oum Kalthoum went from strength to strength. The task of managing her career must have been enormous, and she seems to have shouldered most of the burden herself. Virginia Danielson has written that by the late 1920s, she was handling all her own finances and contracts. After her father's death, she must have taken on even more work. Other people may have been working behind the scenes, too, but if they were, they stayed well out of the public eye. By 1934 Oum Kalthoum was frequently performing at her own theatre on Emad al-Din Street. That summer, when the Egyptian government created a national radio station, she saw a golden opportunity and recorded concerts that were broadcast on the radio every Monday night. The sets were predictably well received, and she soon took over the more coveted Thursday night spot. One magazine writer told his readers that they should cancel all their appointments, stay at home, and listen to the "pure, sweet voice" of the "pride of Egypt." After hearing these shows, listeners gushed with praise and fan letters arrived from across the country. One claimed that the only reason to get a radio was to listen to Oum Kalthoum's voice; another said she was "an angel from heaven . . . whose voice intoxicated me as wine intoxicates a drunkard," adding, "Praised be He, who created this nightingale." A fan in the small Nile Delta town of Simballawein wrote that because he did not own a radio, he had called a friend in the nearby city of Mansoura and listened to the whole performance through his telephone receiver.[20]

Despite her massive popularity and closely guarded private life, even Oum Kalthoum could not entirely overcome the stigma of being a female singer in interwar Cairo. In 1939, when the radio broadcast a series of her concerts performed in Ewart Hall at the American University in Cairo (AUC), some Egyptian evangelical pastors objected. The Egyptian Evangelical organisation "Synod of the Nile" complained that her songs were not appropriate for the Christian institution, especially in a hall that was sometimes used for religious services. Writing to the faculty and trustees of the AUC, they asked the university to bring an end to "such programmes including songs of a nature appealing to degenerate passions." Their appeal included messages of support from other Christian organisations in Egypt, ranging from a Coptic youth group to various other evangelical groups like the Plymouth Brethren, the Apostolic Church of God, and the Canadian Holiness Movement, whose representative Rev. J. C. Black said that Oum

Kalthoum's appearance at the AUC "brings shame to Christianity in a Moslem land."

When the worried AUC administration polled local Egyptians for their opinions about the appropriateness of her show, they got mixed responses. One said that he was "quite confident that the woman Oum Kalthoum has a character above reproach." He added that "during her programmes . . . she maintains complete modesty and proper conduct making no move whatever to objectionable gestures or language." Another agreed that she was "in a class all by herself as a prima donna." Yet another said she was "quite above the ordinary type of Egyptian women singers."

But some disagreed. "This woman is positively bad," one responder stated. "She belongs to the type of woman with which AUC is not supposed to have any contact." Another called her programme "sexual, indecent, degrading, weakening, and effeminate." Many complained about issues of class and respectability. The chief usher, who had been at almost all of the performances, claimed to have been "disappointed and indeed disgusted with the results." He was especially angry about the audience. Many were drunk, around 80 percent were from the "lower elements of the community," and the women were "manifestly of the prostitute class." Even though many young bourgeois Egyptians attended concerts and cabarets, the feeling persisted that the audiences for shows like these were low class. Some also suggested that, for all her superficial virtue, Oum Kalthoum's performances deliberately encouraged bad behaviour. One person claimed that "the words are intentionally ambiguous, primarily to awaken a vulgar response on behalf of the individual."[21]

In 1935 the wealthy banker Talaat Harb—who almost twenty years earlier had dismissed Rose al-Youssef from his theatrical troupe for wearing a swimming costume at the beach—set up Studio Misr in Cairo in an attempt to boost the local film industry. The studio recruited Oum Kalthoum for its first major picture, *Wedad*, a historical romance that took place in the medieval sultanate of Mamluk Egypt. Oum Kalthoum played a faithful slave girl who asks her master to sell her in order to help him out of financial difficulty. It was set to be a lavish production, written by Ahmed Rami and directed by the German Fritz Kramp. Oum Kalthoum, no doubt well aware that she was vital to the film's success, negotiated an impressive contract. She was to receive an upfront fee of 1,000 Egyptian pounds and then 40 percent of the film's subsequent profits, up to a cap of 7,000 pounds. She also maintained significant creative control over the script, insisting that the story remain consistent with "Eastern traditions."[22]

The follow-up to her first movie, *Nashid al-Amal* (Song of hope), was a contemporary story about a virtuous young woman. Forced to bring up her daughter alone after divorcing her villainous, low-life ex-husband, she embarks on a successful singing career that eventually brings her a life of respectable comfort. As the film industry grew in Egypt, Oum Kalthoum proved to be just as successful in adapting to this medium as she was to the radio. Between 1936 and 1947, she starred in seven feature films.

These films were largely star vehicles, primarily designed to showcase Oum Kalthoum's singing voice in extended musical interludes. Virginia Danielson, in her biography of Oum Kalthoum, summarised the films, in which she typically played the roles of "virtuous women who overcame trouble." "The subjects of the film plots were romantic, featuring glamourous characters, exotic settings from Arab history, clearly drawn lines of good and evil, and resolutions in favour of goodness and justice. In each film [she] cultivated sophistication and respectability in her public image and styled herself as an elegant exponent of Egyptian romanticism."[23]

As her career showed no signs of slowing down, Oum Kalthoum

Oum Kalthoum's film *Song of Hope* at a cinema in Jaffa
(Library of Congress, Prints & Photographs Division, [LC-DIG-matpc-17032])

remained in control of her professional and personal life. In 1942 she was also involved in establishing the Egyptian Musicians' Union. Then, despite the misgivings of some members, she ran in the election to become the organisation's president—competing against the male singing star Mohammed Abd al-Wahhab—and won. Over the next decade, she won seven consecutive elections for the presidency and oversaw several initiatives designed to improve life for members, including a campaign for fair wages and a fund to support unemployed, sick, and struggling musicians. The union was designed, in its own words, to "represent all musicians, demand their rights, and defend their existence, considering them all part of one family in which the children share in hopes and struggles alike."[24]

As president, Oum Kalthoum used her long experience in the entertainment industry to help raise the union's profile: She performed at their annual concerts, formed alliances, and built union awareness among fellow artists. She cut a charismatic figure as the union's figurehead. In a series of pictures of her, taken at a meeting of the association of the Musicians, Actors and Cinema Unions and published in 1952, she can be seen smoking a cigarette and gesticulating across the table at fellow delegates.

It is a testament to her amazing management ability that Oum Kalthoum's career trajectory barely wavered throughout her life. In July 1952, when a group of army officers started a revolution to depose Egypt's King Farouk and take power, she moved with the times once again. In that new era, it was unclear which parts of the old order would survive and which would be cleared away; but Oum Kalthoum performed yet another skilful professional sleight of hand that allowed her to flourish. To avoid becoming a remnant of the past age, she went to the main radio broadcasting station to find old recordings of her concerts, and—according to one article published just weeks after the revolution—she "cleansed some of her songs of the sections that were specific to the past age . . . so that they could be broadcast, pure and simple, for a free people to hear."[25]

In 1954, after decades of speculation about her romantic life, she married a prominent dermatologist and long-time fan, Hassan al-Hefnawi, roughly ten years her junior, who stayed with her for the rest of her life. In the 1950s and 1960s, she was without question the most famous woman in the Arab world.

On 3 February 1975 at 6:00 p.m., an announcement from the prime minister of Egypt informed the people that Oum Kalthoum had died. Tributes poured in from musicians, writers, and politicians, including Egypt's leader, President Anwar Sadat. The presidents of Syria and Tunisia, Hafez al-Assad and Habib Bourguiba, sent personal messages expressing their condolences, as did ambassadors from Sudan, Morocco, Saudi Arabia, and Somalia, where people were weeping on the streets of Mogadishu. Even the management at the Sheraton Hotel in Cairo sent a message to *al-Ahram* newspaper to make their grief known.

Her funeral on 5 February 1975 brought Cairo to a standstill. The cortege, led by representatives of Egyptian women's organisations and accompanied by pictures of Oum Kalthoum, floral displays, and a 150-man marching band, set out from the Omar Makram Mosque on Tahrir Square at 11:00 a.m. It travelled through a crowd of onlookers waving white handkerchiefs and was supposed to process about a mile across Tahrir Square and Talaat Harb Square to the Jarkas Mosque. But the turnout was so large that the plans were soon abandoned. The *New York Times* estimated that hundreds of thousands of people were present; *al-Ahram* said 1 million (estimates of the turnout have steadily grown since then and sometimes go as high as 4 million). *Al-Ahram* reported that the crowds managed to take her body off the shoulders of the firemen who were carrying it and take it on a procession of their own that lasted over two hours. Instead of turning towards the Jarkas Mosque, the mourners took Qasr al-Nil Street to Ezbekiyya Gardens and Opera Square. Her body finally reached al-Hussein Mosque, around three miles from Tahrir Square, at 1:15 p.m. After funeral prayers, the body was carried to a grand mausoleum in Cairo's City of the Dead that Oum Kalthoum had constructed for herself many years earlier.

Her funeral was one of the biggest public events in Egypt in the entire twentieth century, perhaps second only to the funeral of President Gamal Abdel Nasser. The display of devotion to the iconic singer, who had risen from the stages of Ezbekiyya in the 1920s, may even have dwarfed the ceremony after Nasser's death. The Lebanese-American visual artist Simone Fattal, who had cancelled a trip to Aswan to be present at the funeral, was quoted in the *Washington Post* that day: "She united all Arabs with her singing and personality, and made us realise the best in our culture. . . . She belonged to the people." The *Chicago Tribune* compared her career to that of the gospel singer Mahalia Jackson, informing its readers that "her popularity transcended the political and social divisions of the Arab world" and that "no Western artist has ever attained such a devoted following."[26]

Of all the women who had public lives in this period, Oum Kalthoum attained the most lasting fame and managed to reflect everything that the new nation of Egypt wanted to see in itself. The day after this huge national event, *al-Ahram* published a cartoon by the poet and artist Salah Jahin. It shows an Egyptian standing at the front of the funeral march, addressing a giant globe dressed in a suit. He is proudly telling this embodiment of the world: "Now you know that the Arabs have other things besides oil."[27]

Chapter 9

"COME ON, TOUGH GUY, PLAY THE GAME"

WHEN MOUNIRA AL-MAHDIYYA DIED in 1965, her funeral was not a huge public event. Only seven people attended, among them the doorman of her building and her local newspaper seller. Her career lasted decades and changed the face of Cairo's nightlife forever, but she spent her final years in relative obscurity, living with her sister after her last husband's death. In her later years she had become more religious and made the pilgrimage to Mecca—according to some, seven times—but she always remembered her glory days. Her dying words were "Don't forget me . . . and tell the newspapers, that Mounira the Queen of Tarab has died with a blameless reputation."[1]

We last saw Mounira in the early 1920s, when she had risen to success first as a nightclub singer and then as the leader of a theatrical troupe, singing songs of the new revolution. As the 1920s went on, Mounira's career as a singer and actress went through several different stages, but she remained one of the biggest stars in Cairo—perhaps *the* biggest. In the first years of the '20s—when Oum Kalthoum had just arrived in the city but was not yet a major star—Mounira spent most of her time abroad, touring the Arab world. She went to Aleppo for a benefit performance, where she made over 100 Egyptian pounds in one night for the city's orphans. She performed in Damascus at an outdoor venue in a neighbourhood also coincidentally called Ezbekiyya. And she went to Beirut, where she performed in several popular shows at the Kristal theatre. The Beiruti public started to think she would never leave—until 1923, when a local magazine announced, "The famous singer who has delighted Beirutis with the skill of her songs, has reluctantly decided to leave the city. She is putting on a series of farewell concerts, having finally decided to go back to Egypt for good. She will say goodbye to Beirut 'and this time, it's serious.'"[2]

She left Beirut but was soon off travelling again, sometimes quite far afield. Once, when the spirit of adventure seized her, she set out from the Levant to Baghdad on a route that crossed the infamous "valley of death," a mountain road thick with bandits on both sides. Her friends tearfully begged her not to go, but she armed herself with a pistol, a rifle, a bag full of bullets, and a sharpened dagger and set off— eventually reaching Baghdad, where she was welcomed with a huge feast. She recalled that during her travels around Iraq, she spent a week enjoying the lavish hospitality of Khazal Khan, then ruler of Arabistan in Mesopotamia, who was abducted by the Shah of Iran a few years later and placed under house arrest.[3]

Mounira's reasons for these long trips, she later admitted, were as much personal as they were professional. Over a decade before, in the early 1910s, she had married the wealthy Mahmoud Gabr Bey, who owned land in the Nile Delta. How or where they met is a mystery (at a nightclub is as good a guess as any), but when she moved into musical theatre and started her own troupe, he became its manager, dealing with finance administration while she focused on the creative side. At first they were a successful partnership, and his name often appeared alongside hers on the posters advertising her shows. But as with so many relationships between performers and their wealthy patrons, things did not stay that way forever. By the early 1920s, it was clear to Mounira that the marriage was falling apart.

Most accounts of the breakup are a little hazy. One story is that, having squandered his own money, Mahmoud was starting to take hers. Other versions insinuated that he was a controlling and perhaps even violent husband. Mounira later described this period as the worst of her life. It was no coincidence, then, that around this time she began doing tours in Syria, Lebanon, Iraq, and elsewhere, later saying it was the only way to escape his tyranny. The situation with Mahmoud made it difficult for Mounira to spend much time in Cairo until May 1924, when Mounira finally managed to get a divorce—after much legal wrangling and giving him a payoff of 1,500 Egyptian pounds. (Egyptian law required a husband's permission for a divorce.) Once she was finally free, she recorded a triumphant new song called "It's Been Thirteen Years," which began:

> It's been thirteen years
> And I can rest after my toil.

and then continued:

> I have suffered in love
> My heart has been burned by it
> People told me of a cure
> I would find the antidote in my singing
> But what truly revived my hope
> Was Beirut, the paradise on the hills.[4]

Another song put her feelings more crisply. The Egyptian historian Ahmed Abd al-Majid, writing in 1970, noted that she summed up her victory in two snappy lines:

> I have done it, I have left the thief
> Long live the lawyer, this woman's saviour.[5]

In the summer of 1924, Mounira was back in Cairo to rebuild her career. At first she moved slowly, doing one-off performances and singing her hits between the acts of other people's theatrical shows, but she had plans for a grand return to the stage before long. She started putting together a new troupe, hiring the best collaborators she could find in Cairo and commissioning a new set of plays for a theatrical run. She hired the prolific and now veteran composer Dawoud Hosni to create her musical scores; he had once taught Fatima Sirri and spent the early years of the 1920s creating his own Arabic operas. For the scripts, she enlisted the young writer Badie Khayri, who had provided many plays and song lyrics for Naguib al-Rihani and Ali al-Kassar. She also instructed him to assemble the finest possible cast of actors and actresses, which happened to include Ihsan Kamel, the Egyptian-Armenian actress whose drug-dealing husband had interrupted a romantic liaison with Youssef Wahbi about ten years earlier.

The first play staged by this new troupe was *al-Ghandoura*, a comic opera set in old Baghdad. It was a simple love story beset by many of the usual difficulties: A merchant called Gamal and his uncle arrive in Baghdad, where they chance to see a beautiful singer (played by Mounira). The young merchant falls in love with her, but his uncle refuses to let him marry her because she is an illegitimate child who does not even know who her father is. As the play unfolds, a series of lucky events reveal to the men that the singer does have a respectable father. His uncle gives Gamal permission to marry her, and everything ends happily.

The title of the play, *al-Ghandoura*, is a strange word. In its feminine form, it is usually translated into English as "pretty woman" or "beauty"; but in its masculine form (*al-Ghandour*), it means something like "fop" or "dandy." As a title for her first play of the new season, it seems very appropriate. Mounira, who was always playing with gender divisions like this, may have been the closest thing to a female dandy in Egypt of the mid-1920s.

Al-Ghandoura opened on 2 April 1925, and Cairo's theatre fans—audiences as well as critics—were thrilled to see Mounira's triumphant, long-anticipated return to the stage. Reviewers loved the play's successful comic interludes but focused on the high standard of Mounira's singing, which she ensured was a central part of the performance. At the end of almost every song, one newspaper wrote, the audience cheered and begged her to sing it again. In one scene, she treated the audience to a special "Baghdadi dance" performed in an impressive costume, studded with real gold coins, that she returned to a bank vault at the end of every night.

The most glowing review of this new incarnation of Mounira's troupe came from her greatest admirer, the lawyer and politician Fikry Abaza. Soon after the performance, he wrote a review declaring that "I was enchanted and felt for the first time in my life, that I was happy." In his view, the play was deeply political. He said that he had seen "democratic love" (a love based on true feelings, not societal strictures) triumph over "aristocratic love" and was elated. At last, he felt that the British occupation, which Egyptians still endured despite their nominal independence, might one day be overcome. He pictured their army leaving Egypt and saw "the flag of Liberty, Fraternity and Equality waving over everyone."[6]

As Mounira's season continued, though, controversies began to arise. On 2 May, she released the next play, *Qamr al-Zaman*, again written by Badie Khayri and with a musical score by Dawoud Hosni. It was advertised to audiences as a fairy tale featuring mermaids, royal castles, and extravagant scenery. Reviews at the time are a bit unclear about the plot; Mounira played the lead role of Qamr al-Zaman, who was shut away in a tower looking out to sea. But audiences did not come for the story; they wanted to see the song-and-dance numbers that had always been an integral part of her theatre. In these dancing scenes, Mounira always had to tread a fine line to avoid offending conservative tastes. In this new play, she crossed that line, creating a minor scandal as she did and falling afoul of those (often sporadically enforced) laws that since at least 1922 had forbidden belly dances on Cairo's stages.

On 6 May, a report was published in an Egyptian newspaper; it said that, in response to complaints by the public, officers from the Ezbekiyya police station had gone to the Printania Theatre, where Mounira was performing, and told her she had to remove any belly dancing from her new play. Her performances, they had warned, would be under police surveillance to ensure she complied. The police found support in the press for this action. If Mounira could get away with these things, people claimed, a contagion of immorality could easily spread through all the theatres of Ezbekiyya. One newspaper said the authorities had a "patriotic duty to eradicate this shameful, forbidden dance." Another article about her plays in the same paper called on the police to restrain "people who make money by destroying our morals and corrupting our habits." Mounira did not comply with official requests to cease, and a few weeks later the same newspaper announced that performances of *Qamr al-Zaman* would be banned.[7]

The day before Mounira premiered her controversial new play, Oum Kalthoum performed for the first time on the respectable stage of the Cairo Opera House. It was around this time that people first started to compare these two singing stars, particularly their diametrically opposed public images. Oum Kalthoum was restrained, bookish, and private. But Mounira courted shock, scandal, and outrage; she let a sense of dangerous fun surround her, flaunted her nonconformity, even built her career around it. Throughout the 1920s, Mounira created a flamboyant celebrity image that kept her in the public eye as new and colourful stories about her filled the press.

In 1927 a journalist from *Rose al-Youssef* magazine enlisted the Cairo-based psychic "Madame Vespasia" to read the palm of Mounira al-Mahdiyya. But Madame Vespasia's palm reading, perhaps more than anything else, was a reflection of the public image that Mounira had cultivated for herself. "Mounira's palm reveals that she is a woman who loves ostentation, luxury and show," Vespasia began; and, she continued, "Mounira is a woman in all senses of the word and has all the contradictions of a woman."[8]

Throughout her career, Mounira had an exceptional ability to market herself to the media. By projecting the image of an eccentric star, just the kind that the press wanted to see, Mounira managed to keep her name constantly in the public eye. She was a woman, she wanted to make clear, who did things differently. When asked by a curious fan why she always wore her heavy coat in the summer but took it off in the winter she replied, smiling, "because I am an *artiste*."[9]

She held late-night poker parties at her house and soon became known as one of the city's most skilful *pokéristes*, even recording a song called *Ya Gada Mazmiz* (Come on, tough guy) that was full of card-playing references. It began with the challenge "Come on, tough guy, play the game and don't try to bluff me, I see you!"[10] She also surrounded herself with a menagerie of animals—from ordinary cats and dogs to more exotic specimens, including weasels (which run wild in Cairo's streets), monkeys, and a snake—and carried a gun in her handbag wherever she went. People began to fear writing bad reviews of her shows because of rumours that she would send a gang of burly men to threaten anyone who did.

As a woman who had started her career in an older world—in those music halls and *cafés chantant* in the maze of alleys to the east of Ezbekiyya Gardens—she was cut from a different cloth than Cairo's new generation of celebrities. In 1925 the Egyptian government started

a competition for performers, awarding cash prizes to the winners in several categories (comedy, tragedy, musical theatre, etc.). Mounira, competing for the musical theatre crown, was asked to perform in the sanitised setting of the Opera House. The contestants had to sing and act while facing hundreds of empty seats in the grand hall. According to reports, Mounira could barely perform in this stale setting without an audience to react to her songs with groans of pleasure or shouts of "Allah!" (though she still won the top prize of 55 Egyptian pounds that year and the year after).[11]

Her apparent total self-confidence, along with a well-honed sense of fun, set her apart from her rivals—as did her extravagant lifestyle. In the mid-1920s, she cemented her reputation for luxury by purchasing, for the vast sum of 2,000 Egyptian pounds (over £100,000 today), a large stationary houseboat on the west bank of the Nile. It had two floors, a large sitting room, and nine elegantly furnished bedrooms. In this apparently decadent setting, Mounira held parties for high-profile guests, serving them fine cognac—whiskey, they claimed, was a poor man's drink. Always on display were the numerous medals she had received from foreign governments, including a gold one from the Italian government for her services to the theatre and "the effect her singing had on Signor Mussolini's heart." She was never afraid to appear louche, dressing in fine clothes and jewellery and ignoring the tutting of her critics. "I made my own money. My mother and father left me nothing. Everything I earned is by my own sweat and toil and it is my right to enjoy every pound of it," she once said.[12]

In her love life Mounira was the complete opposite of Oum Kalthoum. After her divorce from Mahmoud Gabr, she was publicly linked to a succession of men, some of whom she married and then divorced, others whose precise relationship to her was less clear. Almost all the female stars of Egypt in the '20s and '30s seem to have gone

Opposite: Mounira al-Mahdiyya (photo courtesy of Joy Garnett)

through multiple husbands; but as the 1930s began, Mounira may have been the most prolific of all. Many accounts of her partners, real or imagined, were published, and the stories changed so much that it was hard to separate truth from rumour. One issue of a magazine would announce her engagement to someone, and the next issue would publish a hurried retraction.

Some partners in her fleeting romances were more disreputable than others. One of the strangest was Ahmed al-Fiqi Bey, who briefly took Mounira into a strange part of the international demi-monde. As a teenager, Ahmed was sent by his wealthy family to study in Paris, where the children of many prosperous Egyptians went at that time. But instead of studying, he decided to sign up as a dancer at the Folies Bergère and then soon followed another opportunity to Berlin. In Germany his stage name of Ahmed Bey became Achmed Beh, and he found jobs in Berlin's booming film scene. He got a job working behind the scenes on Fritz Lang's *Metropolis* and even had a few minor acting roles in German films like *The Jolly Peasant* and *The Hell of Young Women*, alongside the British actress Ivy Close at the end of her career.[13]

Wherever he went, trouble seemed to follow this aspiring actor and cabaret impresario. An article in *Rose al-Youssef* suggested that he had left Egypt for Europe in the 1920s because, following some unspecified misdemeanour, his situation had become "too hot." The article went on to suggest that the law had caught up with him in Berlin too. The writer even claimed that German police had raided his apartment, discovered an illicit stash of hashish and passports in two different names, and forced him to return to Egypt. However, after his brother had written in to deny the story, the magazine printed a retraction a few weeks later.

Back in Egypt in 1930 (whether or not the law had forced him to return), Ahmed somehow met Mounira. They were married in July, only a few months later (details of their meeting are in very short supply). The couple travelled to Europe for their honeymoon, staying in Berlin and taking the waters at the famous spa town of Carlsbad, but the marriage lasted only a few months. By that summer Mounira was back in Cairo, ready to perform again. And, as she went out in the city to announce her return, observant spectators noticed that her new husband Ahmed Bey was nowhere to be seen.[14]

Like many of Mounira's reported relationships, this one disappeared almost as quickly as it had started. In 1934 Ahmed married Vera Violet, a Hungarian actress based in Cairo.[15] Throughout the 1930s, he worked on the fringes of the entertainment industry—dipping in and out of some rather shady projects, and occasionally at some big venues—with trouble never far behind. In 1936 he landed the job of artistic director at a new cabaret run by the dancer Imtithal Fawzi at the Bosphore Casino, but only a few weeks later, Imtithal was brutally murdered by a local gang. Two years later Ahmed played a small role in the big-budget film *Lashin*, Fritz Kramp's follow-up to Oum Kalthoum's film debut in *Wedad*. Soon after that he went to Europe again and somehow ended up in Vienna during the Second World War, running the casino Bei Achmed Beh. A 1944 film from inside this cabaret shows a succession of women wearing ever-diminishing amounts of clothing while dancing for the well-heeled denizens of Nazi-run Austria—and that may tell us all we need to know. He eventually returned to Egypt at the end of 1946, after nine years in Europe, and sank into obscurity. Throughout the late 1920s and early 1930s, the press constantly brought up Mounira's relationships with a series of men like these, highlighting the striking contrast between her and Oum Kalthoum.

Perhaps unsurprisingly, Mounira became a subject of popular fascination. When she threw a party on her much-storied houseboat, Egypt's political elite rushed to attend. Sometimes there were so many of them that the party on a boat seemed more like a political meeting, and it is probably those guests who gave rise to the myth (fanned by Mounira herself and still told today) that parliament once held a session on the boat. This influential circle of fans followed her professional career closely. One journalist claimed that only people with the noble title of Bey who had served in some office of state were eligible to become part of her *balat* (court) of admirers. After some of her performances, government ministers jumped onstage, hoping to kiss her hands. Fikry Abaza, who had claimed that Mounira's performance in *al-Ghandoura* was the happiest night of his life and was known by some as "the head of advertising for Mounira al-Mahdiyya's troupe," went so far as to write an article begging her to stand for election herself and enter the parliament.[16]

Despite Mounira's counting so many politicians as her fans (or perhaps because of it), it is unclear whether she had any specific political loyalties. In the interwar period, many rival parties fought for electoral dominance, and Mounira mixed with members of all the parties. Journalists speculated, without much evidence, where her true feelings lay; but their assumptions may have involved more projection than fact. The magazine *Rose al-Youssef*—staunchly pro-Wafd, pro–Saad Zaghloul, and anti-colonial—claimed that she was courting members of other parties just for the money and was really pro-Wafd: she was "a *Saadist* in her soul but a Unionist and Liberal Constitutionalist in her pocket."[17]

Throughout the period, Mounira remained difficult to pigeonhole. On the one hand, she was undoubtedly the product of Cairo's modern nightlife with its influences from around the world; but on the other, she was deeply rooted in "traditional" Egyptian culture. Beginning in the late 1920s, her health became an obstacle to her success. A mysterious illness that she could not seem to shake troubled her; she had tried modern medicine and European spa treatments, but nothing had seemed to work. The press reported that she believed the illness to be a product of the "evil eye"—the envy that came upon her when she bought her luxury houseboat on the Nile.[18] Newspapers were fascinated by Mounira's superstitions, noting that she filled both her house and her theatre with incense in attempts to ward off the evil eye.

Nothing, though, excited the journalists more than Mounira's devotion to the popular Egyptian healing ritual of *zar*, which she may have been using to treat her illness. *Zar* is a tradition of spirit-possession and healing found in slightly different forms across much of the Red Sea and in East Africa from Egypt and Sudan to Ethiopia, Somalia, and the Arabian Peninsula. Its precise origins are still debated, but the practice is often thought to have come to Egypt with slaves from sub-Saharan Africa (though this origin story is still the subject of some disagreement). Led by female holy women called *sheikhas*, the rites are a mix of music and animal sacrifice. The goal is to bring forth the spirits that possess some members of the audience and may be the cause of problems ranging from illness to marital difficulties.

The spirits come in many different forms, and regional versions of the practice differ too. Some spirits are male and some female; some are European, some Egyptian; some are from sub-Saharan Africa; some are Muslim, some Christian, some Jewish, and some atheist. They often take the form of outsiders or foreigners, people not part of the community's mainstream. One of the most prevalent spirits in Egyptian *zar* is Yawra Bey, a young playboy who jealously possesses young women and prevents them from getting married. Another is Gado, an African slave who usually possesses hosts when they are in the toilet. Each spirit can be summoned by playing its own specific tune. As the band plays, the spirits that are possessing an audience member manifest themselves. This ceremony allows the *sheikha* to identify those people (usually women) who are possessed and then help them to handle their spirit— its aim is not so much to exorcise these spirits but rather to placate them and allow the possessed to live with them. Mounira's embrace of this practice made her a target for Egypt's chattering classes, many of whom saw *zar* not only as antiquated and irrational but also potentially harmful. They worried about these strange, female-led rituals, which they feared were stopping people from appreciating the benefits of modernity such as science and medicine.

It would, however, be simplistic to see Mounira's rivalry with Oum Kalthoum, which dominated the 1920s, as a competition between modernity and tradition or between antagonistic Egyptian and European (or Western) identities. It was really a clash between two versions of an Egyptian woman. There was an increasing consensus among writers, critics, and others in the industry that popular entertainment should reflect the realities of Egypt and appeal to audiences as Egyptians, but there was much less agreement about what it meant to be an Egyptian. Mounira and Oum Kalthoum offered conflicting approaches to that increasingly relevant topic.

The competition between Mounira and Oum Kalthoum reached its peak in 1927. Early that year, Mounira launched what would be her last major theatrical experiment—an ambitious operatic production of the story of Mark Antony and Cleopatra. Mounira had been working on this project with the gifted but fast-living Alexandrian composer Sayyid Darwish in 1923, but it was derailed when he suddenly died of a heart attack. For their model they had chosen the opera *Cléopâtre*, one of the last works of the French composer Jules Massenet (he died in 1912). The new production was a reworking of the events that had inspired Shakespeare's *Antony and Cleopatra*, starting when Cleopatra and Mark Antony first met and following the course of their love affair. The opera would conclude with their defeat at the Battle of Actium by the forces of the Roman Octavian (later, Emperor Augustus) and, finally, with their respective deaths. Mounira had hired an unknown young Egyptian writer, Salim Nakhla, to translate the libretto in preparation for a theatre performance.

In the early 1920s Mounira had performed a few songs from the play, but it was slow to get off the ground and, after Sayyid Darwish's death, the whole project disappeared, seemingly abandoned. In late 1926 Mounira was back in Cairo and saw her chance to resurrect the opera and dramatise one of the most romantic and exciting times in Egyptian ancient history. Accordingly, she brought in the celebrated poet and songwriter Mohammed Yunus al-Qadi, who had written lyrics to some of the most popular *taqtuqas* of the 1920s, to update Salim Nakhla's original text for its full theatrical debut.

But she still needed a composer for the crucial, unfinished musical parts, and she set her sights on a young singer called Mohammed Abd al-Wahhab. In his mid-twenties, he was a rising star of the Egyptian stage who both sang and wrote his own music. Mounira had been trying to work with him since 1925 without success. But when she offered this project, he could not resist the idea of finishing a work started by the idolised Sayyid Darwish. He agreed to finish the musical score as well as to play the lead role of Antony.

Mounira's final step was to enlist some of the best dancers in Egypt. As in most of her plays, dancing would be central to this production, and she was going to give the audience the best dancers she could find. The stars of her chorus were two famous sisters whose act was called Nina and Mary. The sisters later became famous for singing romantic and comic duets in the cabarets of Emad al-Din Street. They also recorded several popular records with Odeon, including the Charleston-inspired hit "We Are Mary and Nina" and the frankly racist "Black Bottom," which attacked the new jazz-inspired dance crazes of the time. This second song targeted the African American superstar Josephine Baker, accusing her of turning Paris into Khartoum (according to them, a bad thing). The influence of jazz music in Egypt did not always lead to respect for Black culture.[19]

With this all-star team of collaborators, Mounira premiered *Cleopatra and Mark Antony* on 20 January 1927 at the Printania Theatre on Emad al-Din Street. It was all set to be a smash, with "the kind of massive preparation and magnificent staging that is rare to see in Egypt," and at first the critics loved this "innovation in Arabic music and song." Everything about it captivated them. The critic Abd al-Majid Hilmi, with whom Mounira was rumoured to be romantically involved, said, "I saw a performance of *Cleopatra and Mark Antony* last night and the music and songs are still ringing in my ears." One writer even went so far as to say that Mounira was a reincarnation of the Ptolemaic queen herself. "Under Egypt's blue sky, on the banks of the silver Nile, in the land of the Pharaohs, the soul of Cleopatra inhabits the person of Mounira al-Mahdiyya. . . . The only difference is that, whereas Cleopatra's throne was golden and her crown was of pearls, Mounira's throne is people's hearts and her crown is their souls."[20]

But after initially positive reviews, the production began to stutter. Mounira came to resent the young star Mohammed Abd al-Wahhab, who was playing the male lead opposite her. She noticed that in the music he had written, he had given himself the emotional climax of the play—Mark Antony's final song. In fact, he might have given himself all the good songs and left Mounira with the rest. This young, talented novice had ideas above his station; by the spring, Mounira had decided to kick him out of the troupe.

With Mohammed Abd al-Wahhab gone, rumours about who would replace him quickly circulated. One possibility was the young singer Sayyid Shatta, who had spent some time in the court of the pasha of Marrakesh. But then Mounira announced that she would play the male lead herself, laying claim to the play's best songs, and would draft the popular singer Fathiyya Ahmed to play Cleopatra. Her decision was a throwback to the early days of her career, when she took the male roles for herself. For this opera, it had even more symbolism; by playing Mark Antony, Mounira was casting herself as the warrior who fought for the sake of Egypt, not as the queen who awaited defeat at home. Unfortunately, this reshuffle of the cast was no more successful, and by summer the new version had sputtered too. The play was meant to be one of the biggest theatrical events of 1927 and show that Mounira could still compete with rivals like Oum Kalthoum, but it ended up making her look like she was losing momentum.

As Cairo's theatrical season ended, Mounira took the chance to leave Egypt and tour the Levant over the summer of 1927—but this venture did not go much better than her run of *Cleopatra and Mark Antony*. Before she left, Mounira, who was famous for enforcing sartorial elegance in her troupe, bought nice new suits for everyone and insisted they wear them while out travelling. A few months earlier an article had appeared in *Rose al-Youssef* magazine saying that Mounira had taken offence to the moustaches of the male members of her troupe, so she had locked them all in a room with a barber and had all of them shaved. However, once they had arrived in the Levant, the actors totally ignored her instructions. Instead of the nice suits, they went around wearing their old clothes. Even worse, freed from the strictures of home, they ran wild; they got drunk, argued among themselves, and fought with the locals. One of them even sold the jacket Mounira had bought him to pay a bar bill. Another tried to sexually harass a woman who was working at their hotel; when this woman's husband heard about it, he turned up at the hotel with a knife, threatening to stab the actor in the chest. Mounira had to step in herself to calm the man down (the reports do not mention how the victim felt about all this).[21]

Along with these stories of bad behaviour, the trip also produced an especially unpleasant bit of gossip, one that even Mounira would find hard to spin to her advantage. Over the past year, she had become very close to the editor of *al-Masrah* magazine, (Mohammed) Abd al-Majid Hilmi. Their friendship made people suspect that she had used him to plant the rumours about Oum Kalthoum in his magazine, almost causing her father to take her out of Cairo the year before. That summer Abd al-Majid was in the throes of tuberculosis and had been advised by his doctors to take a holiday outside Egypt. When he learned that Mounira's troupe was going on a tour of Syria, Lebanon, and Palestine, he decided to join them.

But when he arrived, according to a later account given by someone calling himself "a grieving friend," Mounira did not welcome him lovingly. Quite the opposite; she was openly hostile. In Jerusalem, she told him that her troupe members were afraid of infection and that he should not stay with them—or even better, leave the city. The anonymous writer claimed that to keep Abd al-Majid away from her troupe, Mounira even tried to persuade the Egyptian consul to force him out of the country. Through all this drama, the trip took a heavy toll on his strength. He did eventually make it back to Egypt but died shortly after his return.[22]

The loss of this beloved young editor and journalist was widely mourned; but the aftermath of his death proved litigious, difficult, and full of allegations about Mounira. His magazine *al-Masrah* (The Theatre), without its main editor, changed its name to *al-Naqid* (The Critic) and published the lurid series of articles about the events in the Levant by an anonymous "grieving friend." The articles claimed that "it was psychological pain, more than physical pain, that did for Abd al-Majid" and that Mounira had been motived by extreme hatred and jealously of Abd al-Majid. The writer claimed, "If she ever bears a grudge against someone she can wait for days or years to get satisfaction. She can coax him and pretend to be submissive until she gets her prey." Frustratingly, the series of articles stops abruptly after the second instalment and the end does not survive. According to *al-Naqid*, Mounira launched legal action against the magazine around this time, and the rest of story was not published. These two events were never explicitly linked, but it is hard to imagine that they were not. *Rose al-Youssef* magazine claimed that when Mounira heard that it had information about her relationship to the late Abd al-Majid Hilmi, she threatened to "send her men round."[23]

Of course, the articles published in *al-Naqid* and *Rose al-Youssef* insinuated that the pair had once been lovers or that Mounira had seduced the young theatre critic. An article published in *Rose al-Youssef* after Abd al-Majid's death claimed that Mounira had accused him of demanding money to print favourable articles about her and her friends in his newspaper. The journalist responded to Mounira's accusation by saying, "Abd al-Majid, may he rest in peace, was not after Mounira's money; he was after something else" (with an implied wink).[24]

After the failure of her ambitious operatic project, *Cleopatra and Mark Antony*, and the scandal surrounding Abd al-Majid Hilmi, Mounira turned away from the theatre and went back to her earlier career as a singer. She was still a star across the Eastern Mediterranean, so although she was having some troubles in Egypt, some of the biggest concerts of her career took place abroad. In August 1928 she put on a now-legendary run of performances in Istanbul. The guest list included some of the most important people in the post-Ottoman capital. Alongside Turkish government ministers, writers, newspaper editors, and aristocracy, the cream of the city's Egyptian residents came to see her sing in the Sarayburnu gardens, overlooking the Bosphorus. But in this list of Turkish and Egyptian elites, the most famous guest was neither a politician nor an intellectual. He was a criminal convicted of attempted murder—Prince Ahmed Seif al-Din, who had recently successfully accomplished a bold escape from an English mental hospital.

Back in 1898, Prince Seif al-Din had walked into the Khedivial Club in Cairo and shot his brother-in-law, Fouad, who survived the attack and went on to become king of Egypt. Not long after the attack, Prince Seif al-Din was declared insane and sent to Ticehurst Hospital, a psychiatric institution outside Tunbridge Wells in England. In the summer of 1925, he launched a daring escape that led to an international manhunt. Secretly travelling down to Hastings, he hopped on the steamship *Devonia*, bound for Boulogne, where his mother and stepfather, who had helped plan the breakout, were waiting for him. From Boulogne they flew to Paris, where they checked into the Hotel des Pyramides—with Seif al-Din disguised as a woman, according to some reports. Once his escape from the asylum hit the newspapers, sightings of this fugitive were reported across Europe: people claimed to have spotted him in Venice, Bulgaria, and a carriage on the Orient Express. It later emerged that he had in fact travelled to Marseilles and then taken a ship called the *Phrygia* bound for Istanbul, where he arrived in mid-September, secured Turkish citizenship, and settled down to a life in the city with all its cultural highlights, including Mounira's well-attended concert.

Mounira's first night in Istanbul was such a success that the Egyptian press soon found out about it. *Al-Ahram* newspaper reported that the crowd had chanted, "Long Live Mounira, Long Live Egypt," and that next morning, when flattering reviews of the show appeared, she had agreed to perform several more nights for the adoring people of Istanbul. At one of these follow-up concerts, the Turkish President Mustafa Kemal Ataturk himself was in the audience. Politically, he had put himself in a tricky situation. At the time, he was attempting to move Turkey away from the Middle Eastern, Ottoman culture of its past: in the same month, he had formally abolished the Arabic script and introduced a Latinised alphabet. Still, he could not be too rude about this great foreign star. In the end he gave a short speech that praised her great singing voice, but added that "the music was a little simplistic and didn't satisfy the progressive Turkish spirit."[25]

In November 1929, back at the Printania Theatre on Emad al-Din Street, Mounira started another extended theatrical season with an Arabic production of the opera *Tosca*, but her new venture lasted only a few months. On 11 January 1930, she fell ill while performing onstage and was forced to cut the run short, later prompting the theatre owner to sue her for damages.[26] In autumn 1930, fifteen years since her first appearance onstage as an actress, Mounira announced that she would be leaving the theatre and devoting herself entirely to music.

At the end of the 1920s new styles of entertainment were becoming popular, and cabarets were taking over from theatres and revues as the most popular night-time destinations on Emad al-Din Street. Mounira, always keenly aware of changes in the entertainment business, decided to open a cabaret of her own. She hired troupes of dancers—Sudanese, Egyptian, and European—and found a stage at the Petrograd Bar and Restaurant, just off Emad al-Din Street (but when a large crack opened up in the floor, she was forced to find alternative premises on Alfi Bey Street). In any case, she had returned to where she had started—the music halls of Ezbekiyya.

Throughout the 1930s, Mounira, then in her early fifties, continued to perform sporadically in Cairo—acting in the theatre of Ezbekiyya Gardens, singing in the Bosphore cabaret, and appearing on the new government radio station. But her name appeared less and less often in Egypt's magazines and newspapers and was replaced by new singers, chief among them Oum Kalthoum. In 1935 she tried her luck in the cinema, producing a film of her old play *al-Ghandoura*. It was not a total flop, but it was not a stunning success either, and she made no more films after it. Mounira's health continued to trouble her throughout the 1930s. It did not help when she was hit by a car on the way to one of her performances and was forced to stop working for several months. By the end of the decade, she was essentially retired.

After the Second World War, Mounira made one last attempt to get back onstage. In the spring of 1948, she reprised some of her classic plays and performed some of her greatest hits at theatres in both Alexandria and Cairo, including Ezbekiyya's opera house. In the audience at one of her shows was the young author Naguib Mahfouz, who would later become Egypt's best-known novelist and win the Nobel Prize for Literature in 1988. At that time he was only in his mid-thirties, and he remembered being one of the few young people in a sea of old music fans who went to relive Mounira's glory days. Feeling very out of place in this crowd, Mahfouz was disappointed to find that the old star's voice had not survived half a century of professional singing and that the icon he heard so much about no longer had the power to move the audience in the same way. "The effects of advancing age were clear. She sang a little and coughed a little; then the show was over. Afterwards, she announced that she would retire from singing."[27]

Mahfouz had a much higher opinion of Oum Kalthoum. In an Egyptian newspaper article in 1943, he said, "There is no voice that can compare with the sublime voice of Oum Kalthoum," and concluded with the grand statement that "through her the bright hope of the future is opened to us, while the radiant joys of the past are rolled up."[28]

Today it is the respectable star, Oum Kalthoum, and not Mounira who is revered as the queen of Arabic music. Mounira gave voice to a different kind of Egypt: It was colourful, glamorous, and transgressive, and with her songs about dark-skinned lovers, her devotion to *zar*, and her troupe of Sudanese dancers, she also made Egypt's connection to Africa clear. Her libertine lifestyle, part of what made her a huge star while she was alive, embodied the edgier and more provocative parts of Egyptian identity that have been pushed out of the mainstream in recent decades.

Chapter 10

ISIS FILMS

AT THE BEGINNING OF 1926, the Turkish writer, actor, and filmmaker Vedad Urfy came to Egypt from Istanbul with a mission—to create a thriving "Eastern" film industry in Cairo. Motion pictures had been popular in the country since 1896, the year after the Lumière brothers had first shown the Paris audience their Cinématographe. By the 1920s Ezbekiyya was full of cinemas showing popular European and American movies as well as home to several entertainment magazines that closely followed developments in global cinema. However, attempts to produce films in Egypt (and there had been a few) had not yet produced anything resembling a film industry.

Vedad Urfy, announcing himself as the artistic director of a new Turkish company called Markus Films, came to Cairo intending to prove that the East could do anything—including cinema—as well as the West. He told the press his company was going to produce three new films based on Egypt's Pharaonic and Islamic history and had already secured the services of the great Hungarian director Michael Kertesz (who later moved to America, changed his name to Michael Curtiz, and is most famous for having directed *Casablanca*).

However, in his eagerness to promote his new venture, Vedad did not reveal the whole truth—or at least he allowed journalists to make certain assumptions about the company without correcting them. Markus Films was not a great Eastern company based in Istanbul. In fact, it had been set up two years earlier in Paris by the Swiss filmmaker Dr. Stefan Markus. A former academic with a PhD in the history of Swiss newspapers in the Helvetic Republic, Markus had recently found work in the exciting new world of cinema. At the same time as Dr. Markus was sending Vedad Urfy to Egypt, he was also putting the finishing touches on a grand new film called *The Cradle of God*. The plot, which he had written himself, involved a man who had lost his faith in God but slowly rediscovers the glory of religion. He was now hoping that Egypt would give him some epic and spiritual inspiration for more films.

But Vedad Urfy was keeping something bigger from the Egyptian press, something that would soon get out and cause the biggest scandal of early Egyptian cinematic history. He had not told them that, besides scouting Egyptian locations and talent, Dr. Markus had agreed to produce a new script written by Vedad himself—an epic biopic of the prophet Mohammed. The two had come to Cairo partly to find an actor who could play the starring role.[1]

The French film company possibly had no idea about the kind of problems that a film like this could cause, but it would soon find out. Islamic orthodoxy was extremely uncomfortable with physical depictions of any prophet, let alone Mohammed, and most religious scholars considered it a forbidden act. So in early May 1926, when articles in the Egyptian press announced that Markus Films was working on a movie about the prophet—and revealed that Youssef Wahbi, the young star who had opened his Ramses Theatre a few years before, had been chosen to play the role of Mohammed—the uproar from religious leaders was no surprise.

Sheikhs at al-Azhar mosque issued a religious opinion (fatwa) confirming that it was forbidden to portray any of the prophets or the companions of Mohammed on the screen. Youssef Wahbi received a letter from the king of Egypt saying that if he went ahead with the film, he would be stripped of Egyptian citizenship. Members of the public were worried about the controversy. One unnamed woman wrote an open letter to Youssef that was critical but not aggressive and begged him to consider, "What curse will God put on you? What divine retribution will there be?" As public outrage reached a peak, all kinds of attacks appeared in the press, and wild speculation was often published alongside fact. In one case, *al-Masrah* magazine claimed to have head shots of Youssef Wahbi in his role as the prophet and said he was using the same costume and makeup that he wore when playing the role of Rasputin. This statement quickly morphed into an accusation that he was trying to compare Mohammed and Rasputin and was then taken up by some sheikhs at al-Azhar, who repeated it in a letter of condemnation they sent to the Ministry of the Interior.[2]

Youssef Wahbi responded to these charges in an open letter to *al-Ahram* newspaper. He began the appeal "as a Muslim man who loves his religion . . . who would sacrifice himself, to the last drop of blood, for his country and his people." He then continued to defend himself and the film, telling readers that the project would create a positive image of Islam and telling his fellow Egyptians that it was a chance "to demonstrate the greatness of our true religion, to prove to the European world that our religion is the most refined, and that Mohammed is the leader of Muslims." He also responded to the rumour that he was going to play Mohammed in the same way he had played Rasputin, saying it was a total lie, spread by people "who hate me and are jealous of me for no reason." In his defence, the photos published in the newspapers exactly matched some that Youssef Wahbi later published in his memoirs showing him in the role of the Moroccan rebel leader Abd al-Krim; and since Youssef was working on a play about him at the time, they were almost certainly not photos of him as Mohammed (or as Rasputin), but as Abd al-Krim.[3]

Vedad Urfy publicly also defended himself from the attacks, assuring people that the film was not intended to denigrate the prophet. Just as Youssef had, he affirmed his own love of Islam. As a Muslim who loved the prophet, he said that writing the script had been an honour, and he was prouder of it than anything he had ever done. To help alleviate the situation, he told the newspapers he had made sure the company would hire Islamic scholars to confirm that all details of the film were correct. Anyway, he concluded, this was not part of the Markus Films project to start a Middle Eastern film industry; instead, it was intended for Western audiences, who knew nothing about Islam and, in fact, frequently belittled it. If anything, Vedad Urfy said, it would be a powerful defence of Islam to the people of Europe. If Egyptians did not think the film was appropriate for their own country, the national censorship system could always prevent it from being shown.[4] None of these arguments convinced the Egyptian public. In the end, the uproar ensured the film was never made. Youssef Wahbi dropped out, other problems emerged, and the whole project became unsustainable. The great director Michael Kertesz, whom Dr. Markus claimed to have hired, had either been stringing him along or had never really agreed to work on the project. Each time work was about to start, the company would announce a delay in production due to Kertesz's schedule. In June, Dr. Markus discovered that he had gone to work for Warner in California, and Markus Films had lost its most bankable name. The idea soon vanished without a trace, and Youssef Wahbi went back to making plays as if nothing had happened.

Vedad Urfy's first attempt at starting an Egyptian film industry had failed. But his desire appears to have been genuine, and he did not give up; he decided to stay in Cairo and keep working on the mission. A few months after the Mohammed film fiasco (in either late 1926 or very early 1927), he met the young Egyptian actress Aziza Amir. Together the two began work on a new film that would be remembered, after another series of controversies, as the first Egyptian feature film.

In what is now becoming a predictable feature in the story of an actress from this period, Aziza Amir had come to Ezbekiyya in the 1920s with a somewhat murky history. People said she had been born in 1902 somewhere in the Nile Delta, but they disagreed on exactly where and on whether she grew up rich or poor. When she was young Aziza had, so the rumours said, been married and then divorced (perhaps twice) and moved to Cairo to become an actress. In the mid-1920s she "moved from house to house," as one magazine euphemistically put it, until she ended up living with the cotton magnate Elie Edrei.[5]

Elie, who at that point had not yet met Fatima Rushdi, showered Aziza with gifts. Some people said she had gotten so rich during their relationship that she built herself a house in the exclusive neighbourhood of Garden City with his money. When Aziza and Elie eventually split up, it only made for more gossip, and competing versions of the breakup appeared. A story in Youssef Wahbi's memoirs claimed that Elie was a heavy drinker and fanatically controlling, so Aziza was forced to flee the house secretly in the middle of the night, eventually taking refuge with Youssef Wahbi. If this account was true, it raises further uncomfortable questions about Fatima Rushdi's relationship with Elie Edrei and the unpleasant insinuations by the press that she liked a man to use force. But other people took Elie's side, claiming that he simply grew tired of Aziza and ended the relationship himself.

Aziza's own story of her early life mentions none of these events—neither the first husband nor the alleged string of affairs. Although the stories of her relationship with Elie Edrei were reported independently and in different places, Aziza never talked about it. In a short set of serialised memoirs in the late 1920s, she told the story of a well-educated girl who had the means to travel around Europe just after leaving school. She implied that her home life was comfortable and largely uneventful. The bare facts of these different accounts might be broadly compatible, but in spirit they are polar opposites, and the less respectable version often won out.

There were stories about the affairs and love lives of almost all actresses in the 1920s, but in the mid-1920s Aziza Amir was a particular target. And although she did not respond to any of the rumours directly, she had little respect for the journalists of the time. In an interview in 1927, she expressed a general sense of frustration about all the reports in the press and the people who wrote them: "They have bad intentions," she said, adding: "I know myself better than they know me and I don't need them. I'm fine as long as the ordinary people of my country love and support me. Those are the people I rely on, after God and my own hard work."[6]

It is only after late 1924 that anything definite can be said about Aziza Amir's life. That was when she entered the world of mainstream theatre, answering an advert posted by the Ramses troupe looking for actresses. She was accepted in the company, took the stage name Aziza Cleopatra, and acted in some minor roles. Despite showing promise, Aziza found these early years difficult. She was troubled by what she referred to as a nervous illness (perhaps something like depression) and often was bedridden for weeks on end. Her condition meant that theatre acting, with its constant schedules, never quite suited her; after joining the Ramses troupe, she acted in only three plays before leaving in 1925. Her illness continued to affect her for over a year after she left, and it eventually led to a month's stay at a Berlin sanatorium in summer 1926.[7]

When she got back from Europe—having adopted the stage name Isis, after the Egyptian goddess—Aziza returned to the Cairo stage with the house troupe of the Ezbekiyya Gardens theatre. It was there that she first met a wealthy young aristocrat called Ahmed al-Sharii, who came from an important family with major landholdings in the fertile Nile valley south of Cairo; in April 1927 they married.

In the late 1920s, the theatre was the obvious place for an ambitious young actress to find steady work, but Aziza had other ideas. She had always been more interested in the screen than the stage. When she was young, films were an obsession; she went to the movies whenever she could, and at home she re-created the main scenes, acting them out in front of her mirror. She used all her spare money to buy illustrated magazines and cut out photos of the latest film stars: Lillian Gish, Pearl White, and Mary Pickford. During her earlier enforced breaks from the stage, she had even bought a Pathé Baby video camera and managed to put together a short film with her friends (who included some of Egypt's best-known stars, the stage actress Nazla Mizrahi and the singer Salah Abd al-Hayy). She even held a small private screening on her houseboat, *Zaza*.

In the winter of 1926–1927, Aziza Amir and Vedad Urfy found each other; these two young movie obsessives, both ambitious to create a thriving film industry in Egypt, seemed like the perfect match. Aziza found Vedad's passion infectious and immediately considered him capable of making the kind of film she wanted to act in. He also saw the perfect collaborator in her—he thought she was a great actress, but he also saw in her a spark of creativity and "the kind of intelligence that few actors have." Before long they had agreed to work together on a new Egyptian film. Vedad Urfy would be the artistic director, in charge of the production, but the company would be called Isis Films, after Aziza's Pharaonic stage name, and she would be the star.[8]

As the figurehead of Isis Films, Aziza proved to be both hardworking and charismatic. The magazine *Rose al-Youssef* used its trusted palm reader, Madame Vespasia, to give its readers a sense of her character. "The sun rules this woman, who gives off a lot of heat and whose power affects everyone around her," the article began; it then went on to say, echoing Vedad Urfy's judgment on her intelligence, that "her heart is quick to enflame but her mind is balanced and precise." Aziza gave interviews herself and vigorously promoted the new company. During one meeting with a journalist from *al-Masrah* magazine, she chain-smoked his cigarettes (she smoked a lot but famously never bought her own) and told him all about the great things coming in her future. Despite the breaks she had taken as a result of her nervous condition— or perhaps because of them—she boasted about her stamina. When the journalist asked her if she had stopped acting onstage to pursue the cinema, she rounded on him: "I know what you're thinking. You're making fun of me but you have no right. You think that I am weak and that I can't do two jobs at the same time. That's wrong. I am very strong indeed. I'm stronger than you if I have to be." Then she grabbed his hand to prove how strong she was, and he relented.[9]

By 1927 Aziza was also quite a wealthy woman, and the press was full of stories about her luxurious villa in Cairo's Garden City. Whether this prosperity came from family wealth or, as some sug-gested, Elie Edrei's large coffers, we can only speculate. In any case, with the money—soon to be augmented when she married Ahmed Sharii in April—financing the company was not difficult for someone as dedicated to the cause as Aziza was. Isis Films began work on its first silent feature early that year, using the working title *The Call of God*. Vedad Urfy had written the screenplay, whose locations ranged from the pyramids of Giza and Saqqara to the streets of Cairo. Aziza would play Layla, the lead character. It was the story of a tragic affair in an Egyptian village, where Layla is betrayed by her lover, cast out of the village, and eventually dies. After completing this film, Aziza and Vedad planned to produce a succession of local films centring on the greatness of the Arabs and the glory of the pharaohs.

Opposite: Aziza Amir (photo courtesy of Lucie Ryzova)

Excited and full of energy, Aziza threw herself into the filming process. At the Saqqara pyramids, she ran barefoot through scorching hot sand riddled with broken glass. After several takes her feet were burnt and bleeding, but as her account of the production made sure to say, she was happy. Making a film in a historic location like Saqqara, with its famous step pyramid, she recalled, gave her strength to go on. Every now and then, she was thrilled when a group of tourists, intrigued by the activity, came over and she could tell them the story of Isis Films.

When filming was done, Vedad took the movie reels and set to work putting together the finished product. The production went through several stages, and no prints survive, so any account of the plot is partially guesswork. It is safe to say that it was a tragic tale, set against a background of traditional Egyptian village life, with a supporting cast of archaeologists, Bedouins, and aristocrats. The story revolved around Aziza's character, the poor young woman Layla, who falls in love with a man from her village called Ahmed, played by Vedad Urfy. She soon gets pregnant with Ahmed's child, but he almost immediately betrays her, running off with the daughter of a Brazilian Egyptologist. Layla, pregnant and alone, is cast out by her conservative village and goes to live with an old Bedouin woman, the only person who takes pity on her. Eventually Layla decides to leave even the Bedouin woman and walks off into the desert until she comes to a main road, where she collapses on the ground, heavily pregnant, thirsty, and exhausted. Then a car approaches, driven by a local aristocrat who (as we know from the beginning of the film) is in love with her. He takes Layla back to his house, where she gives birth to her child but dies shortly afterwards.

As Vedad was putting the finishing touches on the title cards, Aziza was excited to know what her landmark film would look like. Before sending it to the Ministry of the Interior for approval to show it in public, the two decided to have a private screening for a few friends, writers, and journalists. But when Aziza finally saw her work onscreen, she was horrified. The story was incomprehensible; one scene bore no relation to the next, and she was convinced that no one who watched it would be able to follow the action. *Rose al-Youssef* magazine described it as "a farce dressed up as a national project." Despite reassurances from her friends, Aziza knew that if she did not take drastic action, her money and effort would have been wasted and the film career she had dreamt of for so long would be over before it started. "I no longer felt anything, everything around me turned dark, darker than a cinema hall . . . the despair almost killed me," she recalled a few months later.[10]

Aziza quickly identified the main culprit for the terrible state of the film—Vedad Urfy and his editing. She wasted no time correcting the error, dismissing Vedad from the company and deciding to remake the film herself. With two other actors from the film and her new husband Ahmed Sharii, she turned the basement of their Garden City house into a production lab and spent what was supposed to be their honeymoon reediting the existing footage and shooting several new scenes. Aziza discarded the old title, *The Call of God*, and christened her new film *Layla*, after the character she played in it. After months of fevered efforts to create a new film from the ashes of the last, *Layla* premiered on 16 November 1927 in the Metropole Cinema, behind the grand Cicurel department store near Emad al-Din Street, where it was hailed as the first Egyptian film.[11]

For months after the film's release, newspapers were filled with arguments between Vedad and Aziza as each accused the other of a litany of offences. Vedad claimed that Aziza had added a scene to the film featuring an indecent belly dance; Aziza responded that the scene had been Vedad's idea. She also claimed that Vedad had been living in her basement and sponged off her throughout the filmmaking. Vedad, for his part, claimed that Aziza's apparently new film, *Layla*, was essentially the same as the old *Call of God*. Aziza challenged him to put the two films together and let an audience decide. By then, of course, it would have been impossible because she had used the old footage to make her new film. Today, even prints of Aziza's version, *Layla*, are practically unlocatable.[12]

But when all was said and done, *Layla* was a smash. Audiences packed in to see this landmark in the history of Egyptian cinema that had been brought about by Aziza Amir, the young actress whose past was shrouded in a combination of rumours and silences. Many critics said the film had its weaknesses, but a few flaws could be forgiven in this, the first truly Egyptian film production. More than anything, everyone agreed that it was a momentous national event. But in an open letter, Aziza told people that she wanted go much further: "This is just my first step and there are more to follow. I hope that God helps me accomplish them successfully in a way that satisfies myself and my fellow countrymen."[13]

Aziza was right that one of the most important effects of her early attempt at Egyptian filmmaking was to convince people it could be done. In the last years of the 1920s, about a dozen new films followed *Layla*. Vedad Urfy, despite his calamitous role in both the biopic of the prophet Mohammed and in *Layla*, kept working at both writing plays and making films. In 1929 his new production company, called Oriental Films, began making a film called *The Tragedy of Life*, starring Vedad himself alongside the popular Turkish cabaret dancer Efranz. But even before it could be shown, it entered the history books with the dubious honour of being the first Egyptian film banned by the censors. It was the story of a nightclub dancer, her rich Egyptian lover, and the scandal that ensued—but it never saw the light of day. The censor's office deemed it to contain "scandalous vices" and refused it permission to be shown. Apparently, among other faults, they tried to show a belly dance onscreen, and they put a respectable Egyptian student in a scene that "did not conform with the morals of the country." One can only imagine what that meant.[14]

In 1928 Aziza started working on her second film, *Daughter of the Nile*. It was an ambitious and expensive production featuring scenes from all over Egypt: from the luxurious Winter Palace Hotel in Luxor, where Agatha Christie would write *Death on the Nile* a few years later, all the way up to Stanley Beach at Alexandria, and including plenty of scenes among ancient Egyptian ruins. The story was adapted from a play Aziza had starred in the previous year, *Ihsan Bey* (written by Mohammed Abd al-Quddus, the well-loved and eccentric actor who was briefly married to Rose al-Youssef in the late 1910s).

Aziza was to play the main character—Mufida, the daughter of a wealthy aristocratic family, who has fallen in love with a poor but charming archaeologist. Her mother, though, wants her to marry the wealthy Mahmoud Bey, who has just returned from studying law in Paris. Mufida reluctantly agrees. Predictably, their relationship turns out to be a terrible failure. After the birth of their daughter, Mahmoud neglects his wife, squanders his money, and is obsessed with his belief that Egyptian women are backwards compared to Europeans. As her unhappy marriage grinds her down, Mufida rekindles her relationship with the young archaeologist. But her husband finds out, divorces her, and takes custody of their daughter. Mufida's spirit is broken by these events, and she eventually becomes a patient in a mental hospital. After four years, she escapes and goes straight to see her daughter, but the girl does not recognise her. The film ends when Mufida commits suicide, throwing herself in the Nile.

A pattern was starting to emerge in Aziza's films. It was not just their ostentatiously tragic plots, ending with the death of the female protagonist. She was also making a political point: a critique of modern Egyptian gender roles, which often forced women to marry against their will and indulged Egyptian men's obsession with foreign women. Both of these films end with the sad deaths of women who had been wronged both by their lovers and the society around them.

Egyptian filmmakers of the late 1920s were still at a major disadvantage when compared with many others in the world: Egypt had no sound-recording technology. The world's first talking film, *The Jazz Singer*, had been released in America in October 1927, around the same time that Aziza was preparing to screen *Layla* for the first time. By 1928 sound films imported from abroad were being shown in Egyptian cinemas, and suddenly—after all their work to start a local film industry—Egyptians were stuck with making silent films in the age of the talkies. Before long, Egyptian filmmakers were in a mad rush to be the first to make an Arabic talkie.

Aziza was desperate to make a film with her own dialogue, saying the difference between the talkies and silent movies was like the difference between humans and animals. However, with no sound stages in Egypt to make a film, she looked abroad for her next two projects after *Daughter of the Nile*. For the first she went to Istanbul and teamed up with the great Turkish actor and director Muhsin Ertuğrul to make *The Streets of Istanbul*, the first Turkish talking film, about two brothers who are in love with the same cabaret dancer. She played a minor Egyptian character in the film, which was released in 1931. Although most of the dialogue was in Turkish, the Egyptian press billed Aziza as "the first Egyptian actress whose voice featured in a talking film."[15]

Sometimes Aziza's projects involved more hype than substance—not uncommon in the early days of cinema across the world. While she was working on the Turkish film, the press was also full of reports about her second project—an Arabic talking film that Aziza herself was producing in France, where the technology was available. A few working titles were making the rounds in the press—sometimes it was *In Cairo . . .*; sometimes it was *The Tunisian Woman*—and throughout the early 1930s, constant updates were issued about the progress on her talking film. Little, however, was revealed about the plot or cast, and by 1931 reports were starting to grow sceptical, suggesting that the film existed primarily in Aziza Amir's imagination. This ill-fated project, like so many, did not seem to get off the ground, and the press quickly stopped mentioning it.

With this, Aziza bowed out of the race to make the first Arabic talkie, leaving others—including Youssef Wahbi, the French-trained tragic star George Abyad, and Fatima Rushdi—to fight it out. For fans of hair-splitting, the singing duo Nina and Mary, who had come to prominence in the chorus of Mounira al-Mahdiyya's *Cleopatra and Mark Antony*, technically released "the first talking reel in the Arabic language": on 11 January 1932, a short film of their song-and-dance act premiered at the Ramses Cinema in Ezbekiyya alongside the French film *Les Amours de Minuit* (The lovers of midnight), starring Danièle Parola.[16]

But in March 1932, soon after Nina and Mary's film premiered, Youssef Wahbi's *Sons of the Elite* went down in history as the first Arabic talking feature film. The plot, based on a play Youssef had written a few years before, dealt with a theme that was prominent in Egyptian stage and screen productions at the time—Egyptian men marrying foreign women. Whereas earlier films by Aziza Amir had portrayed this from a woman's point of view, Youssef's play took a decidedly male perspective. It was inspired by a famous murder case that took Egypt by storm in the early 1920s: The rich Egyptian playboy Ali Fahmy (said to have courted the young Fatima Rushdi) had been killed by his French wife, Marguerite Alibert. She was said to have been a high-class courtesan to wealthy clients, including Edward VIII when he was still Prince of Wales. She met Ali Fahmy in Egypt, where they had a passionate affair that swiftly turned into a difficult marriage, through-out which the couple fought frequently and sometimes violently. Their many quarrels came to a bloody end in the early morning of 10 July 1923. In suite 41 on the fourth floor of the Savoy Hotel in London, Marguerite shot three bullets at Ali, who stumbled into the corridor and died in a pool of blood.

The subsequent trial set both Cairo and London on fire. Mar-guerite Fahmy's case hinged on her acting in self-defence against a violent, threatening, and abusive husband. The racial element to her defence—the supposed depravity of "Oriental" men—quickly became a significant part of the trial and the newspaper reports. Marguerite's lawyer, Sir Edward Marshall Hall, played on the prejudices of the English court, describing Ali Fahmy, in the moments before he was shot, as "crouched like an animal, like an Oriental." Depictions like this of Egyptian men found their way back to Cairo, and many people there were deeply insulted. When the verdict came in, Marguerite was acquitted, and Egyptians saw the entire affair as a reflection of British control of their country—another example of how cheap Egyptian life was to the British.[17]

This prominent, high-profile trial and the scandal surrounding it inspired Youssef Wahbi to write his play, *Sons of the Elite*, for the Ramses troupe's 1929–1930 season. In his hands it became a morality play intended to show the dangers of Egyptian men marrying foreign wives. Youssef was not writing from a neutral standpoint on this matter. He also had a deep personal stake in the case because in the late 1920s he had divorced his own foreign wife—the American opera singer Louise Lund, whom he met while studying in Italy—and married Aisha Fahmy, sister of the murdered Ali Fahmy. Youssef said in his memoirs that not long after he had moved into Aisha Fahmy's magnificent villa on the banks of the Nile, he made a chance discovery in a forgotten drawer of a wardrobe: a cache of letters, written in French and wrapped in a red silk ribbon, between Marguerite Alibert and her secret lover. Enraged by the revelation of Marguerite's unfaithfulness and determined to win justice for the man who would have been his brother-in-law, he poured his anger into a new script.

Youssef's work always showed a flair for the melodramatic, and the plot of *Sons of the Elite* was no different. It tells the story of Hamdi Bey, a wealthy man who runs away from his wife to marry a French woman—played in the film by the French actress Colette Darfeuil, whom Youssef had met in the famous Parisian nightclub La Croix du

Sud. Once in France, Hamdi discovers that his new wife is having an affair. In a fit of jealousy, he kills her lover; but the murder is discovered and he is sent to prison. Over a decade later, having served his sentence, Hamdi returns to Egypt to find that his old family has forgotten him, and his young son does not recognise him. Devastated and remorseful, he lies down on a railway line and waits for the train to come and kill him.

A comparison of Youssef's film with Aziza Amir's earlier ones reveals the difference between projects where women had creative control and those where men did. The films are similar in many ways: they are melodramatic, their plots revolve around marital problems and affairs, and they all end with the death of the main character. However, in Youssef Wahbi's film, women primarily function as metaphors for either the seduction of Egyptian men by foreign pleasure or the stability of the traditional Egyptian family; in Aziza Amir's, women are people—exaggeratedly virtuous and mistreated, perhaps, but still people.

The new Egyptian film industry, which came to dominate the acting business by the early 1930s, enabled many other female stars like Aziza Amir to rise. One of the first to grab the attention of the Egyptian public was Bahiga Hafez. A tall, thin, impeccably dressed woman with thick black hair, Bahiga was rich and well educated (she spoke French and Turkish with ease). People were amazed that a refined aristocrat from a wealthy Alexandrian family had the courage to become an actress when the vast majority of performers were from the margins of Egyptian society. Women of the working class had, by necessity, always moved more readily in traditionally male spheres; but elite women had until quite recently spent their lives largely secluded in the home.

Bahiga had not grown up wanting to be a film star. Thanks to her musical family, she had been playing both Arabic and European styles of music since she was a child. In the 1920s, while still in her late teens, she was composing and selling her own work to record companies in Egypt. However, when she tried to go to the elite bastions of Arabic music in the country—the Oriental Music Club and the recently founded Conservatoire of Arabic music—she encountered significant hostility. She asked for funding to pursue her work and was told that they did not appreciate the kind of music she was writing. "My way of adapting Arabic tunes to a Western rhythm did not please this conservative group," she complained. She saw "a hostility in artistic circles to all those who are tempted by innovations, to free Eastern music from the unchangeable rules which hold it captive," but it is hard not to suspect an undercurrent of sexism too.[18]

Bahiga broke into the film world in 1928, when the young director Mohammed Karim started work on the film *Zeinab*, an adaptation of a popular novel set in the Egyptian countryside about three men competing for the love of a peasant girl. Mohammed Karim had met Bahiga at a party and thought, for some reason, that this young musician from a wealthy and influential family would be the perfect woman to play Zeinab, the symbolic embodiment of a downtrodden Egyptian peasant. Some critics at the time noted that Bahiga was a strange choice for the part, but she threw herself into the film and found freedom that she had never experienced in the elite institutions of Arabic music.

In 1928 she gave an interview to the feminist activist Ceza Nabarawi in the French-language women's magazine *L'Égyptienne*, published by the Egyptian Feminist Union. In the article, Bahiga was held up as a model for the new generation of Egyptian women, "not made for a quiet and peaceful life, but for a free and eventful existence." When asked about her reasons for becoming an actress, she replied that it was her "desire to smash these heavy chains which prevent me and every other educated Egyptian woman from showing the world they are no less capable or productive than women in the West. I am a supporter of women's freedom . . . to do honest work instead of spending their time imprisoned in the house."[19]

Bahiga's aristocratic background did not always work to her favour, particularly when Egyptian filmmakers were striving for the appearance of authenticity. According to later accounts, she was originally chosen for the lead Egyptian female role in Youssef Wahbi's film, *Sons of the Elite*, playing the honest Egyptian woman whose husband deserts her in favour of a French mistress. However, she was cut out of the project during the filming, in part because her elite Alexandrian background had made her Arabic weak and often infused with French, Turkish, and Italian. The director later recalled that she "stuttered, made mistakes in the dialogue, pronounced some Arabic words wrong." As someone who had been attacked, even disowned, by members of her family after she became an actress, having her background used against her must have stung.[20]

But Bahiga was not going to let this snub hold her back. Soon after being dismissed, she sued Youssef Wahbi, the film's producer, for breaking her contract—and won. Then she set up her own film company, Fanar Films, intending to produce musical films that she would score herself. Her first effort was the 1932 film *The Victims*, whose plot had all the hallmarks of a movie from this period. The victims of the title are a couple who are in love but cannot get married. The female lead (Bahiga) is then forced to marry an unpleasant man, and after a troubled life does not confess her feelings to her real love until he is on his deathbed. This film has extra spice because the man Bahiga loves is a noble coastguard officer and the man she marries is an unscrupulous drug smuggler whose dealings lead to an exciting police chase around the pyramid at Saqqara. Bahiga herself wrote the score for the film.

In the 1930s the rise of the film industry, coupled with a global economic crisis, dealt Cairo's live theatres a hard blow. Theatrical troupes became less interested in attracting audiences and more interested in artistic ideals, much to the delight of those who had been crying out for theatre to move in that direction. In 1935 the government created and funded the Egyptian National Troupe, designed to be Egypt's equivalent of the Comédie Française. However, because this new troupe focused on serious high drama and disdained so-called commercial theatre, it only pushed audiences further towards the cinema. The first production by the National Troupe captured its flavour. It was *The People of the Cave*, a new play by a young Egyptian writer called Tawfiq al-Hakim, who was earnestly trying to create a new, uniquely Arabic form of tragedy. Audiences were either overwhelmed or bored by the experiment; many of them fell asleep during the performance. Egyptian theatre was starting to lose its spark.

Cinema, on the other hand, only grew more vital and successful with locally made productions that appealed to local audiences. It is hardly surprising, then, that many of the women who became famous in the '20s as singers, dancers, or actresses began to follow the audiences (and the cash) into the new film industry. This trend only increased as big money started investing in the business. In 1935 Talaat Harb—whose interest in the entertainment industry went back to the 1910s, when he had funded the Okasha Brothers' troupe (and unceremoniously fired Rose al-Youssef for wearing a swimming costume at the beach)—opened Studio Misr. As the first large-scale studio in Egypt, it fulfilled Talaat Harb's dream of giving Egyptian filmmakers their own state-of-the-art workplace. Located in Giza, it was furnished with the best filmmaking equipment and staffed by a diverse crowd of people. They were primarily Egyptians but also included a notable number of Germans, many of them recent refugees from the Nazis.

In the 1930s and 1940s, audiences flocked to Emad al-Din Street not for the plays, but for the films. The lives of the stars were no less fascinating and could fill another book of their own, but these celebrities no longer spent most of their lives in Ezbekiyya. They filmed in Studio Misr and came to town only for their premieres. During the 1940s, in the words of one British writer, they lived "in a colony on the Mena Road to the Pyramids and constitute the sophisticated fringe of Egyptian society, drinking, marrying and occasionally murdering with something of the heady enthusiasm of Hollywood in the twenties."[21]

But if cinema changed Ezbekiyya and Emad al-Din Street, it still owed something to its musical and theatrical history. The Egyptian film industry is now the biggest and highest grossing in the Middle East, producing hundreds of films including screwball comedies, big-budget action films, historical epics, and much more. Yet it is not fanciful to say that its roots are in the world it left behind. Long before moving to Studio Misr and the Mena Road, Egypt's stars learned their craft in Ezbekiyya. They had acted in its theatres, talked and drank in its bars and cafés, danced and sang in its cabarets. The new cinema still carried the old Egyptian entertainment industry in its DNA.

Chapter II

MADAME BADIA'S CASINO

ALONGSIDE THE CINEMA, the other major contributor to the decline of live theatre in Cairo was the creation, at the end of the 1920s, of a string of new venues on and around Emad al-Din Street known as *salas*. This Arabic word, from the Italian for "room," had been used before to describe performance halls. But these nightspots were new and different; within a few years of their creation, these venues completely changed Emad al-Din Street, replacing the revue theatres that had been popular since the 1910s. Essentially, *salas* were cabarets exclusively fronted by female singers or dancers, with shows that combined popular Arabic songs with short comic skits and featured touring variety performers from around the world. The model was so successful that they became the go-to spot for devotees of Cairo's nightlife.

The woman most responsible for this new phenomenon was a comic actress, singer, and dancer from Damascus. Her name was Badia Masabni, and her story has a lot in common with other female stars in '20s and '30s Cairo: her personality was larger than life, and she was adored by fans, denounced by conservatives, and obsessed over by the press. More than anyone else, though, she appears to have realised that while her celebrity could be beneficial, it could also be unstable. Even while reaching the highs, she was always expecting the next low. To stand apart from the rest of society, as many well-known women did, could make her a target; and if she fell, she knew that no one else was going to pick her up.

Badia was a famous comic actress and singer in Cairo during the mid-1920s; but in 1926, when she opened the first *sala* on Emad al-Din Street, she became a superstar. Inside the *sala* the décor, like the entertainment, was a mix of European cabaret and Arabic music hall. She "adorned it with decorations in the eastern style and brought in the finest furniture," and for 10 piastres, audiences saw a programme of entertainment in the classic style of an inter-war variety show. "She hired the famous singers and the most eminent musicians" to perform, and she "sang the most enchanting songs to beautiful tunes, as well as *taqtuqas* from Egypt and Syria, and danced an Eastern dance in breath-taking clothes which she imported herself from Paris."[1]

Badia's act was supported by an array of performers from across the Middle East—Egyptians, Levantines, Armenians, Iraqis, and more. Through two decades of operation, she also gave breaks to local performers who went on to become some of the biggest stars of the mid-twentieth century, including the dancers Tahiyya Carioca and Samia Gamal and the singer Leila Murad, who became a superstar in Egypt's 1940s film industry. Alongside Arabic-speaking acts, a huge variety of European performers reflected the tastes and makeup of the Egyptian public at the time. She scoured Europe and the Middle East in search of talent, earning herself the nickname "Carnarvon of the Music Halls" (after the famous British lord who had invested so much time and money in the search for Tutankhamen's tomb).[2] On just one of her trips abroad she recruited Turkish singers, a Hungarian ballet troupe, and a Spanish dancer called Rosita Montenegro. Rosita later found small roles in French films like *Ernest the Rebel*, a comedy about the misadventures of a ship's accordion player in South America, and

Badia Masabni (centre) with her troupe (photo courtesy of Lucie Ryzova)

The Puritan, a crime drama based on a novel by the Irish writer Liam O'Flaherty.

Of all the people Badia brought to Egypt, one of her most intriguing finds was the dancer Efranz Hanem. Discovered in the Levant and of either Turkish or Armenian descent (newspapers in Egypt could not decide which), Efranz soon became very popular. In the few years after her arrival in Cairo, Efranz can be found in a surprising number of places: acting in Vedad Urfy's banned film *The Tragedy of Life*; touring in South America with Youssef Wahbi; even discovering customers dying in nightclub toilets. A sense of danger always accompanied Efranz. Stories circulated about the time she spent performing in Aleppo, and they weren't always savoury. One actor who was touring in Syria got to know Efranz a little, but he wrote to *Rose al-Youssef* magazine and said their friendship had ended when a friend of hers attacked him one night with a knife. Almost as soon as she had settled in Cairo, the Egyptian authorities tried to have her expelled "because of the numerous fights she caused." She was only saved when the actor Naguib al-Rihani personally intervened to keep her there. Unfortunately, like so many of the other women in interwar Egypt who did not write their memoirs and have not been the subject of much research, Efranz has all but disappeared from history, her life only told through a few colourful anecdotes.[3]

Badia's *sala*, populated by this strange cast of characters, was an instant hit. As much as anything else, it was a triumph of marketing. Her success was a result of combining two cultural traditions of entertainment, the Arabic and the European, both of which were still extremely popular in Ezbekiyya at the time her *sala* opened.

The Arabic music halls and so-called *cafés chantant* that had flourished in the maze of streets east of Ezbekiyya Gardens were still going strong in the 1920s. Many European travellers looking for what they hoped was an authentic night of "Oriental entertainment" wrote essays about these places and sent them to newspapers at home. These writers eagerly described the crowds that drank, cheered, and clapped in smoke-filled music halls: middle-class city dwellers in Western suits and tarboushes, sheikhs from villages, people of many nationalities—Greek, Sudanese, Egyptian. One visitor saw this diversity among attendees as "one of the most amazing features of the democracy which is Islam."[4]

Above all, the audiences were fascinated by the performers—and none of them attracted more interest than Tawhida, a veteran singer and dancer in the music halls around Clot Bey Street and the red-light district since the late nineteenth century. In 1897 she had married a Greek man called Emmanuel ("Manoli") Joannidis, who owned both the Wataniyya café and the Thousand and One Nights music hall, located down an alley in Ezbekiyya and round the back of a mosque. She was still singing there, one of the last stars of that generation, until the hall burned down in 1927.

Tawhida's act stayed rooted in the older Arabic music hall traditions. She wore the extravagant jewellery common for all dancers in the late nineteenth century. The one-time music critic of the local English-language newspaper *The Sphinx* described, with awe, the "heavy gold bangles completely covering her arms and ankles, and solid gold chains round her neck," reminiscent of traditional dancers of the previous century. She even fashioned a classical Arabic heritage for herself by telling people that although she was Christian, she was descended from the great freethinking Muslim scholar and physician of the ninth and tenth centuries, al-Razi.[5]

In 1926 the young American travel writer Eleanor Early went to see Tawhida perform and was captivated: "Sometime after midnight Tawhida was escorted to the stage and lowered tenderly into an enormous chair. . . . Then, when all was still, she began to sing." The set included, in the words of this enthusiastic visitor, "Oriental love songs—beautiful things, rich and throbbing. There were many verses, and they told of desert love, and fighting men, and dark-skinned girls." When that section of the performance was over, she "danced until she was exhausted." Seeing that she was about to collapse, audience members "leaped from the wings and helped her into her chair. When the applause had quieted others came. Six of them carried her off the stage, chair and all."

For travellers, Tawhida was unspeakably exotic—they found it particularly unusual that a woman who was so old and overweight could be so popular. Eleanor Early was astonished to see that she had "more suitors than any young girl." Later, when taken backstage, Eleanor asked for advice about how to stay beautiful. Tawhida's answer was simple: "cook everything in oil, she counsels, and drown your sweets in honey. To be loved, she said, a woman must be nice and fat." For younger Egyptian audiences, however, performers like Tawhida were a little old-fashioned. In 1927 *Rose al-Youssef* magazine published a picture of Tawhida with the caption, "Tawhida, the famous singer that our fathers and grandfathers told us about." The writer went to on describe her customers, belonging to an older era, who watched her "with a shisha pipe in one hand and a glass of cognac in front of them."[6]

European-style cabarets in Cairo—like the Kursaal and the Casino de Paris, rivals to the Arabic-speaking *cafés chantant*—thrived even before Badia Masabni opened her *sala*. But these venues were not aimed at an Arabic-speaking Egyptian audience; ordinary locals would have felt unwelcome there; and some places, like the nightclub in the Continental Savoy Hotel, did not even admit locals. These nightclubs were designed to offer European-style entertainment in European languages, and they hired acts that spent only a few months in Egypt and then left for another stop on the global music hall circuit.

The simple genius of Badia's *sala* was to create a hybrid of these two venues. For lovers of Arabic music and dancing, it offered a sophisticated night out, not a seedy remnant of the past. For devotees of the European cabaret, it let them see a different kind of show with a strange and "exotic" twist. Thanks to its broad appeal, the *sala* managed to attract a curious mix of guests that included young students, foreign visitors, and the Egyptian aristocratic elite. A report in *Rose al-Youssef* magazine, published not long after the *sala* opened, noted that the Sufi sheikh and renowned religious scholar Mohammed al-Ghunaymi al-Taftazani "was a frequent visitor to Badia Masabni's *sala*, sneaking through the back door and putting his robe over his head. . . . The sheikh goes in and sits in a private room where he can see the singing and dancing onstage, without anyone else in the *sala* seeing him."[7]

Badia also repurposed some other ideas that she picked up from Ezbekiyya's nightlife for her *sala*. The most high-profile of these was her women-only performances. For a long time, theatres in the city had been putting on shows that only women were allowed to attend, specifically for those who either did not want to watch a play with men

تياترو وقهوة «ألف ليلة وليلة»

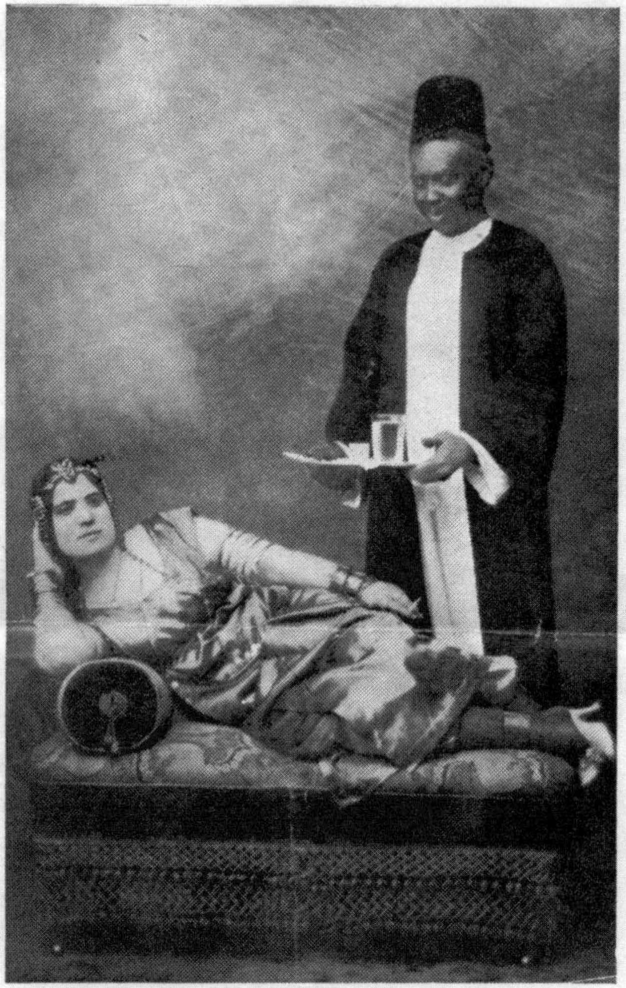

السيدة توحيدة المطربة المبدعه

مطبعة البشلاوى

ذكرى ليالى الانس يامؤنسى
تعيد للقلب البعيد القصى
سروره فاقبل لتذكارنا
هدية المخلص للمخلص

in the audience or were worried about their reputation being harmed if they were seen at such a performance. Badia adopted the women-only strategy too, instituting her own exclusively female Tuesday afternoon matinee. It was a canny move that drove yet another wedge between her *sala* and the seedier music halls in the maze of streets to the east of Ezbekiyya Gardens, where very few women besides the performers were seen.

Soon after Badia opened her cabaret, *al-Masrah* magazine sent a woman to write a report about these female-only shows. The anonymous writer loved it, complaining about how hard it had been for a woman to see music hall acts like this before—that is, "if she wanted to preserve her honour and protect her eyes from the sight of human insects" (by which she meant men). Finally, there was a chance to watch a cabaret show in a roomful of women without a man in sight. The writer informed readers that Badia especially had enchanted the audience with her singing, dancing, and extravagant outfits. She had just one complaint: that this refined new venue had physically enshrined a dangerously "aristocratic" ethos. She had noticed one seating area that had been cordoned off and was reserved for important women; its chairs alone were covered in expensive silk. As "one of those women who has embraced democracy and the era of the constitution," the writer said, that kind of discrimination and social segregation didn't seem right to her.[8]

Badia's journey to become one of the leading lights of Cairo's nightlife began in Damascus, where she was born in the 1890s to a prosperous Christian Levantine trading family. Her father owned a soap factory and used its proceeds to support his seven children (four sons and three daughters), insisting on educating his girls as well as boys. The first few years of Badia's life were bourgeois and comfortable; but in common with the life stories of many of these stars, everything changed when her father died and his profitable factory burned down. In Badia's early childhood, the family went from modest wealth to poverty, barely managing to survive in their house in the old city of Damascus. More disasters followed. One of her brothers died of a fever; someone broke into their house and stole her mother's jewellery, leaving them with almost nothing of tangible value. As if this were not enough, another brother, who could have helped support the family, became a serious alcoholic.

Badia was only seven years old at the time, but she got on well with her heavy-drinking brother. When he was in his favourite bar, where he sat more often than not, she used to come in to say hello, and he would give her little presents like sweets and even clothes. But one day she went to the bar and did not find him sitting in his usual spot. The owner recognised the girl and called her in, saying her brother was sitting inside. But he was not; the man was just trying to lure her into the bar. As soon as they were alone, he shut the door; in her memoirs this event is couched in euphemism, but the clear implication is that he raped her.

She went home crying and told her mother exactly what had happened—a decision she later regretted. Her mother was so furious that she found the local community leader (the Sheikh al-Hara) and took him to the bar, where together they apprehended the bar owner. He was put on trial, found guilty, and given a short sentence. But for Badia, the stigma of this event, as well as the trauma, lasted much longer. In the tight Orthodox Christian community of Damascus, no one forgot the scandal. Badia soon stopped going to church, discouraged by the looks she received. She could barely talk to anyone in the city anymore.

For the next few years, the family went on the move. The situation in Damascus became so unbearable that Badia's mother decided to take the family halfway across the world to Argentina. Her choice was not as random as it might seem. At the turn of the twentieth century, many people from the Levant were emigrating to the Americas, fleeing poverty and hunger and looking for new opportunities (though Badia did not say how they could afford the cost of tickets). They settled in Buenos Aires among the large Arabic-speaking immigrant community on Reconquista Avenue. Badia went to school, learning to read and write in Spanish, while the others worked as peddlers selling goods around the city. They might have stayed there permanently had a letter not arrived from their family in Syria with news that Badia's grandmother had died and left the family a significant (but unspecified) sum of money. So, almost as quickly as they had come, they left Argentina.

Typical of the family's luck, they soon found their golden inheritance was not as large as they were expecting. They were still poor, and now they were back at square one. Badia's memoirs describe an itinerant life of moving around Syria and Lebanon in search of work, comfort, or support. For a young Badia the threat of the sex trade loomed especially large. In one story given particular prominence in her memoirs, she remembered narrowly avoiding being trapped in a brothel run by a Greek madam and forced into prostitution. She only escaped when one of the other women in the brothel took pity on her—because she had clearly been tricked into being there—and helped her sneak out. Even Badia's mother was briefly arrested, apparently erroneously, on suspicion of trafficking her own daughter.

Finally, in the early 1910s, Badia and her mother gave up on Syria and Lebanon and decided to try their luck in Egypt. Badia's mother had an uncle there, and they hoped he might take pity on them; armed with nothing but his name, they moved into a hotel in Ezbekiyya. Badia, who was by then around twenty years old, decided this venture was a dead end—they did not even know where in Egypt their relative lived. She found instead the amazing variety of entertainment on offer in the city. In the theatres of Cairo, Badia entered a new chapter of her life—and with it all the glamour of the entertainment industry, personal ambition, lucky breaks, wealthy (possibly exploitative) lovers, and powerful patronage that were a common thread woven into the stories of other women in Egypt's nightlife.

She started to explore the streets of Ezbekiyya, and soon found herself in the audience of a play staged by the great tragic actor George Abyad. He had recently returned from Paris, where he studied theatre for many years at the expense of the Khedive Abbas Hilmi II. The great new hope of Egyptian theatre, he was putting on shows all over town. As she watched the play, Badia's gaze was drawn to the women onstage, dancers and singers whose fine dresses and jewellery sparkled under the lights. Then she looked down at her own cheap, worn-out dress and began to dream about being up there onstage herself, looking as wonderful as the performers did. It was on that night, as she remembered it, that she fell in love with performance, just as Rose al-Youssef had done when she walked through the streets of Ezbekiyya dressed as Mary Tudor.

In the following weeks, Badia went back to the theatre again and again. Through a chance meeting in the audience one evening, she was taken backstage to meet the members of George Abyad's troupe personally, and she miraculously talked her way into a part in their company. They even paid for a tutor to give her lessons in reading Arabic (as a child, she had only learned to read in Spanish) so that she could follow the scripts.

Soon after Badia had landed the job, her mother, who had by then given up on finding her uncle, decided to go back to Damascus. Rather than returning to the Levant herself, Badia stayed in Egypt alone; free of her mother's supervision, she devoted herself entirely to the enter-

tainment business. She left George Abyad and took up an offer from
a smaller troupe that specialised in touring the Egyptian countryside,
travelling from town to town and putting on shows. For the first time,
she was given the opportunity to play leading roles. She recalled in her
memoirs that theatre became a kind of wish fulfilment. While acting
the parts of wealthy and successful women, she imagined herself tri-
umphing over those who tried to hold her back; when she played a
woman defeating the people who would take advantage of her poverty,
she felt revenge against the bar owner who had abused her when she
was just a girl.

Around this time, Badia also paired up with a wealthy lover, Sayyid
Zaki, who had been a long-time fan of the troupe. After the tour, he
took her to Cairo, paid for her hotel room, and they went out to the
theatres and nightclubs of Ezbekiyya. One night it was the Arabic version of *Romeo and Juliet*; another night, it was the legendary Tawhida
singing at the One Thousand and One Nights music hall. Of all the
stars performing in Cairo at the time, Badia was particularly obsessed
with Mounira al-Mahdiyya, going to her shows almost every night and
memorising as many of her songs as she could.

Badia relished the comfort and luxury of living with Sayyid Zaki
in Cairo and at his country estate. But she realised that if times ever
got tough, as she knew they could, she would need income to support
herself. Determined to preserve her independence above all, she left
Sayyid Zaki and his life of relative ease. And in 1914 she was back
in Beirut, where she planned to introduce the city's audiences to the
songs she had learned in Egypt. In her young life she had travelled
from the Levant to South America and then to Cairo. Now Badia was
back in the Levant, this time as an entertainer with her own power
and agency.

In Beirut, Badia immediately made her way to the city's only large European-style cabaret, run by a French woman called Madame Jeanette, where she was hired to perform the Mounira al-Mahdiyya hits she had learned in Egypt. As Badia honed her nightclub act, the First World War was just beginning, and life in Beirut was not easy. The Ottoman Empire, which controlled the region, had entered the fighting alongside the Central Powers. As the war went on, problems that had been brewing in the region for some time became crises. This period is now mostly remembered for the famine that ravaged the whole area; during the war, an estimated 500,000 people died in Greater Syria—around 15 percent of the country's inhabitants. In Beirut alone, the population decreased by more than half due to death or emigration. The local Arab population was growing increasingly resentful of Ottoman control and pushing for greater autonomy; for their part, the Ottomans responded violently to any opposition, arresting and executing many key dissenters.

Badia had come back to a land of war, famine, and rebellion. Amidst all this, she became a mother after a neighbour told her that a young orphan had been dropped off at a local convent. Badia went over there straight away and adopted the girl, raising her as a daughter and taking her along to performances across the region. The girl, named Juliette, later became a star at Badia Masabni's cabaret in the 1930s, under the stage name "Blonde Layla."

Despite the severe wartime conditions (much worse than those in Cairo), the cabarets of the Levant appeared to flourish, if Badia's memoirs are anything to go by. For the next few years, she sang and danced her way around the region, going from one music hall to another and often back again. First she left Madame Jeanette's music hall, taking another singer with her, to form a short-lived cabaret of their own. Later she moved to the small *L'Astre d'Orient* music hall on Place des Canons (now Martyrs' Square) in Beirut. As the war escalated, she travelled longer distances—to places like Damascus and Aleppo. On those tours she gained experience as a professional singer and made contacts that would prove useful once she returned to Cairo to open a cabaret of her own.

As the First World War ended and the Ottoman Empire collapsed in the Levant, Badia kept performing as usual. By 1922 she had been touring across the Levant for almost ten years. In Jerusalem, for instance, the influential Palestinian oud player and memoirist Wasif Jawhariyyeh fondly remembered Badia's singing, dancing, and outlandish outfits—she would wear a pistachio-seller's costume as she sang a suggestive *taqtuqa* about nuts and a milkmaid's outfit when she sang one about starting the day with a glass of "creamy milk." In his memoirs, Wasif (great-grandfather of British MP Layla Moran) saw in Badia a potent symbol of the wild atmosphere of post-war Palestine—full of music, dancing, drinking, drugs, lock-ins at Jerusalem bars, and joking until dawn.[9]

After the war, Badia's life could have taken many different paths. She was one of the most famous music hall *artistes* in the Levant, had performed with its best musicians and in its finest cabarets, and easily could have spent the rest of her life there as a singer and performer. But Cairo's entertainment industry still had a strong pull, and a chance meeting in Beirut in 1922 would bring her back to Emad al-Din Street. That year, Naguib al-Rihani, star of the Franco-Arab revue and creator of Kish-Kish Bey, was on an extensive tour of the Levant. When members of the troupe heard that Badia, the young actress some of them knew from her work in Cairo, was now one of the best singers in the city, they went to find her. They asked her to join their company for the rest of the tour and then come back with them to Egypt. She quickly accepted the offer and was soon back on the stages of Ezbekiyya where her career had begun—this time with a decade of theatre experience behind her and a young daughter, Juliette, at her side.

In early 1923, in a world that had vastly changed in the decade since she was last in Cairo, Badia stepped onstage for her comeback as the prima donna in Naguib al-Rihani's troupe. Her first play, *Happy Nights*, was a comic adaptation of tales from the Arabian Nights, consisting of several interwoven stories full of fantastical scenes of genies, demons, and harems, including a popular parody of Aladdin. One reviewer lavished praise on her "graceful movements, harmonious action, and beautiful voice," pleading for the author of the play to write a few extra songs for Badia so that the audience could go home satisfied. In another of her performances, the audience applauded so long and so hard after one of her songs that she immediately sang it again.[10]

Within a year or so, Badia was regarded as one of the best comic actresses in the city. She had admirers across the country, including some very wealthy people who attended her performances and gave her the usual extravagant gifts. One of these rich fans had even rented an apartment for her, which she happily moved into. Cairo, in short, was immensely productive for Badia both professionally and financially. She soon had enough money to hire her daughter a private tutor from the Lycée Français in Cairo.

She was also developing a close relationship with the troupe leader Naguib al-Rihani, an idle but charismatic rake with an expressive face and a pencil moustache. Naguib had grown up in a middle-class Christian family but fell in love with the theatre as a teenager and spent his early years moving between different jobs, performing whenever he could. Never very attached to hard work, he preferred to spend evenings with friends, a bottle of cognac, a pack of cigarettes, and some falafel sandwiches, talking and telling stories. He was famously witty and was used to dominating a room with jokes or stories about his scrapes as a poor young actor. He was also a well-known womaniser, but Badia had been captivated by his charm, and in September 1924 they were married in Cairo.

The next summer the couple went on a theatrical tour of South

America, the first Egyptian troupe to travel such a distance to perform. After a month on the ship to Brazil, they visited several cities with Arab immigrant communities like the one where Badia had lived as a child—São Paulo, Rio de Janeiro, Montevideo, Buenos Aires—and crowds of the diaspora welcomed the Arabic-speaking troupe when it arrived. Naguib later recalled that South America had as many Arabs as Egypt had Greeks. There were enough Arab communities to support the career of yet another imitator of Naguib al-Rihani's famous Kish-Kish Bey, who seemed to pop up wherever he went.

For Badia and Naguib, it soon transpired that a mutual love of theatre was not enough to sustain a marriage. Among friends they were well known for their high-spirited joking, but in private their personalities were a bad match. Badia was hard-working, active, and needed a busy social life. Naguib was idle (or "bohemian") and more than a little selfish. Rumours that he had other lovers started to circulate. He left her to spend nights at home alone—something she was not used to—while he played billiards in cafés and bars. Before long, they began arguing about the theatrical troupe too. She said he did not work hard enough, had no financial sense, and was ruinously lazy. He thought she was too uptight. In their more heated fights, he declared that she couldn't tell him what to do with his company, because she was just a dancer.

It is hard to pinpoint the moment that ended the marriage, but in 1926 they separated. In an interview for *Rose al-Youssef* magazine, Badia described Naguib's discovery of a series of secret letters from her fans and admirers across the Arab world. After reading their declarations of love, Naguib saw the letters as evidence of her unfaithfulness and left her. In her later memoirs she described a slow build-up of arguments and recriminations that came to a head when, during a routine argument about the theatrical troupe, he slapped her. Physical violence was the last straw; she left him.

After the separation, they stayed officially married (the Orthodox church had strict rules on divorce), but Badia left Cairo for a while to regroup. When she returned she received an unpleasant surprise: as she recalled in her memoirs, she went to her house and discovered that Naguib was sleeping with Claire, the French tutor who had been hired for Juliette. Indeed, by 1927 Naguib had made Claire the troupe's manager, and the name "Mademoiselle Claire" was plastered across the company's adverts.

Badia, while spending the summer in Alexandria, had a rebound of her own. She ran into Sayyid Zaki, her old flame—the two had met years ago while Badia was touring with Ahmed al-Shami's troupe in the 1910s. They stayed at the Beau Rivage Hotel in Alexandria for a while; but soon, even more convinced of a woman's need for independence since the break-up of her marriage, she left him. She had no worries about money: at the end of 1924, *al-Tiyatru* magazine had estimated her personal wealth at 10,000 Egyptian pounds, and by 1926 it may have been much more. A strong pattern of fraught love lives was evident in the stories of female stars during this period, and Badia's story was no exception. In an interview with a Lebanese magazine a few years later, she championed the benefits of a life without a husband: "Being single is better for dancers, singers, and *artistes* because singledom is freedom and freedom is priceless."[11]

It is sometimes hard to know what to make of Sayyid Zaki's role in Badia's life. His chance appearances, which gave her time to recover before going out into the world again, are so convenient that at times he seems more like a literary device than a real person. But he did exist. In 1930 *Rose al-Youssef* magazine reported that he had collapsed in the toilet of the Bosphore Casino following a night of heavy drinking. Efranz, that mysterious Turkish (or Armenian) dancer, found him in the bathroom and dragged him out, but she was too late; one of his carotid arteries had burst, and he died soon after.[12]

In late summer 1926, using money she had saved—including some from her wealthy admirers—Badia bought a large hall that was for sale on Emad al-Din Street. That fall she opened Sala Badia, which would influence Cairo's nightlife scene for decades to come. She worked hard building her own brand, living extravagantly at her fashionable cabaret and luxurious villa—her whole lifestyle drew crowds to the *sala*. The club was opulent, yes; but equally important, it was fun. Champagne and whiskey flowed among the excited clientele, and the "house was in constant uproar, actors or no actors."[13]

Badia always kept her mind on expansion. She brought her nephew, Antoine, from Lebanon to help with administration (he later married her daughter, Juliette). As her venue became more established, her classic cabaret-style shows began to include more unorthodox performers, no doubt picked up on her many travels. Her entertainments variously featured Mrs. Mary, a female weightlifter; Mademoiselle Erika Wahl, "the eccentric dancer"; Buck and Chick, the Kings of Lasso; and Martonn, a quick-change artist who "could neither sing nor dance, although he tried both." She even enlisted an Italian company with a performer who "appeared on stage in women's clothes and did the nimblest and most skillful dance that was possible" and a man who, impersonating a frog with both his voice and his body, "wore frog-coloured clothes and crawled along the floor slowly like a frog."[14]

But Badia also had competition. In 1928 a new venue, the Kit Kat Club, was launched and quickly became a fabled decadent night spot for Cairo's elite—and shook up the city's cabaret scene yet again. George Calomiris, a wealthy hotelier who owned the National Hotel in downtown Cairo, had ploughed his cash into the Kit Kat, making it the most ostentatious and talked-about venue in town. It was an open-air cabaret located near the Nile and built on land once owned by Henri Meyer, the wealthy Swiss sewage magnate. Meyer's old villa still survives a few hundred meters from the Nile and operates as the Swiss Club. The main entrance to the club incorporated the enormous triumphal arch that Meyer had erected to commemorate Napoleon's victory at the Battle of the Pyramids.

At the centre of the sprawling Kit Kat Club was a large terrace, laid out with tables and chairs, where customers could enjoy dinner and drinks. While they ate and drank, they might watch a selection of dancers and singers, some of whom had performed in the music halls of Paris and London, or see a film on the newly installed cinematograph. The complex had two different stages, one on the "illuminated floor" and another in the so-called Moorish pavilion. In its early days, the Kit Kat featured bands that included the Rector's Club Orchestra, led by the Belgian jazz pianist Marcel Raskin and including a young French guitarist-banjo player called Loulou Gasté, who later became a prolific songwriter in France.

Al-Ahram newspaper excitedly announced the arrival of the Kit Kat Club: "Tonight will be a memorable one for the residents of Cairo because tonight the Kit Kat Club will open. . . . Its location on the banks of the Nile is one of great beauty, and there we will spend our summer nights breathing the cool, soft air." A private bus service was engaged to take customers from Ezbekiyya on the roughly three-mile trip between the club and Opera Square. The Kit Kat made such an impact in its first year that when Edward, Prince of Wales, visited Cairo later in 1928, he went to the club and was entertained by its dancers. Edward's visit was later made infamous when he teed off from the top of the Great Pyramid.[15]

Partly in response to the success of the Kit Kat, Badia opened her second Cairo venue in 1930: Casino Badia was a grand open-air complex also on the banks of the Nile next to the English Bridge, roughly where the Sheraton Hotel stands today. The word *casino* did not imply gambling; it was just the term used at the time for the cafes, clubs, and restaurants on the river, where people went in the summer to feel the cool Nile breeze. From 1930 onwards, she would leave her Emad al-Din Street *sala* every summer for her casino by the river, which soon incorporated a cinema, a theatre, and a dance hall with a cabaret show starting at midnight. The place soon became so famous that people started referring to the English Bridge as Badia's Bridge.

By the early 1930s, the success of Badia's ventures was increasingly clear, and a torrent of *sala* imitations spread across Ezbekiyya. These places were always fronted by enterprising women. Fatima Rushdi's sisters Insaf and Ratiba were among the first to open a similar venue, called Insaf and Ratiba's Sala, on Emad al-Din Street. Soon after, an actress called Mary Mansour started another *sala* on the same street. She not only sang and danced but, along with a troupe of comedians, acted in short skits—with titles such as "The Women's Police" and "Tutankhamen"—satirising modern Egypt. Mounira al-Mahdiyya, in 1930, opened Sala Mounira on Alfi Bey Street. Even Tawhida, the singer from the old-style Thousand and One Nights music hall, opened a *sala* on Emad al-Din Street later that summer. However, Tawhida's new venue did not last; by December, one journalist disparagingly noted that "the size of the audience could be counted on the fingers of one hand."[16] Before long, so many women were opening their own *salas* that people found it hard to keep up. In the early 1930s one magazine complained that the line-up at the Bijou Palace on Emad al-Din Street changed so quickly that the sign of one *sala* had barely been posted on the front of the building before a new owner had taken over. Throughout Ezbekiyya, this decade was a new era of cabarets.

Summer spots by the Nile were thriving too—venues lined the river from the Giza tramway stop to the Kit Kat Club. In 1931 the actor and theatre impresario Youssef Wahbi rented a plot of land and began work on Ramses City, his own entertainment park designed to compete with Casino Badia and the Kit Kat Club. The project took two years, but when he eventually opened Ramses City in 1933, it offered a vast array of entertainment from cinema to circus acts, including a "wall of death where a motorcyclist rides at full speed round a circular perpendicular wall," bars and music halls, and a theatre that he gave over to Mounira al-Mahdiyya's troupe.[17]

The owners of these summer cabarets must have felt that they were worth pouring money into: In 1931 George Calomiris financed an extensive renovation of his Kit Kat Club, adding new furnishings, another entrance, and a new stage featuring an illuminated arch above a raised platform for a band or orchestra. In 1934 Badia also upgraded her casino, hiring the architect Aziz Abdel Malek, designer of many of Cairo's cinemas and cabarets, to totally redesign her casino, landscape the grounds, and build a huge new stage.[18]

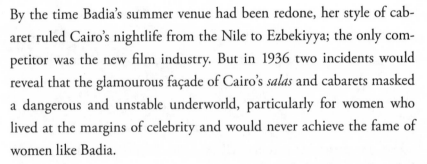

By the time Badia's summer venue had been redone, her style of cabaret ruled Cairo's nightlife from the Nile to Ezbekiyya; the only competitor was the new film industry. But in 1936 two incidents would reveal that the glamourous façade of Cairo's *salas* and cabarets masked a dangerous and unstable underworld, particularly for women who lived at the margins of celebrity and would never achieve the fame of women like Badia.

The first incident was the brutal murder of the dancer Imtithal Fawzi just before she performed at her own club on 22 May 1936. Imtithal, whose career began as a dancer in Badia's troupe, had been quite successful. She was getting small parts in films such as *The Runaway* (starring Fatima Rushdi), the story of a deserter from the Ottoman army in First World War Palestine. Keen to advance her career and capitalise on the current trends, Imtithal decided to open her own *sala*. She went into partnership with Mary Mansour, who by then was a veteran performer in the world of *salas* and music halls. The two women rented a performance space at the top of the Bosphore Casino, near the train station and a short walk from the top of Emad al-Din Street. The property had been newly renovated by one of Egypt's best architects, Hassan Fathy, and Imtithal agreed to take charge of its administration.

Sadly, Imtithal soon discovered the underworld of protection rackets—and worse—that pervaded Ezbekiyya's nightlife. On opening night, a man approached Imtithal. His name was Fouad al-Shami, and he was a *futuwwa*—head of a local gang that controlled the area, known by locals as "the emperor of Faggala and Ezbekiyya."[19] Fouad made two demands: He declared that members of his gang should be able to drink for free in her new club and that Imtithal would have to pay him regular protection money, as most other venues in the area did. If she did not, he said, her business would not succeed. Still, she flatly refused his demands—a brave decision, perhaps partly motivated by her inability to pay their large fee.

Not used to their demands being refused, the gang started a campaign of intimidation. The bullying went slowly at first; sometimes a gang member would come into the club, order the most expensive drinks on the menu, and refuse to pay. Then, in person and on her home phone, gang members started explicitly threatening to harm Imtithal. She still did not pay; instead, she went to a local police station and reported what was going on. The policemen's reaction would later come back to haunt them. Instead of helping her, the officers told her that they weren't bodyguards; their job was to investigate crimes only after they had happened.

On the night of 22 May, one member of the gang, Hussein Ibrahim Hassan, turned up at the Bosphore Casino and sat in the back row of seats to watch the show. Just before going onstage, Imtithal went to get a drink from the bar. The manager of the Bosphore Casino had just spoken to her about what she was going to sing. As he left, he saw her lean down to kiss a little boy and assumed it was her brother. Before she could make it to the stage, Hussein Ibrahim Hassan, brandishing a broken bottle, walked up to Imtithal and stabbed her in the throat. She immediately fell to the ground. One lurid report claimed that Hussein then picked up her still-lit cigarette from the floor and began to smoke it. Imtithal's mother, who was also in the *sala* that night, rushed to help her daughter, but there was nothing she could do. Imtithal died on her way to the hospital.

This cold-blooded murder of a young dancer provoked an uproar in the local press and a wave of mourning. Imtithal was described as a popular and well-liked figure in Ezbekiyya. Zaki Tolaymat, the distinguished actor and (now ex-) husband of Rose al-Youssef, had been Imtithal's close friend, perhaps even lover, published a tribute in the magazine *al-Musawwar*. When the newspapers reported that Imtithal had a young daughter who had been left without a mother, sympathy for her only increased. On the first day of the trial, a significant number of Cairo's women arrived at the courthouse, where the staff had greatly underestimated the public interest. Three benches in the courtroom had been set aside for women. Even so, many of them were forced to stand in the aisles. The next day, the number of seats for women was doubled.

After emotional speeches from the lawyers and several accounts of the gruesome details of the case, the verdict came in. The gang members managed to avoid the hangman's rope, but they did not escape prison. Their leader, Fouad al-Shami, and the murderer, Hussein Ibrahim, were given life sentences with hard labour; four others were given shorter sentences of ten or fifteen years with hard labour. Reports of the trial said that tears fell from Fouad al-Shami's eyes as he was led away.[20]

In the wake of this crime, extravagant descriptions of all kinds of criminal activities perpetrated by these gangs and criminal strongmen began to emerge: extortion, prostitution, and violence. In Ezbekiyya the gangs spent most nights in the cabarets that paid them protection money and gave them free drinks. It was even rumoured that performers paid the gangs extra to beat up journalists who gave them bad reviews. The gangs also tried to extort money from any particularly wealthy or illustrious men who were seen frequenting the cabarets. Newspapers published guides telling readers how to spot these men. But they were not always easy to find. Reports (showing their bourgeois prejudices) informed readers that some were rough-and-ready working-class thugs, but others blended in with polite society, did exercises to build their muscles, and dressed in sharp suits with silk shirts; some were Egyptian and others were European.[21]

In the weeks following the murder, the public also turned on the police, who had been so glaringly incompetent in their handling of Imtithal's complaints. *Rose al-Youssef* magazine published a full-page cartoon of a tearful Imtithal Fawzi walking into a police station where officers are yawning or sleeping at their desks. She begs the sergeant to help her, and he just tells her, "When someone is dead, come and tell me about it."[22] In Ezbekiyya, customers in a bar drew attention to the city's war on drugs—a war that often focused on Ezbekiyya bars. One customer complained to the Egyptian press, saying that Thomas Russell, former police chief of Cairo and now head of the Narcotics Intelligence Bureau, should stop worrying about opium, hashish, and cocaine and start caring about people's lives.

In the wake of Imtithal's death, a wave of violence against female dancers and performers was unleashed. Both Mounira al-Mahdiyya and Badia Masabni received threats, Mounira by letter and Badia over the phone, demanding that they send money or face the same fate as Imtithal. In the Nile Delta town of Faraskur, a popular singer and dancer was found murdered in her own home.[23]

Just days after the incident at the Bosphore Casino, *al-Ahram* newspaper reported another murder in Cairo. The victim was one of Badia Masabni's former dancers, Ayousha Nabil, who was killed by her lover. As a young girl growing up in Cairo, Ayousha had been attracted by the lights of Emad al-Din Street and signed up as a dancer at Sala Badia. Moving from one cabaret to another, she had made her way amidst Cairo's buzzing nightlife. In one of these clubs Ayousha met a young student called Hussein Gamal al-Din, who started to court her. Using a large inheritance from his recently deceased father, Hussein sent her expensive gifts and eventually proposed to her. She accepted.

This marriage was short-lived. Hussein soon began to feel jealous of his new wife. She knew a lot of people in Cairo's nightclubs and would often say hello to them across the room, and he interpreted those greetings as flirtation. After only a few months, he divorced her. Ayousha, left with no savings or independent income, was forced to support herself again. Unable to make enough as a dancer, she turned to sex work to make ends meet. During one police raid on a brothel, she jumped out of the window to escape arrest and broke her leg. In desperate need of money, she got back together with her ex-husband, whereupon the pair quickly fell back into their old habits of drinking late into the night in the city's bars and clubs. But this time, the atmosphere was different. He behaved bizarrely—suddenly getting angry and threatening her and then calming down again.

Late one night the couple went back to a hotel room on Soliman Pasha Street after drinking in a nightclub. When they were alone in their room, he opened a bottle of wine and poured each of them a glass. It is unclear whether Hussein had planned what happened next or had acted in a moment of anger. The hotel owner heard screams coming from their room and opened the door to find Ayousha lying on the floor covered in blood. Turning to the owner, Hussein said, "I killed her. It's done. She's dead." The owner slammed the door in his face and called the police, who arrived soon after. When they opened the door, they found Hussein lying on the floor too, also covered in blood. "It's better to die like this than on the gallows," he told them before being rushed to hospital, where he passed away the next morning. At her autopsy, it was discovered that Ayousha Nabil had been stabbed twenty-eight times.[24]

As the 1930s continued, Badia held firm to her reputation as the queen of Cairo's nightlife. She made herself a small fortune and launched a whole new generation of singers and dancers. But if life had taught her anything, it was that nothing lasts forever. In 1936 her throne started to shake after a series of professional failures and personal betrayals. In 1935, with an eye on where the entertainment business was going, she decided to stake her future in the film industry. She had made a few short films in the early 1930s to showcase her singing and dancing acts, and some of them were screened as far away as New York. Apparently partly influenced by her husband's former lover Claire, who had remained Badia's friend despite all that had happened between them, she stopped performing in cabarets and started working on her own feature film; it would be called *The Queen of the Music Halls*. It was a dance-filled extravaganza with an unusual plot centred around a cabaret owner (Badia), her absent husband, and several other men who planned to seduce her.

She started her own production company and poured thousands of pounds into the film as well as many months of her life. When it was finally released in 1936, Badia's star vehicle was a flop. Up against Oum Kalthoum's first smash hit film *Wedad*, a historical drama set in Mamluk Egypt, Badia's film could not compete; it quietly sank without a trace. Badia did not try to defend the finished product. She blamed the editing; the sound was inaudible, the story was confusing, the montages were bad, and some of the most expensive scenes that she had lavished her money on did not even make the final cut. In short, Badia was broke. Even worse, she had borrowed money all over town, and if she did not pay it back soon, she would be forced to declare bankruptcy.

Devastated at the failure of the movie and faced with mounting debts, Badia became depressed and suicidal: in an attempt to kill herself, she drank most of a bottle of whiskey followed by a large handful of aspirin. In her memoirs she recalled that she would have succeeded had her nephew Antoine not heard her crying and called a doctor. From then on, nothing went quite right for her. For some reason, the press started publishing short news items about dancers leaving Badia's troupe. One of her stars, Tahiyya Carioca, left in February; then Juliette also went, joining a troupe set up by Badia's estranged husband, Naguib al-Rihani.

In March 1937 things got worse when one of Badia's old dancers, Beba Izz al-Din, took control of Sala Badia. According to Badia's memoirs, the move was the result of a campaign of deception and treachery. She alleged that her nephew Antoine, who was having an affair with Beba, had secretly sold the cabaret to her for a ridiculously low price as part of a plot to cut Badia out. He had even converted to Islam in order to marry Beba after deserting Badia's daughter, Juliette. Upon hearing the news, Badia rushed straight to Emad al-Din Street to confront Beba, but one of the workers blocked her at the door. He asked her, "What are you doing here? It doesn't belong to you anymore, it belongs to 'the lady' now." According to Badia's dramatic account of the scene, the worker slapped her in the face—and she, fired up with rage, grabbed a chair and threw it at him; then, taking another chair, she threw it at "the lady."[25]

Beba, who kept using the name Sala Badia despite the alleged scandal, seems to have gone from strength to strength over the next couple of years. Her line-up included the usual assortment of dancers and singers, as well as "a bit of smutty humour, a bit of politics, a bit of patriotism, 'European,' 'ancient Egyptian,' and 'Arab' dances." The house was full every night: "They come in from the Delta and from the south, from the Desert in the west and from the oases in the east, to see her."[26]

Badia, on the other hand, was still on a downward trajectory. She did not return to Emad al-Din Street until 1938, when she opened a *sala* in a new theatre called the Alhambra. The season was not a success, and *Rose al-Youssef* described the performances as "the weakest programme that Badia has put on since she started working in the *salas*." Badia quickly stopped the run and went on a tour of the Levant instead.[27]

During the Second World War, Badia's fortunes were revived after a number of very bad years. Cairo was once again full of foreign soldiers, as well as countless spies, intriguers, and troublemakers. Badia, perhaps seeing that these new arrivals could be very good customers, immediately threw herself behind the Allied cause and mocked the Axis powers. In May 1940, *Rose al-Youssef* published an article saying that Adolf Hitler had sentenced Badia to death in absentia after she performed a series of sketches in her club, one criticising Nazi aggression against smaller states and the other depicting the actions of the Gestapo in Germany. "This man who had terrified the whole world," the article said, "is afraid of a monologist." In autumn of 1940, Badia opened a huge new venue overlooking Opera Square. This "Casino Opera," which included an American Bar, a restaurant, a theatre, and a roof terrace, quickly became one of the most popular night spots of the war. An American reporter described it as a "huge, barnlike place . . . jammed to the doors nightly with laughing, shouting soldiers from the four corners of the empire, trying for a few hours to forget the war." As Badia performed her famous anti-Nazi sketches, dancers dressed up as soldiers or air hostesses proclaimed an imminent Allied victory.[28]

But once the war was over and the lucrative customer base was gone, her fortunes began to wane again. In 1950 she retired from the cabaret business. She had been performing for forty years and running cabarets for over twenty. She sold the Opera Square Casino to her old enemy Beba Izz al-Din and left the country—Badia had a habit of forgiving people who had wronged her. As so often happened, scandal followed Badia's departure from Egypt. She had apparently not realised that selling her cabaret would lead to a large tax bill. In late 1950, instead of paying the taxes, she fled Egypt for Lebanon and left behind, according to one newspaper, $200,000 of debt.[29]

After leaving Egypt, Badia found that her luck was only a little better, and her later life was marred by more deception and loss. Another marriage, this time to a much younger Lebanese man (amidst speculation that she had only done so to escape Egypt), ended in a couple of months. At first she had been excited that a younger man might still find her attractive, but she soon realised that he was only after her money. He even demanded a payoff from Badia before he would agree to a divorce. Her account of these years sometimes makes for difficult reading. Suspicion runs through her memoirs, but in her last two romantic involvements with men, she appears irrationally distrustful about the influence of unidentified Jewish women. She claimed, for instance, that this Lebanese con artist was not acting alone but was under the influence of his unnamed Jewish lover.

In the late 1940s, she also attempted to reconcile with her estranged husband Naguib al-Rihani and claimed to have been thwarted by another unnamed Jewish girlfriend. Badia said that after Naguib died in 1949, she went to his funeral and saw this girlfriend ostentatiously crying during the service. Naguib al-Rihani's love life was notoriously complicated, so it is hard to tell which woman Badia had singled out. Some rumours intimated that he was romantically involved with the young Jewish actress Nagwa Salem just before his death. It is also tempting to think it might have been the young actress Camelia

(Lilian Cohen), who was pictured weeping at Naguib's funeral; she had been linked to several men across Cairo, from King Farouk to the poet and songwriter Kamil al-Shinawi. Still, the most likely candidate was the Jewish woman known only by her first name, Victorienne—who Naguib's long-time writing partner, Badie Khayri, said had nursed Naguib in his final years. Had it not been for Naguib's Jewish lover, Badia continued to think in her later years, she would have made peace with her ex-husband.

For someone who had spent most of her life working with Jewish musicians and actors, helping to launch the careers of so many Jewish stars—including Layla Mourad, Negma Ibrahim, and Semha al-Boghdadi—and was so quick to support the anti-Nazi cause during the war, it is uncomfortable to see her, in these memoirs, repeatedly turning her suspicions in that direction. Why, in any case, did she need to find someone to blame besides the men?

At the end of a life constantly fractured by betrayal, exploitation, and abuse, Badia appears to have given way to paranoia and bitterness. The events of these final years cannot help but puncture the romantic image of her glory days on Emad al-Din Street. After her final divorce, unable to return to Egypt for tax reasons, Badia left the entertainment industry altogether. She settled down in a farm shop and dairy in the Lebanese countryside. For a woman who reached the peak of fame, glamour, and celebrity in the global city of Cairo, her story has a strangely rural ending.

Act III

CURTAIN CALL

Chapter 12

THE SECOND REVOLUTION

I n 1950, a fourteen-year-old Palestinian boy and his friends sneaked into Badia Masabni's casino by the Nile to see the famous dancer Tahiyya Carioca perform. He was Edward Said, who would become a professor of English Literature at Columbia University in New York and a leading cultural theorist of the late twentieth century and is now best known as the author of *Orientalism*. Writing decades later, his memory of that evening was still vivid. Tahiyya danced to a song called *Mandil al-Helou* (My darling's handkerchief), "whose innumerable verses celebrated the woman who draped it, cried into it, decorated her hair with it, on and on for almost a full hour." The adolescent Said was extremely impressed: "The beauty of her dance was its connectedness: the feeling she communicated of a spectacularly lithe and well-shaped body undulating through a complex but decorative series of encumbrances made up of gauzes, veils, necklaces, strings of gold and silver chains, which her movements animated deliberately and at times almost theoretically."[1]

Cairo was two years away from the revolution of 1952 that would change Egypt—its nightlife and all—forever. The dancer Edward Said so admired would soon have to navigate a new post-colonial world

Opposite: Tahiyya Carioca (Getty Images)

inspired by the politics of socialism, Arab nationalism, and the Non-Aligned Movement. Tahiyya saw the popularity of Cairo's cabarets and revue theatres fade, and she witnessed the dawn of a new historical period. In the 1950s Egypt would finally gain the full independence that many had wanted for so long. However, as Tahiyya and others would find out, the path to progress did not always run smoothly.

Although from a later generation, Tahiyya's story has much in common with the biographies of the earlier stars of Emad al-Din Street. She was born around 1920 into a lower middle-class family living in the Nile Delta. Her family moved between Ismailia, on the Suez Canal, and a small town called al-Manzalah. Her memoirs touch on familiar themes: a father who died while she was young, a turbulent childhood, fantasies of escape, and a lucky break that brought her to the stages of Emad al-Din Street.

After her father's death, Tahiyya lived with members of her large extended family, staying first with her half-brother Morsi, who sent her to a local Christian school. When it was discovered that she, although Muslim, was sent to pray with the nuns, Morsi immediately withdrew her, and she was sent to live with Ahmed, another half-brother, and his Maltese wife. Tahiyya remembered those years as the worst of her life. Ahmed threatened her, beat her, and kept her trapped in the house while she spent her days dreaming about how to escape this tyrant.

She felt her only hope lay in a young woman who sometimes attended their family gatherings and whom she called Auntie Souad, though her precise family relationship to Tahiyya is a little unclear. And then Tahiyya had a stroke of luck; she discovered that her Auntie Souad was none other than Souad Mahasen, a dancer from Cairo's cabaret scene. Every time they met, Souad joked that Tahiyya should come with her to the capital, and one day Tahiyya decided to take the chance. In 1934, aged about fourteen, she crept out of Ahmed's house by herself, took the train to Cairo, and made for Emad al-Din Street. She spent around a year moving between different troupes until, in the summer of 1935, she joined Badia Masabni's troupe and started performing at Casino Badia by the Nile.

As Tahiyya was rising in the world of dance, Egypt was heading for two significant political changes. The first was the death in 1936 of King Fouad, who had reigned for almost twenty years, and the succession of his son. Farouk was only sixteen when he came to power, but magazines and newspapers quickly published hopeful articles about the new future heralded by his reign, accompanied by triumphant photos of the athletic young king. In May of that year, the new king returned to Egypt from his school in England, landing first in Alexandria and then heading for Cairo to visit his father's tomb in the citadel.

The second major political event, in the same year, was the signing of a new Anglo-Egyptian Treaty. It was touted as a concrete step towards Egyptian independence, and the first clause bluntly stated, "The military occupation of Egypt by the forces of His Majesty the King and Emperor is terminated." Now the Egyptians had the right to form and control their own army, a significant move towards national self-determination. The much-resented system of capitulations, under which foreigners were not subject to the laws of Egypt but to their own "consular courts," was also to be abolished.

Although the treaty was a major advance for the Egyptian nationalist cause, the British had still left a number of stipulations alongside the concessions. The Suez Canal, for instance, was to remain under British control "until such a time as . . . the Egyptian Army is in a position to ensure by its own resources the liberty and entire security of the navigation of the canal." This condition was to be assessed after twenty years. The other important clause stated that in case of war (or international emergency), the Egyptians would give control of all their "ports, aerodromes and means of communication" to the British, even if it meant imposing martial law to ensure the arrangement.[2]

Meanwhile, on Cairo's stages, Tahiyya was working in Badia Masabni's company during two of the worst years of Badia's life—1936 and 1937, in which she made the flop film *Queens of the Music Hall*, went bankrupt, and attempted suicide. Still, the experience managed to instil a love of dancing in the young Tahiyya. Badia was famous for her serious and rigorous approach to the art of dance, and Tahiyya remembered her shouting words of encouragement during rehearsals: "When you are dancing, forget everything. . . . Forget yourself. Close your ears and don't listen to anything that is being said in the *sala*. Let your mind, your heart, and your soul be in your legs if you really want to be a proper dancer."[3]

Another extremely influential person in this early part of Tahiyya's career was Isaac Dixon. Badia's main trainer and choreographer at the time, he was a mysterious figure about whom very little is known. He took it upon himself to train Tahiyya personally, giving her the stage name Carioca (after a popular song-and-dance number in the smash hit Ginger Rogers and Fred Astaire film *Flying Down to Rio*). Although Isaac Dixon was one of the most important choreographers of mid-twentieth century Egypt and worked in many great films of the 1940s and 1950s, he totally disappeared from the record after 1956. Few details of his life now survive—his nationality and even the correct spelling of his name (Dixon or Dickson) are still debated.

When the Second World War broke out in 1939, the entertainment scene that Tahiyya was just getting used to changed completely. Egypt did not formally join the war itself, and Cairo was never really on the front line; the most violence it experienced was during occasional air-strikes. But in following the conditions of the Anglo-Egyptian Treaty, the Egyptian government handed over control of its military infra-structure to Britain. Cairo became an important administrative base as well as a place for troops fighting in the Western Desert to take a break.

"The first thing that men on leave from the desert were interested in when they reached Cairo was a binge," wrote Pennethorne Hughes, a BBC producer doing war work in Cairo as director of broadcasting.[4] The audiences of Emad al-Din's cabarets swelled as Cairo played host to an array of people ranging from poets and writers to soldiers, adventurers, and *artistes*. Some of Britain's most famous writers passed through Cairo, including Lawrence Durrell, Patrick Leigh Fermor, and Olivia Manning. The photographer Cecil Beaton and politician Randolph Churchill were all brought there, one way or another, by the war. There was such an active literary scene among the English visitors that a poetry journal, *Personal Landscape*, was founded in Cairo in 1942 and continued publication until 1945.

Many in this group of writers have now achieved legendary status; but when they were in Egypt, they spent their time in much the same way as everyone else. They sat in restaurants, they drank, and they went to cabarets. The main difference was that, unlike everyone else, they wrote poetry about it. Two members of the *Personal Landscape* circle composed their own sultry poems about nightclub dancers. A co-founder of the group, Bernard Spencer, described a dancer's act:

And as the music built to climax and she leaned
Naked in her dancing skirt, and was supreme, . . .[5]

Another poet, Terence Tiller, was lecturing at Cairo University during the war. He wrote an equally suggestive poem on the same theme, which describes a dancer's arms as "snakes," her breasts as "alive and writhing," and her thighs as "gimlets of oil."[6]

The famous Josephine Baker also came to entertain the troops. She had visited Cairo once before in 1934 to perform for a few nights on a stage in Ezbekiyya Gardens. On that trip she had visited Badia Masabni's *sala* in the company of the passionate cabaret-goer Baron Édouard-Jean Empain. He was the principal owner of the Paris Metro and also operated the Heliopolis Palace Hotel in Cairo, where he had a large villa. Baker also went to see the pyramids with an Egyptian journalist, rode a camel called Sarah Bernhardt, and promised to return to Cairo soon. In 1940, she performed a concert in support of Franco-Egyptian cooperation, "the first Free French gathering in a country that had not yet recognised de Gaulle's government."[7]

Cairo's strategic importance meant that even if it saw no front-line fighting, its alcohol-soaked entertainment palaces were rife with espionage. Several dancers were employed by many different parties and tasked to find whatever information they could about the enemy by any means they had at their disposal.

At the elegant and elite Kit Kat Club, a favourite haunt of British officers, a dancer called Hekmat Fahmy subtly pumped her tipsy admirers for information, even convincing some soldiers to send her letters once they got to the front. She would then pass the information on to an Egyptian-born German, Johannes Eppler, who had—using his Arabic name Hussein Gaafer for cover—created a small operations room on a Nile houseboat. According to Major A. W. Sansom, one of the British officials involved in the operation, the British learned the details of this German spy ring through a rather unlikely source. Eppler, whose life seemed to consist more of drinking, dancing, and carousing than actual spying, had been sleeping with a young French cabaret dancer who went by the name of Natalie. As the British began to get wind of suspicious activities taking place on Eppler's houseboat, they rounded up a number of his associates, including Natalie.

On questioning her, they discovered that she was not just a cabaret dancer. She was also working as a spy for an underground Zionist organisation, and she revealed that Eppler was a German agent. Natalie told the British that Eppler and his accomplice had been sending messages through a secret radio transmitter and that they used a code hidden in a copy of Daphne du Maurier's novel *Rebecca*.

Tahiyya Carioca also had a minor part in this story. In his later memoirs Eppler claimed that in 1940, to divert suspicion from his activities, he decided to rent an apartment in Sharif Pasha Street, parallel to Emad al-Din Street. He then started "cohabiting with the bellydancer Carioca, at the time the toast of the Badia Massabni [*sic*] Oriental Theatre." Eppler was an extravagant storyteller, and his tale may be a little overblown, but he rationalised their living arrangement by claiming that it was designed to stop people being suspicious if he went away on a mission and was absent from his apartment for a long time. After all, he would not be expected to spend all his time with his mistress, and "how many other sons of rich fathers were doing the same!"[8]

Tahiyya spent the rest of the war in the world of Cairo's partly seedy, partly glamourous, partly desperate nightlife, dancing in cabarets and private parties alike and performing before some of the country's elite. She made her way into the film business, starring as a dancer in Aziza Amir's 1944 "song-and-dance super-production," *The Magic Cap*.[9] And through a friendship with the actor Sulayman Naguib, the son of a distinguished poet and civil servant, she got a series of high-prestige gigs: in the Opera House, at the exclusive Gezira Club, even for King Farouk.

To dance in front of Farouk in the 1940s was a dubious honour. The stories of his wartime nights in Cairo, full of gambling and adultery, were becoming legendary. From the strapping young prince of 1936 he had quickly become a portly, sybaritic king. He became known for driving around Cairo in his red Cadillac convertible and for his obsession with collecting—almost anything, from antiquities to smutty playing cards. He was also linked with a string of different women, though some British officials were sceptical about his ability to maintain so many sexual relationships and gossiped among themselves that he was, in fact, almost impotent. The British ambassador in Egypt, Miles Lampson, wrote to Foreign Secretary Anthony Eden that although Farouk enjoyed the company of cabaret *artistes*, he had the sexual capacity of "a man of fifty or fifty-five" and "the greatest difficulty bringing the thing off at all!" Lampson even said that there was "talk of an operation to rectify the faulty glands."[10] In February 1942 the British also demonstrated his political impotence by rolling their tanks onto the lawns of the royal palace and forcing him to appoint a new government of their choosing.

The war ended in 1945 but, as with the First World War, the cessation of global hostilities did not bring an end to tensions in Egypt. The British military presence in the country—particularly around the Suez Canal—the apparently useless King Farouk, and the corruption of the Egyptian political class all fuelled resentment. Radical parties started to exploit the situation: in particular, the Muslim Brotherhood (an organisation formed in 1928 and dedicated to freeing Egypt from foreign influence by increasingly violent means) and the fascist-inspired nationalists of the Young Egypt Party.

In 1948, when the state of Israel was formed, it provided the spark that ignited a fire across the country. Egypt's army—which had somewhat tentatively joined the Arab forces to find that they lacked training, military intelligence, and in some cases working equipment—suffered a series of humiliating defeats. The political fallout was dramatic: Egypt's leaders and military establishment lost credibility. The Muslim Brotherhood, which had passionately opposed the establishment of a Jewish state, started a campaign of bombings and political assassinations.

In 1948 the Brotherhood was accused of murdering, among others, a prominent judge, the Cairo chief of police, and Prime Minister Mahmoud El Nokrashi. Then, in February 1949, Hassan al-Banna, founder of the Muslim Brotherhood, was also assassinated (Brotherhood members weren't the only ones stoking this political violence; they were just the most prominent).

For Egypt's Jewish community, these geopolitical events beyond their control would have devasting effects. Just a few decades before, Jews had been considered a normal part of the nation and were involved in politics, business, journalism, and of course, the entertainment industry. Egypt was certainly not free of anti-Semitism before 1948 (stereotypes, particularly about Jewish stinginess, can be found in many places), but according to a 1949 report by the American Jewish Committee, that bias "did not appear to be a national vice."[11] But soon outbursts of anti-Semitism and accusations that Egyptian Jews were sympathetic to Zionism left many of them feeling afraid and unwelcome. A series of bombs, blamed on extremist groups like the Muslim Brotherhood, targeted Jewish businesses. Waves of emigration began, ending any significant Jewish presence in Egypt—the active Jewish community in Egypt shrank from an estimated 80,000 in 1948 to only a few hundred by the end of the 1960s.

But the politics of the post-war period were not all violent or reactionary. A huge variety of political movements were competing to win followers and make themselves heard—among them liberals, socialists, and progressives. It was a vital time for Egypt's feminist movement. The foundation for a new era of activism had been laid in part by the successes of Hoda Shaarawi's mainstream feminism as well as the work of countless singers, dancers, and actresses who had also proved that women could be successful public figures. Now they were building on the huge steps taken in the '20s and '30s and starting to push for more direct political recognition.

In 1951 the young feminist activist Doria Shafik, head of the newly formed political group the Daughters of the Nile Union, grew tired of slow progress and decided to take the issue of women's participation in politics directly to the government. At the head of a large protest made up exclusively of women, she marched to the Egyptian parliament. According to newspaper reports, the women entered the complex and started "shouting slogans, scattering leaflets, blowing automobile horns and puncturing tyres." Doria headed for the office of the president of the senate and, seeing that he was absent, was undeterred. She picked up his telephone and called him, saying that she was in his office and had a list of demands: First, the right to vote (which women in Egypt did not yet have), and second, the right of women to run for political office. By the end of the call, he had agreed to at least consider these demands—a minor victory, but a start.[12]

Tahiyya Carioca missed much of the political turmoil after the war. As the British and Allied forces declared victory, she left Cairo for California. Her companion was a young American soldier, Gilbert Levy from New Jersey, whom she had met at one of her wartime concerts— "I whistled loudest," he joked to the press.[13] The two were married in Los Angeles in 1946, and Tahiyya attempted to start a career in the American film industry. She attracted the attention of a Hollywood agent, Wynn Rocamora, who saw the potential of an Egyptian dancer who had acting experience in Egyptian films. He began promoting her, saying that she would play the part of Salome in a new film version of the story. But despite the high hopes that she might have had for her Hollywood career, it was not to happen. She stayed only a few years in America. As with many GI brides, her marriage failed, and her American film career never got off the ground.

She returned to Cairo in 1947, just as Egypt's political troubles were reaching a peak. Nonetheless, she found the film industry back home an easier target than Hollywood and got starring roles in a string of successful films: *I Love to Dance, Long Live Art, Love and Madness*, and the 1949 film *Mandil al-Hilou* (My darling's handkerchief), in which she played two characters—one is a dancer, the other an ordinary woman who lives with her mother; but, crucially for the plot, the women look exactly alike. When Edward Said saw Tahiyya perform in 1950, she was dancing to the title song of this last film.

During this period, Tahiyya also began to explore left-wing political causes: people were calling for national liberation and better conditions for the working class while also standing against the prejudice and reactionary nationalism espoused by groups like the Muslim Brotherhood and Young Egypt. She was especially attracted to a new political group called the Partisans of Peace. This Soviet-sponsored endeavour, formed in 1950 as part of a larger umbrella organisation called the World Peace Congress, included many prominent leftists from across the world: from the East, Soviet author Alexander Fadeyev and historian V. P. Volgin; from the West, Paul Robeson, Louis Aragon, and Pablo Picasso. The Partisans of Peace spoke out against war, atomic weapons, and the formation of NATO, calling for a new, peaceful world order (as it was conceived of by the Soviets).

In Egypt, the Partisans of Peace hardly resembled a communist cell. If anything, the organisation looked like a prototype of non-aligned third-world politics whose members did not see why they had to be dragged into the West's growing conflict with the Soviet Union. And if there was to be a new global war, they certainly did not see why they should fight on behalf of colonial and imperialist Britain, whose shackles they were still trying to escape. Undeniably, there were communists in the group's ranks; most prominent was the so-called Red Pasha, Kamel al-Bindari, the former Egyptian ambassador to the USSR who had been instrumental in creating the Partisans of Peace. However, the movement included people of many different political persuasions: an assortment of liberals, leftists, and even Islamists. Some of its best-known figures were members of the country's old ruling elite and were far from radical Marxists. There was Ibrahim Rashad Pasha, a long-time proponent of the cooperative movement that aimed to create systems to allow workers and ordinary people to work together and pool resources for the greater good; another supporter was Ceza Nabarawi, the prominent women's rights activist and cofounder of the Egyptian Feminist Union. Thirty-year-old Tahiyya Carioca joined the movement in 1950, shortly after it was formed, as part of a drive to recruit artists, writers, and public personalities to spread their message. Before long, she was hosting meetings and political discussions at her house.

Those meetings are described in the memoirs of a young member of the Partisans of Peace: Nayla Kamel (née Mary Rosenthal) was born to an Egyptian-Jewish father and an Italian mother in Cairo but had changed her name upon marrying Saad Kamel, a left-wing activist. Nayla recalled that she and Saad had started to attend salons at Tahiyya's house. She was apparently a consummate host, serving *mezzes* as well as whiskey and a home-made Arabic pudding called *balouza*. The first part of the evening always started seriously—people read and critiqued articles written by members of the group. As the night went on, they started raucous sing-alongs to hits of the great Sayyid Darwish. Nayla remembered the evenings as an intoxicating combination of pleasure and politics.

Over the next few years, political change flooded across Cairo, and many groups like the Partisans of Peace were swept along in its wake. In 1951 the Egyptian government officially annulled the Anglo-Egyptian Treaty, armed guerrilla groups were formed, and well-armed and well-trained Egyptian partisans (*fedayeen*) began openly fighting the British in the Canal Zone. In January 1952, the British launched a fierce reprisal against the only enemy they could find, opening fire on a group of Egyptian soldiers and killing around fifty people in what became known as the Ismailia Massacre.

On 26 January 1952, Egyptians protested against the British military in Cairo. One Egyptian police officer was sitting on the terrace of Badia Masabni's old Casino Opera in Ezbekiyya having a drink with a dancer. When a group of protestors saw the police officer, they were incensed and shouted something at him to the effect that while he was having a fine time in Cairo, his compatriots were dying in the Canal Zone. "He retorted sharply," said one British security official in his account of the riots, "and the girl with him sneered at the demonstrators." The altercation soon became physical, and by around noon a group of about thirty or forty men with large quantities of paraffin had piled up the furniture on the street and were getting ready to torch both the building and its contents. By one o'clock the casino was on fire, and the demonstrators were moving on to other targets. Within a few hours, almost the whole of Ezbekiyya was ablaze.[14]

The crowds torched buildings that seemed obviously foreign—among the targets were cinemas, department stores, hotels, and the main branch of Barclays Bank. They also torched Tommy's Bar, a popular hangout for British soldiers as well as, for some time, the daily watering hole of the surrealist art movement Art and Liberty. The most high-profile casualty was Shepheard's Hotel, a Cairo establishment for almost a hundred years, on whose terrace tourists had mixed with international royalty. The *Manchester Guardian* would report a few days later that "virtually every cinema, cabaret, restaurant, bar, and wine shop in the centre of the city was destroyed."[15]

Various attempts to identify culprits followed. Some blamed communists, others the Muslim Brotherhood; some suspected it had been staged by either the British or the Egyptian king as an excuse to crack down on their enemies. The British had their own suspicions that Egyptian police had been secretly told not to stop the protestors' rampage. The Minister of Interior, in a piece of rather tortured logic, declared that "the people who precipitated the events in Cairo are bad elements, and of course communists are bad elements" (clearly implying that communists had "precipitated the events").[16]

But the strongest evidence pointed to the ultranationalist Green Shirts, who were now active as the Socialist Party but whose ideas were largely unchanged from their earlier incarnation as the fascist Young Egypt Party. They had both the means and the motives to target foreign businesses, and what's more, witnesses had reported seeing prominent members of the group in Ezbekiyya that day. Their leader, Ahmed Hussein, was quickly arrested and accused of being one of the prime instigators of the destruction.

Hussein's own publications contained plenty of evidence to support his arrest. Until it was banned a year earlier, his party's newspaper, Young Egypt, had included some inflammatory rhetoric against "imperialist" businesses (meaning British-owned or doing business with the British). The newspaper articles called on people to boycott the British-owned Rivoli Cinema and withdraw their money from Barclays Bank (both structures burned that day). A 1951 article in the party paper asked, "How is it that the cabarets are crowded with people until the early hours of the morning and how is it that tens or hundreds of thousands of people can pass their time in the cinema as if there isn't a war going on the Canal Zone?"[17]

There is a certain irony to Ahmed Hussein's alleged involvement in the destruction of Ezbekiyya. As a young student, he was obsessed with the theatre, putting on plays at his school and even acting as an extra at the Ramses Theatre. In his memoirs, he recalled that he once tried to drop out of school and join Youssef Wahbi's troupe on a tour of North Africa. He had run away from home, with ten Egyptian pounds in his pocket, and turned up at the stage door begging for a place in the troupe. Youssef had told him bluntly that it would not be possible, and the young Ahmed Hussein had left with a severely dented ego. His revenge on Egypt's theatrical scene came in early 1952.

After police investigations and a short trial, in March 1952 Ahmed Hussein was sentenced to eighteen months in prison for disseminating his seditious articles. The other charges against him were connected with inciting the riots and carried the death penalty; but the hearings, complicated by legal wrangling and hunger strikes by Hussein, were frequently postponed and eventually forgotten.

A few months after this chaotic event, a group of army officers— known as the Free Officers—took matters into their own hands by launching a coup against the rakish King Farouk. It was a bloodless affair, and Farouk left Egypt with no great fuss in July, bound for exile. After the revolution General Mohammed Naguib was installed first as prime minister and then as president, but was soon replaced by the young and charismatic Colonel Gamal Abdel Nasser, whom many rec- ognised as the power behind the takeover. Farouk would be remem- bered (fairly or unfairly) as an ineffective playboy king more devoted to his own pleasure than his people. When the Egyptian military auc- tioned his possessions, they offered a special treat for those who spent enough money: a closed exhibition of his vast stash of pornography.

The early years after this revolution were full of contradiction and confusion. Few people wanted to return to the chaos and misrule of the previous years, and almost everyone agreed that change was needed. But they were unsure about what to expect from these new rulers and how they wanted to change the country. Leftists like those entertained by Tahiyya at her salons had a particularly complex relationship with the new government. They were pleased, for instance, when one of the new government's first acts was to pass a series of land reforms designed to break up the old feudal estates and empower the peasants. Likewise, almost all the left-wing organisations were united on the need to rid Egypt of imperial control once and for all.

Yet, many things would cause left-wing Egyptians to doubt the

aims and motives of these army officers. Just a few weeks after the revolution of 1952, cotton workers went on strike in the town of Kafr
al-Dawar, near Alexandria, to protest the dismissal of a number of
workers and to demand better pay and conditions. The strikers may
have hoped that the new administration would support them, but it
did not. After reports of rioting at the factory, the army moved in to
stop it, and several people were killed in the violence. Shortly after this
incident, the new Egyptian government tried and then executed two
of the strike leaders. The Free Officers blamed communists for these
disturbances and announced the creation of a state security department to fight what they saw as the dual threats of "communism and
Zionism." Not much later, police arrested forty-two people—including
the French novelist, playwright, and communist party member Roger
Vailland—"on charges of spreading communist propaganda in Egypt."
Over the next few years, the new government introduced more authoritarian policies and arrested many left-wing activists (and other people
deemed subversive) on vague political charges.[18]

Tahiyya Carioca, who found herself in the strange position of being
a famous dancer and film star as well as a member of a communist-
supported group, had her own ambivalent relationship with the new
government. After the revolution she was publicly optimistic about
the future and was quoted in *al-Kawakib* magazine as saying that the
leader of this new movement had "put an end to oppression and weak-
ness and brought this people, striving for life, out of the darkness and
into the light."[19]

But trouble quickly came her way after a trip to Bucharest with the
Partisans for Peace delegation to the World Festival of Youth and Students for Peace and Friendship in August 1953. The event featured a cultural programme and sightseeing tours as well as various sporting events.

It was attended by 30,000 to 40,000 people from as many as eighty countries. Tahiyya went, as part of a fifty-strong delegation from Egypt, to display her dancing skills; a women's basketball team and a young cartoonist were also delegates. When they arrived in Romania, Tahiyya was a big hit as she danced through the streets of Bucharest surrounded by crowds of people. A young Egyptian writer, Ahmed al-Hadari, who later went on to become one of Egypt's best-respected film critics, was at the festival with his camera and managed to capture some grainy footage of Tahiyya onstage. Wearing a bra and a long dress flecked with silver that shimmered in the light, she danced as she held aloft a translucent scarf, moving it over her body as the audience looked on.

In early November, soon after returning from the Youth Festival in Bucharest, Tahiyya became a casualty of the new regime's paranoia. She was arrested in a sweep of communist activists, picked up from her apartment along with two others: her then husband Mustafa Kamal Sidqi (a member of the Free Officers before he had failed to support their programme), whom she had married after returning from America, and Sharif Hatata, a communist who a few years earlier had escaped from prison, where he had been incarcerated for being a member of the banned party. A cache of subversive pamphlets was discovered in Tahiyya's house, and later accounts claim that one included an anti–Free Officers slogan: "One Farouk has gone and a lot of new Farouks have come."[20]

After her arrest on slightly unclear charges, Tahiyya was sent to a women's prison and was welcomed as a hero. Her fellow Partisan of Peace Nayla Kamel, who had been caught in the same sweep, was in awe. She recalled that the guards were so starstruck by Tahiyya that they arranged all kinds of favours for her, including bringing extra supplies such as sugar, whole milk, and even cocoa. Every morning the guards opened her cell door so that she could go out and exercise. Tahiyya claimed that if her limbs didn't move, they would waste away and she would never be able to dance again.

Tahiyya's own account of her imprisonment, published after her release in February 1954, was not so light-hearted. In an interview with *Rose al-Youssef* magazine she said, "The cell was small and the sunlight barely came in and the air was fetid" and complained that political prisoners were not separated from ordinary criminals. She had written memoirs while in prison, and they had been confiscated; "but," she added, "I have memorised everything in these memoirs so that one day I can publish them. Then society will get to know something about the life that people lead behind walls in the twentieth century, in these advanced times when liberators expound their theories all around us of how to improve people's lives." Then, she continued (appropriately for an article entitled "When Tahiyya Carioca Turns Out to Be a Communist"), "and I think that the people who are trapped by walls of bad luck should get their share of this better life too."[21]

In March 1954, almost immediately after Tahiyya's release from prison, the feminist activist Doria Shafik embarked on a sit-in and hunger strike to demand women's rights. Doria was incensed because the council that had been formed to write the country's new post-revolutionary constitution included no women. She marched into the chairman's office in the Journalists' Union and said she would not eat again until her demands were answered: female suffrage, female representation in parliament, and the appointment of women to the new constituent assembly. Before long, eight other women joined in the strike, which instantly became a press sensation. Doria received messages of support from women around the country as well as from outside Egypt. When she began to feel very weak a few days into the strike, a *Manchester Guardian* reporter asked Doria whether she worried about how her children would feel if she died. She replied, "I prefer to die for Egypt's women rather than to live for my daughters."[22]

After a week, the exhausted Doria was moved to a nearby hospital. There, lying in her sickbed, she received written assurance from the new government that the revised constitution guaranteed full women's rights—and she ended her strike. In 1956, when the constitution was promulgated, it not only gave women the right to vote but also guaranteed equal rights for women and declared that no one could be discriminated against because of their sex.

Tahiyya, who had attended meetings of Doria Shafik's Daughters of the Nile Union, was cautious after her time in prison. Nonetheless, she managed to provide some support for these protests. She sent a telegram directly to those responsible for the new constitution, asking them to accede to Doria's demands; and according to one newspaper article, she visited the women on hunger strike. During the rest of the 1950s, Tahiyya kept up her political activism but, perhaps remembering her time in prison, showed little public opposition to the new government or the Free Officers. On 15 October 1955, for instance, she joined a troupe of dancers dressed in military uniforms and paraded through the streets asking people to donate money to a project called Armament Week. The event had been designed to raise money for the Egyptian army and also, no doubt, as a propaganda effort in support of the troops. The dancers brought the show to the gates of the Soviet Embassy, hoping to convince the Soviets to support Egypt's soldiers, but they were unceremoniously turned away.

The political contradictions of the Free Officers' rule became most apparent in 1956. Nasser announced on the radio that he had nationalised the Suez Canal. Soon after, Egypt was attacked by a tripartite force of Britain, France, and Israel that tried to regain control of the important international shipping route. At this decisive point in history, the new Egyptian president managed to emerge victorious, protecting Egypt's ownership of the Suez Canal from foreign interference while also cementing his own power. The moment had great symbolic importance not just in Egypt, but across the world. Britain had been forced to back down from its former colony and accept that things had changed since the early twentieth century. Those on the Egyptian left were ecstatic about this triumph over imperialist powers, although many left-wing activists were serving long prison sentences on political charges. Strange happenings ensued in which prisoners celebrated and wrote letters of congratulation to Nasser, the head of the very government that had jailed them.

In the years following the Suez crisis, people without Egyptian citizenship began to leave the country in droves. The British and French were expelled, as were many of the remaining Jews. When Nasser launched a programme of nationalisation in 1961, many more people left. If, over the preceding decades, people had debated about what being Egyptian meant, the government of the Free Officers had an extremely restrictive answer—and in the years that followed, Egypt became a much less diverse society and Cairo a much less diverse city.

Politically, women had made huge strides forwards in the 1950s. However, for female performers, much had stayed the same. Tahiyya's private life was still scrutinised with the same lustful fascination, as reporters obsessed over how many times she had been married—some counted the number of her husbands as high as seventeen. Tahiyya was aloof and disparaging about this old question but it didn't stop people asking it. When she was asked at one of her parties in the early 1950s about her love life, she replied, "I don't need anyone to help me live, I am perfectly capable on my own. But I don't like to live in sin, so if I like someone, why shouldn't we get married?"[23]

Even Edward Said, who came back to Cairo in 1990 to meet Tahiyya for an article in the *London Review of Books*, repeated that old question:

She sat up straight, one elbow cocked provokingly at me, the other arm gesturing rhetorically in the air. "Many times," she retorted, her voice taking on the brassiness one associates with a lady of the night. Her eyes and her tone seemed to add: "So what? I've known lots of men."

When her friend the filmmaker Nabiha Loutfy, who had brought Said along for the meeting, asked her which of her husbands she had loved or which ones had influenced her, she gave a damning answer: "'None at all,' she said harshly. 'They were a shabby lot of bastards'; a declaration followed by a string of expletives."[24]

The prudish, quasi-puritanical disdain of the modern entertainment industry, which had existed since the nineteenth century, did not disappear with the revolution. In 1957, Rufus C. Lewter, a young African American medical student in Egypt, found out for himself that many people still worried about the corrupting effects of Cairo's nightlife. Rufus Lewter was an aspiring doctor who had graduated from Howard University, served as a lab technician in the United States Army, and tried in vain to enrol in American medical schools. When no American college would accept him, he decided to study abroad and eventually selected Ain Shams University in Cairo. Although he was a veteran and therefore eligible for funding under the new GI bill, he found himself—like so many other African Americans at the time—unable to access the money. When Nasser was informed of Rufus' presence in Egypt, he enthusiastically agreed to grant him a four-year scholarship. "If America doesn't want to educate you, I will," he promised.[25]

By night, Rufus started making a bit of extra money showing off the new rock 'n' roll dance crazes to enthusiastic Egyptian audiences. He was almost immediately successful, getting work at nightclubs like the Casino Abdine, on the grounds of Farouk's old palace, and at L'Auberge des Pyramides. In 1957 he was chosen to emcee one of the biggest rock 'n' roll dance nights Egypt had ever seen, which featured acts from five different clubs around town. However, when one busybody in the Ministry of the Interior got wind of these dances, outrage followed. Rock 'n' roll, as well as being "against public morals," was slammed as a dangerous import from imperialist America. In the summer of 1957, a campaign was begun to ban these rock 'n' roll nights, in much the same way that belly dancing had been forbidden in the 1920s. As the *New York Times* sarcastically reported, "Egyptian authorities have nipped at least one 'imperialist plot' in the bud. They have banned rock 'n' roll."[26]

The next year, Tahiyya and her fellow dancers came up against a similar puritanism. In mid-May 1958, Sulayman Rushdi, the "head of public morals," announced that beginning in June, dancers would be prohibited from wearing revealing costumes. Outfits showing bare stomachs or bare shoulders would be banned, and any dancer wearing them would be investigated by the morality police. Dancers immediately came together to protest. One of them joked, "Do you want me to wear an abaya [a loose-fitting black robe often worn by conservative women]?" When the American journalist Charles Arnot interviewed her about this ban, Tahiyya said, "It just won't be the same Egyptian dance any more. All the charm and beauty and art will be gone— killed. This silly unfair regulation is being imposed by unartistic people who understand nothing of dance or art." Eventually, the dancers made such a storm over this decision that the Bureau of Morals backed down. The day after the ban was supposed to go into effect, Tahiyya appeared before a group of important visitors and diplomats in a decidedly revealing costume.[27]

As Egypt moved through the 1950s and into the 1960s, the entertainment industry changed along with the rest of the country. It would be wrong to say that the old world of interwar Ezbekiyya had totally disappeared, but it had certainly been radically altered. Cinema, radio, and soon television became dominant forms of entertainment. Many cabarets survived, but they were not as central to the city's cultural life as they had once been. The Nasserist government still supported the arts, boasting that Egypt could "publish a new book every six hours, stage a new play every week and build a new hotel every 15 days."[28] But the type of theatre performance had changed completely. Plays influenced by Brecht and Ionesco replaced the revue theatre, farce, and music hall; drama became more intellectual and less popular. Then as now, men were more likely to be judged highbrow, serious, or intellectual, so women were often pushed out of the creative process (at the same time, they were becoming *more* prominent in public life as a whole). Cairo was now a city populated by a whole new cast of characters: Soviet advisors, African liberationists, and activists from across the third world. At that time, the arrival of a star and actress like Sarah Bernhardt was not what made the headlines; rather, it was a visit by Malcolm X. Edward Said's visit to Casino Badia as a child had become a memory from a different era.

Today the bright lights of Ezbekiyya have faded. The old music halls and bars that were popular in the late nineteenth and early twentieth centuries have disappeared. Only the shells of a few buildings survive, and none of them offer the entertainment they used to. On Emad al-Din Street, theatres and cabarets gave way to cinemas, and most of those are now abandoned or stand empty, playing films to a handful of people.

But if you know where to look, some traces of the old world still survive. The Ramses Theatre where Youssef Wahbi launched his troupe has been renovated several times since 1923 and is still open for business, as is the theatre of Naguib al-Rihani. Its interior is reminiscent of how it must have looked almost 100 years ago. Lavishly decorated with gilt statues holding up a blue-and-gold ceiling, the auditorium has wide stalls, a small mezzanine, and is flanked by boxes for audience members who can afford them.

Most of the cabarets and dance halls have long since moved out to the Pyramids Road in Giza or to five-star hotels, but a good number remain in Ezbekiyya and downtown Cairo, hidden behind nondescript doors or in narrow alleys. In these small, smoke-filled venues, the *takht* has been replaced by a Casio keyboard and a microphone with exaggerated reverb, and an exclusively male crowd throws five-pound notes to a succession of dancers. The only place attempting to replicate the atmosphere of interwar Emad al-Din Street is the grand Scheherazade Cabaret, which still holds nightly shows on the site of the old Printania Theatre.

But the stars of Cairo's nightlife in the '20s and '30s influenced women in ways that can still be felt. They live on in actresses such as Yousra, who recently called on filmmakers to break society's taboos in their work, not just talk about it. They are evident in the career of dancer Fifi Abdou, a social media sensation with over 6 million Instagram followers: she is famous for her long Facebook Live videos, in which she answers questions from fans and sends messages of love across the world. Fifi was recently profiled in *Vogue Arabia* and shared her view on the struggles of the performing life in words that any female star of interwar Cairo might have used: "The artist is a candle that burns from the intensity of pain to give light, hope, and happiness to the audience."[29]

Conclusion

HOW TO END A STORY

A FUZZY HAZE OF NOSTALGIA, both in Egypt and abroad, surrounds the lost golden age of Cairo in the 1920s and 1930s, and in looking back it can feel like the "old" Cairo was a wild cosmopolitan playground of fun and glamour. Sometimes it was, but things were never quite that simple. Interwar Egypt had many faults—British colonial control, poverty, inequality, and more. The revolution of 1952 proved that the older system was unsustainable. I have tried to tell the history of Cairo's nightlife through the eyes of the women who made it what it was—the first generation of modern Egyptian celebrities who lived through that legendary period. They enjoyed the opportunities it allowed and faced the stark realities of prejudice and exploitation.

In a world that was trying to impose one image on them, these women fought to shape the way their stories were told, in all their complexity. But the question remains: How does it all end? On 6 December 1962, Tahiyya Carioca's theatrical troupe started a run of their new play, *Shafiqa al-Qibtiyya*, based on the life of the legendary nineteenth-century dancer. In it, Tahiyya played the lead role in a story that had already become a cliché: A rebellious young girl defies her family to perform onstage; she becomes a star, and the play follows her through years of fantastic success, torrid love affairs, and decadent parties. The play concludes, as these stories almost always do (certainly on the mid-century Egyptian stage), with Shafiqa's inevitable fall from glory and tragic death. She is seen wandering the streets and then dies in the arms of the son who never knew she was his mother.

An uncomfortable pattern often emerges in the biographies of extraordinary, independent women regardless of their nationality, age, class, or profession. With a tragic force that sometimes feels inescapable, their lives end in decline, loss, and humiliation. At the end of her life, we are told, Fatima Rushdi was forgotten and alone. So was Mounira al-Mahdiyya. Badia Masabni gave in to bitterness in a little shop somewhere on the road between Beirut and Damascus. Even Tahiyya Carioca experienced a version of this familiar story: in her old age she stopped performing and found religion, and later pictures show the once carefree dancer wearing a black veil—a religious statement that some people enthusiastically (if simplistically) interpreted as a rejection of her former career.

Tragic endings to the stories of exceptional women are almost cliché, not just in Egypt but across the world. The biographies of Marilyn Monroe, Virginia Woolf, and Jean Rhys all follow this pattern. The scenes of decline, neglect, or suffering that are a feature of almost all of them have a strong emotional pull, but they also veer close to misogyny. There is an implicit cautionary message for other women: Rebel now, and you will have fun while it lasts; but punishment always lies in wait. Men will leave you; your children will hate you; and you will die forgotten and alone. We are all encouraged to marvel at these stars and their flouting of society's norms—but not to copy them. People can write the stories of their own lives, but nobody ever gets to write the end; someone else always has to finish it for them. Is it possible to end the story of these women without resorting to the familiar pattern of the old narrative?

To change the ending, we need to find another way to see these stories. This applies as much to the story of cosmopolitan Cairo in the '20s and '30s as it does to the story of the women who lived there. This need not be the story of a lost golden age nor of great lives that end in tragedy. After all, in early twentieth-century Cairo, life was never likely to be easy for these women. They faced disparagement, prejudice, even violence, and they were sexualised by men who wanted to either possess or police their bodies. For most people, especially women, the golden age of Cairo was no utopia.

Nonetheless, in the years after the 1919 revolution, Egypt offered something intangible but vital: possibility. The female stars whose lives are set down in this book represent the promise, hope, and opportunity of the interwar period. There was a space for women to make their voices heard. Some triumphed, some failed, and some fell afoul of the law while doing it, but all of them were navigating a new world. That sense of possibility is what makes this period so compelling. Perhaps audiences back then saw the possibility in these women, and it helped make them famous. Injustice and oppression were always present during those years, but so was the belief that things could get better. Optimism was particularly clear at the margins of society, in dance halls, theatres, and cabarets where *artistes* from Egypt, Greece, Italy, Syria, Palestine, Turkey, and beyond came together to create, and where anything could happen. One moment, a mournful love song; next, a bawdy political satire; next, a man writhing around on the floor, impersonating a frog.

Looking back at the Middle East of the '20s and '30s, it can feel as if you're on another planet—one remote from the wars, authoritarian governments, and repression of today. In the twenty-first century hope seems to have been stamped out, for the most part, by those in power. Life in the interwar period of the twentieth century remains so seductive because many of its people were convinced that the world could, and would, improve. The women of interwar Cairo who made their way into the limelight were fighting to exert their power and be heard. Their struggles and successes remind us not that things were perfect, but that they can always be different.

ACKNOWLEDGMENTS

This book would not have been possible without the help of archivists and librarians across the world, including the National Library of Egypt, American University in Cairo, American University of Beirut, British Library, Columbia University, New York Public Library, Penn Libraries, King's College Cambridge Archive, National Archives of the UK, NYU Abu Dhabi (particularly Ozge Calafato, Jasmine Soliman, and Jonathan Burr at Akkasah Center for Photography whose photo is used on the UK cover), and many more. I am very thankful for their help. Likewise, I am grateful for the support of Columbia University and the Society of Authors' Michael Meyer Award, as well as the Levantine Heritage Foundation (especially Craig Encer and Philip Mansell), and the NVIC in Cairo (especially Ifdal Elsaket) who allowed me to speak about this topic over the past few years.

So many people have helped in different ways, sacrificing their time, reading chapters, finding sources, and giving other support. I cannot thank them all, but they include Alaaeldin Mahmoud, Alex Jacobs, Andrew Franklin, Anna Girling, Esmat Elhalaby, Heba Farid, Heba Gowayed, Joy Garnett, Kevin Dean, Kevin Eisenstadt, Lucie Ryzova, Marilyn Takefman, Nikhil Krishnan, Peter Cherry, Peter Stothard, Randa Ali, and Tom Hardwick.

To be a man writing about so many fascinating women, I sometimes worry if I have done them justice (the final verdict will always be the readers', not mine). This book owes a huge amount to some other amazing women. To Marilyn Booth and Olga Taxidou, my PhD supervisors, with whom I had many fruitful discussions about Egyptian theatre (sorry I haven't turned my dissertation into a book yet). To my editors, Lynn Gaspard at Saqi Books and Alane Mason at Norton, who have supported and improved this project. To my mother, Mary Beard, who not only contributed enormously to my intellectual formation but has given countless comments and suggestions as I wrote this book. Finally, to Pamela Takefman, without whom I could not have written this book. It is for her.

NOTES

INTRODUCTION: THE PAST IS A SET OF OLD CLOTHES

1. Luwis Awad, *Awraq al-'Umr* (Pages from my life) (Cairo: Maktabat Madbuli, 1987), 550–51.
2. George Seferis, *Collected Poems* (Princeton, NJ: Princeton University Press, 1981), 304–5.
3. *L'Égypte Nouvelle*, 6 October 1923, viii; Louis Touraine, "Au Cabaret" (At the cabaret), *Le Magazine Egyptien*, 22 October 1927, 24.
4. *Variety*, 31 March 1937, 68.
5. *Al-Kawakib*, February 1951, 83.

CHAPTER 1: "PARDON ME, I'M DRUNK"

1. Li Guo, *The Performing Arts in Medieval Islam: Shadow Play and Popular Play in Ibn Daniyal's Mamluk Cairo* (Leiden, Netherlands: Brill, 2012), 164.
2. Curt Prüfer, "Drama: Arabic," in James Hastings, ed., *Encyclopaedia of Religion and Ethics*, vol. 4 (Edinburgh: T & T Clark, 1911), 874.
3. Edward William Lane, *An Account of the Manners and Customs of the Modern Egyptians* (Cairo: American University in Cairo Press, 2003 [based on the definitive 1860 ed.]), 352.
4. Ibid., 315; 341–46.
5. *Harper's Bazaar*, 23 February 1884, 119.
6. From a lecture by James Sanua, titled "Ma Vie en Vers et Mon Théâtre

en Prose" (My life in verse and my theatre in prose), published in *Abou Naddara*, 6 August and 7 September 1906; reprinted in Philip Sadgrove, *The Egyptian Theatre in the Nineteenth Century* (Reading, UK: Ithaca Press, 1996), 172–85. Quote from p. 174.

7. *The Saturday Review*, 26 July 1879, 112; Sanua, "Ma Vie en Vers et Mon Théâtre en Prose."

8. *Al-Hilal*, 1 November 1906, 117–18.

9. The memoirs ran sporadically in *al-Ahram* from 31 July to 21 September 1915. They were republished in Fuʿad Rashid, *Tarikh al-Masrah al-ʿArabi* (The history of Arabic theatre) (Cairo: Dar al-Tahrir, 1960). These two quotes from *al-Ahram*, 31 July 1915.

10. *Al-Ahram*, 20 August 1915.

11. Hafiz Hassanayn, *Siyahat al-Azbakiyya fi-l-Azjal al-Fukahiyya* (A tour of Ezbekiyya in comic verse) (Cairo: al-Matbaʿa al-ʿUmumiyya, [n.d.; c. 1900]), 3.

12. Douglas Sladen, *Oriental Cairo: The City of the "Arabian Nights"* (London: Hurst & Blackett, 1911), 108–13.

13. *Al-Manar*, 5 August 1902, 360.

14. The story appears in Muhammad al-Muwaylihī, *What ʿIsa ibn Hisham Told Us*, ed. and trans. Roger Allen (New York: New York University Press, 2015), 1–117. Quote from pp. 84–85.

15. *Nashville American*, 19 June 1899, 17.

16. *Egyptian Standard*, 18 November 1907.

17. Mahmud al-Bulaqi, *Mufrih al-Jins al-Latif wa-Suwwar Mashahir al-Raqqasin* (Joy of the fairer sex and pictures of famous dancers), 2nd ed. (n.p., 1904), 13–14.

18. Two versions of this song can be found online: https://soundcloud .com/esmatnemr4/jveezvp6fewi and https://soundcloud.com/ahlawi-1/ baheyya-al-mehallaweyya-yalla-ya-habibi-neskar-raqs-shafiqa-v1-odeon. Another version is available in the National Library of Egypt.

19. *Al-Ahram*, 17 February 1935, 9.

20. These can be found in Abbas Hilmi II Papers (Durham, UK: Durham University), HIL/15/1–553.

21. HIL/15/81.

22. HIL/15/21–22.

23. Albert Lantoine, "La Danse à l'Exposition" (Dance at the exhibition), in *Revue Franco-Allemande*, 10 July 1900, 95–99; *L'Exposition en Famille: Revue Illustrée de L'Exposition Universelle de 1900*, 5 June 1900, 159.

24. *Al-Ahram*, 21 September 1905.

CHAPTER 2: FROM QUEEN OF TARAB TO PRIMA DONNA

1. UK National Archives, FO 141/669/3.

2. C. R. Ashbee, *Fantasia in Egypt*, King's College Cambridge Archives, CRA/3/5, 21–27.

3. *Al-Masrah*, 30 May 1927, 14–15; 25.

4. *Al-Masrah*, 24 May 1926, 23–25.

5. Ali Jihad Racy, *Musical Change and Commercial Recording in Egypt, 1904–1932*, PhD dissertation, University of Illinois at Urbana, Champaign, 1977, 169, citing Sabri Abu al-Majd, *Zakariyya Ahmad* (Cairo: al-Mu'assassah al-Misriyya al-'Amma, n.d.), 74.

6. Oscar Preuss, "Round the Recording Studios," in *The Gramophone*, March 1928, 411–12.

7. Mounira al-Mahdiyya, "Asmar Malak Ruhi," in *Cafés Chantant du Caire*, vol. 2 (France: Les Artistes Arabes Associés, 1996).

8. *Egyptian Gazette*, vol. 19, 20 January 1905.

9. Hector Dinning, *Nile to Aleppo* (New York: Macmillan, 1920), 261.

10. John Jensen, *Letter About Cairo Riots and Gallipoli Landing*, 1915, State Library of South Australia, D 7720 (L).

11. Iziz Fathallah, ed., *Salama Hijazi* (Cairo: Shuruq, 2002), 168.

12. For example, *al-Minbar*, 10 March 1916, 3 (in Egypt's National Theatre Centre's series of reprinted historical articles about Egyptian drama, *Silsilat Tawthiq al-Masrah al-Misri*, hereafter referred to in notes as STMM; vol. 7, 137).

13. *Al-Basir*, 13 January 1916 (STMM, vol. 7, 24).

14. Gérard de Nerval, *Voyage en Orient* (Paris: M. Levy, 1867), 88–89.

15. Joseph McPherson, *Moulids of Egypt* (Cairo: Nile Mission Press, 1941), 84.

16. Dinning, *Nile to Aleppo*, 273–75.

17. H. R. Barbor, "An Arab Music Hall," *Saturday Review*, 30 March 1929, 427–28.

18. Muhammad Taymur, *Hayatuna al-Tamthiliyya* (Our theatrical life) (Cairo: Matba'at al-I'timad, 1922), 176.

19. *Al-Afkar*, 8 April 1917, 2 (STMM, vol. 8, 110–12).

20. Sayyid Ali Isma'il, *Masirat al-Masrah fi Misr* (The path of theatre in Egypt)*: 1900–1935* (Windsor, UK: Hindawi, 2017), 333.

21. *Al-Afkar*, 27 March 1917 (STMM, vol. 8, 92–93).

22. Ibid., 92–93.

23. *Al-Afkar*, 1 April 1927 (STMM, vol. 8, 97–98).

24. Kamil al-Khula'i, *al-Aghani al-Asriyya* (Modern songs), (Cairo: Matab'at al-Sa'ada, 1921), 97.

CHAPTER 3: "COME ON SISTERS,
LET'S GO HAND IN HAND TO DEMAND OUR FREEDOM"

1. Naguib Mahfouz, *Bayn al-Qasrayn* (Palace walk) (Cairo: Maktabat Misr, 1956), 17.

2. Rose al-Youssef [Ruz al-Yusuf], *Dhikriyyati* (My memoirs) (Cairo: Ruz al-Yusuf, 2010 [first printing 1953]), 30–31.

3. Fatima Rushdi, *Kifahi fi al-Masrah wa al-Sinima* (My struggle in the theatre and cinema) (Cairo: Dar al-Ma'arif, 1971), 35.

4. Guy Thornton, *With the Anzacs in Cairo* (London: H. R. Alleson, 1917), 63; quote on p. 81.

5. W. N. Willis, *Anti-Christ in Egypt* (London: Anglo-Eastern 1914), 41.

6. *The Advertiser* (Adelaide), 27 July 1925, 15; Thomas Russell, *Egyptian Service* (London: John Murray, 1923), 180–81; Willis, *Anti-Christ in Egypt*, 29–33.

7. *Al-Dunya al-Musawwara*, 23 April 1930, 15.

8. Abd al-Wahhab Bakr, *Mujtam'a al-Qahira al-Sirri 1900–1951* (Cairo's secret society 1900–1951) (Cairo: al-Arabi, 2001), 140 (citing *al-Musawwar*, 4 January 1950).

9. LSE Women's Library 4/IBS Box FL113; Francesca Biancani, *Sex Work in Colonial Egypt* (London: Bloomsbury, 2018).

10. *Egyptian Delegation to the Peace Conference* (Paris: Published by the Delegation, 1919), 12–13.

11. *Further Correspondence Respecting the Affairs of Egypt and the Soudan: January to June 1919* (London: British Foreign Office, 1920), 67.

12. Russell, *Egyptian Service*, p. 191; William T. Ellis, "Egypt Peril to East," *Washington Post*, 25 June 1919, 4; *Further Correspondence Respecting the Affairs of Egypt and the Soudan*, 72.

13. UK National Archives FO 371/3714/467; Ellis Goldberg, "Peasants in Revolt—Egypt 1919," *International Journal of Middle Eastern Studies* (May 1992): 261–80.

14. Joseph McPherson, Memorandum on the Egyptian Situation. Miscellaneous documents, booklets, and memoranda on various subjects submitted to [Milner] Mission while in Egypt. UK National Archives FO 848/8.

15. Huda Shaarawi, *Harem Years: The Memoirs of an Egyptian Feminist*, trans. Margot Badran (New York: Feminist Press, 1987), 133.

16. Russell, *Egyptian Service*, p. 209.

17. William T. Ellis, "Cairo Mad with Joy," *Washington Post*, 21 June 1919, 4.

18. Iziz Fathallah et al., ed., *Sayyid Darwish*, vol. 2 (Cairo: Dar al-Shuruq, 2003), 415. In this modern version, the word *Jews* (Yahud) had been changed to *soldiers* (Junud). Whoever was behind that alteration ought to be ashamed, on a number of levels.

19. Ibid., 429–30.

20. Kamil al-Khula'i, *al-Aghani al-Asriyya* (Cairo: Matab'at al-Sa'ada, 1921), 120.

21. Habib Zeidan, *Majmu'a al-Aghani al-Sharqiyya* (Anthology of Eastern songs) (New York: n.p., n.d.), 152; Ziad Fahmy, *Ordinary Egyptians* (Cairo: American University in Cairo Press, 2011), 116.

22. Abd al-Azim Ramadan, ed., *Mudhakirrat Sa'd Zaghlul* (Saad Zaghloul's memoirs), vol. 6 (Cairo: GEBO, 1996), 347–48.

23. *Hansard*, House of Lords, 28 February 1922, vol. 49, column 237.

24. *Manchester Guardian*, 19 September 1923, 8.

CHAPTER 4: DANCE OF FREEDOM

1. George Duncan and Billy Brooks, "Letter from Cairo, Egypt," *Chicago Defender*, 7 June 1924, 13.

2. "Uncle Tom's Cabin." *The Observer*, 25 August 1878, 4.

3.   *Chicago Defender*, 11 March 1922, 7.

4.   *Chicago Defender*, 24 May 1924, 13.

5.   *Al-Ahram*, 3 March 1924, 1.

6.   *Al-Ahram*, 17 March 1924, 5.

7.   Lord Lloyd, *Egypt Since Cromer,* vol. II (London: Macmillan, 1934), 95.

8.   *Al-Nil*, 30 April 1921, 12 (STMM, vol. 10, 166).

9.   *Al-Fukaha'*, 5 January 1927, 14.

10. *Le Magazine Egyptien*, 28 August 1928, 12–13.

11. *L'Egypte Nouvelle*, 13 October 1923, v; *Variety*, 3 July 1935, 18.

12. *L'Egypte Nouvelle*, 23 February 1924, iv; *al-Ahram*, 21 August 1929.

13. LSE Women's Library 4/IBS/6/034; Francesca Biancani, *Sex Work in Colonial Egypt* (London: Bloomsbury Academic, 2018), 91; National Archives FO 841/306, case 12.

14. *Al-Dunya al-Musawwara*, 4 December 1929, 9.

15. *Al-Liwa' al-Misri*, 21 August 1923 (STMM, vol. 13, 105); *al-Muqattam*, 23 January 1923 (STMM, vol. 12, 57–58).

16. *Al-Nil*, 8 October 1921 (STMM, vol. 10, 319).

17. *Majallat al-Nil al-Musawwar*, 21 July 1923 (STMM, vol. 13, 56–57); *New York Herald*, 9 August 1925; *Ruz al-Yusuf* [Rose al-Youssef], 25 January 1932, 20–21.

18. Habib Zaydan, *Majmu'a al-Aghani al-Sharqiyya*, 4.

19. Nabil Bahjat, ed., *al-A'mal al-Shi'riyya li-Shaykh Yunus al-Qadi* (Poetic works of Sheikh Yunus al-Qadi) (Cairo: Firqat Wamda, 2012), 322.

20. Frédéric Lagrange, "Musiciens et Poetes en Egypte au temps de la Nahda," PhD diss., Université de Paris VIII, 1994, 676—77; author unknown, text from Polyphon catalogue, 1929.

21. Lagrange, "Musiciens et Poetes en Egypte," 695–96; text by Muhammad Ismail from *Baidaphon nouveau catalogue général des cantatrices* (Cairo: 1928), 28.

22. *Ruz al-Yusuf* [Rose al-Youssef], 18 August 1927, 14.

23. *Al-Ahram*, 3 January 1925 (STMM, vol. 16, 73).

24. *New York Times*, 5 December 1893; "'Coochers' Stopped by Police," *Variety*, 19 October 1904, 4.

25. *Al-Ahram*, 31 May 1916, 4.

26. *Al-Ahram*, 15 May 1927, 4.

27. Joseph McPherson, *Moulids of Egypt* (Cairo: Nile Mission Press, 1941), 84.

28. *Chicago Defender*, 20 January 1923, 13.

29. *Ruz al-Yusuf*, 1 February 1926, 14; and 31 March 1926, 8.

30. *Ruz al-Yusuf*, 6 January 1927; *al-Naqid*, 12 December 1927, 16.

31. For example, Said Shimi's reports make occasional references to homosexual relationships, involving both men and women, including a daughter of the Khedive Ismail; see, for instance, Durham University Library, Abbas Hilmi II Papers, HIL 15/482, 15/73. In Luwis Awad, *Awraq al-'Umr* (Cairo: Maktabat Madbuli, 1987), 472–73, the author also mentions rumours of homosexual relationships among those in Cairo's literary circles who frequented the cafés of Emad al-Din Street and elsewhere.

32. *Samir al-Afkar*, 23 February 1924 (STMM, vol. 14, 202–203).

33. *Samir al-Afkar*, 1 March 1924 (STMM, vol. 14, 238–41).

34. *Ruz al-Yusuf*, 19 June 1928, 20–21; 26.

35. Ibid.

36. *Ruz al-Yusuf*, 24 December 1929, 20.

37. *Ruz al-Yusuf*, 19 June 1928, 20–21; 26.

CHAPTER 5: "IF I WERE NOT A WOMAN, I'D WANT TO BE ONE"

1. *Al-Tiyatru*, December 1924, 17.

2. *Ruz al-Yusuf* [Rose al-Youssef], 28 February 1938; reprinted in Rashad Kamil, ed., *Min Dhikriyyati al-Ṣahafiyya bi-Qalam Ruz al-Yusuf* (Cairo: Ruz al-Yusuf, 2016), 51–57.

3. Rose al-Youssef [Ruz al-Yusuf], *Dhikriyyat* (Cairo: Ruz al-Yusuf, 2010 [first printing, 1953]), 26.

4. *Al-Minbar*, 14 February 1916, 2 (STMM, vol. 7, 66).

5. *Al-Watan*, 16 March 1916, 2 (STMM, vol. 7, 168–69).

6. *Al-Ahram*, 10 March 1923.

7. *Al-Afkar*, 12 March 1923 (STMM, vol. 12, 172–73).

8. *Al-Siyasa*, 26 March 1923 (STMM, vol. 12, 224–25); *al-Muqattam*, 27 March 1923 (STMM, vol. 12, 228–31).

9. *Al-Masrah*, 1 August 1927, 15.

10. *Ruz al-Yusuf,* 26 October 1925.

11. al-Youssef, *Dhikriyyat,* 103–104; 151.

12. *Ruz al-Yusuf,* 16 November 1925.

13. Madiha ʿIzzat, "My Days with the Grand Dame of Arabic Journalism," in Rashad, Kamil, ed., *Ruz al-Yusuf: Sayyida Hurra Mustaqilla dhat al-Siyada* (Rose al-Youssef: a free, independent woman, in control) (Cairo: *Ruz al-Yusuf* [n.d.; 2010s]), 211.

14. *Ruz al-Yusuf,* 29 October 1956; Rashad, ed. *Ruz al-Yusuf,* p. 160; al-Youssef, *Dhikriyyat,* 218.

15. *Ruz al-Yusuf,* 16 November 1925, 6; 21 December 1925, 2.

16. *Ruz al-Yusuf,* 12 March 1929; 30 April 1929.

17. *Ruz al-Yusuf,* 14 December 1931, 20.

18. al-Youssef, *Dhikriyyat,* 218.

19. Fathi Ghanem, "Lan Tamut" (She will not die), *Sabah al-Khayr,* 14 April 1958, in Kamil, *Min Dhikriyyati al-Ṣahafiyya bi-Qalam Ruz al-Yusuf,* 144–46.

20. There are a few different versions of this story (some say she went to the cinema, others that she went to an agricultural exhibition ground). My version is based primarily on Ahmed Baha al-Din's and Ahmed Kamil Mursi's, reproduced in Kamil, *Ruz al-Yusuf,* 43–44 and 88–90.

CHAPTER 6: SARAH BERNHARDT OF THE EAST

1. Sharon Marcus, *The Drama of Celebrity* (Princeton, NJ: Princeton University Press, 2019), 14.

2. Fatima Rushdi, *al-Fanan Aziz ʿId* (Cairo: GEBO, 1984), 48.

3. *Al-Musawwar,* 17 November 1933.

4. *Al-Masrah,* 31 May 1926, 25; 28 February 1927, 11.

5. *Al-Mumathil,* 30 December 1926, 13; *al-Masrah,* 28 March 1927, 20.

6. *Ruz al-Yusuf* [Rose al-Youssef], 28 April 1927, 13; 21 July 1927, 11.

7. Fatima Rushdi, *Kafahi fi-l-masrah wa-l-sinima* (Cairo: Dar al-Maʿarif, 1970), 67.

8. *Ruz al-Yusuf,* 22 May 1928, 19.

9. *Al-Ithnayn*, 16 November 1936, 10; Maria Elena Paniconi, "Italian Futurism in Cairo," *Philological Encounters* 2 (2017): 159–79. Quotes from p. 172 trans. Paniconi. Morpurgo remembers the performance as taking place in 1928, but public shows did not start until 1929.

10. *'Iraq*, 11 June 1929, from Ali Muhammad Hadi al-Rabi'i, *al-Furuq al-Masrahiyya al-Misriyya fi-l-Iraq: Firqat Fatima Rushdi* (Egyptian theatrical troupes in Iraq: Fatima Rushdi's troupe) (Sharjah, UAE: Arab Theatre Institute, 2019), 72–77; *al-Dunya al-Musawwara*, 10 July 1929, 22.

11. Youssef Wahbi, *'Ishtu Alf 'Am*, vol. 3 (Cairo: Dar al-Ma'arif, 1976), 210–17.

12. *Al-Nahda* (Haifa), 12 April 1930, 2; *Miraat al-Sharq* (Jerusalem), 24 May 1930, 4.

13. *Palestine Post*, 4 May 1933, 6.

14. *Zaqzuq wa-Zarifa*, 14 October 1930, 8.

15. *Ruz al-Yusuf*, 29 August 1932; and 18 July 1932, 28.

16. *Variety*, 21 March 1933, 52.

17. *Ruz al-*, 15 July 1930, 19.

18. *Al-Ahram*, 1 September 2007, 9.

CHAPTER 7: THE SINGER, THE BABY, AND THE BEY

1. *Al-Masrah*, 26 December 1926, 9.

2. *Al-Masrah*, 10 January 1927, 17.

3. *Al-Tiyatru*, June 1925, 20. Legal proceedings between Fatima and Odeon were reported in *Journaux des Tribunaux Mixtes*, 7–8 May 1926, 18.

4. *Al-Masrah*, 10 January 1927, 19.

5. Ibid.

6. *Ruz al-Yusuf* [Rose al-Youssef], 19 May 1926, in Rashad Kamil, ed., *Maqalati al-Sahafiyya: Bi-Qalam Ruz al-Yusuf* (Cairo: Ruz al-Yusuf, 2017), 56–58.

7. *Al-Masrah*, 11 April 1927, 25.

8. *Al-Ahram*, 11 March 1931, 9.

9. *Ruz al-Yusuf*, 31 August 1931, p. 19.

10. *New York Times*, 26 January 2005; "High-Profile Paternity Case High-lights Risks of Common-Law 'Urfi' Marriage in Egypt," *Voice of America*, 31 October 2009, https://www.voanews.com/archive/high-profile -paternity-case-highlights-risks-common-law-urfi-marriage-egypt, accessed 24 June 2020.

CHAPTER 8: STAR OF THE EAST

1. Muhammad Shuqayr, ed., *Mudhakirrat al-Anisa Umm Kulthum* (The memoirs of Miss Oum Kalthoum) (Cairo: Dar Akhbar al-Yawm, 2018), 40.

2. *Al-Masrah*, 23 May 1926, 15; Mahmud Awad, *Umm Kulthum allati la ya'rifuha ahad* (The Oum Kalthoum that nobody knew), 3rd ed. (Cairo: Dar Akhbar al-Yarm, 1987), 25.

3. *Al-Ahram*, 27 July 1922.

4. Shuqayr, ed., *Mudhakirrat al-Anisa Umm Kulthum*, 54.

5. Awad, *Umm Kulthum allati la ya'rifuha ahad*, 55–58.

6. *Aghani wa-taqatiq wa-Qasa'id al-Anisa Umm Kulthum* (Songs, taqtuqas, and poems of Miss Oum Kalthoum) (Cairo: n.p., n.d. [1926?]), 17.

7. *Al-Masrah*, 25 April 1927, 12.

8. *The Sphinx*, 1 January 1921, 235.

9. Khalil al-Misri and Mahmud Kamil, eds., *Al-Nusus al-Kamila li-jami' aghani kawkab al-Sharq Umm Kulthum* (Complete texts of all the songs of Oum Kalthoum, Star of the East) (Cairo: Muhammad al-Amin, 1975), 93; 100.

10. *Al-Masrah*, 8 March 1926, 11.

11. *Al-Masrah*, 30 November 1925, 9.

12. *Al-Ma'rad*, October 1931, 20.

13. *Ruz al-Yusuf* [Rose al-Youssef], 7 February 1928, 20.

14. *Kawkab al-Sharq*, 11 May 1925 (STMM, vol. 17, 318–23).

15. Virginia Danielson, *The Voice of Egypt* (Chicago: University of Chicago Press, 1997), 64; *al-Masrah*, 2 August 1926, 26, and 16

August 1926, 16; Ratiba al-Hifni, *Umm Kulthum* (Cairo: al-Shuruq, 1994), 51–52.

16. *Ruz al-Yusuf*, 8 August 1932, 24.

17. *Ruz al-Yusuf*, 4 February 1930, 21.

18. *Ruz al-Yusuf*, 31 December 1929, 19.

19. *Filastin* (Jaffa), 4 July 1933, 7.

20. *Al-Sabah*, 8 June 1934, 31; 15 June 1934, 31; and 6 July 1934, 30.

21. "Memorandum Concerning the Singing of Um Kulthoum in Ewart Memorial Hall, April 15th 1939," from American University in Cairo, *Minutes of the Meetings of Council*, vol. 17, 24 September 1938–17 June 1939 (available at the American University in Cairo's digital collections). The letter of complaint from the Synod of the Nile is reproduced a little earlier, in minutes dated 13 April 1939.

22. Danielson, *The Voice of Egypt*, 89.

23. Ibid., 90; 88.

24. *Al-Musiqa wa-l-Masrah*, February 1949, 933.

25. *Al-Kawakib*, 5 August 1925, 9.

26. *Washington Post*, 6 February 1975; *Chicago Tribune*, 6 February 1975.

27. *Al-Ahram*, 5 February 1975, 7.

CHAPTER 9: "COME ON, TOUGH GUY, PLAY THE GAME"

1. *Al-Musawwar*, 19 March 1965.

2. *Al-Ma'rad*, December 1923.

3. *Al-Masrah*, 25 April 1927, 18–20; 2 May 1927, 18–20.

4. Nabil Bahgat, ed., *al-A'mal al-Sha'riyya li-Shaykh Yunus al-Qadi* (Cairo: Wamda, 2012), 313.

5. Ahmad Abd al-Majid, *Li-Kul Ughniyya Qissa* (Every song has a story) (Cairo: Anglo-Egyptian, 1970), 123.

6. *Al-Ahram*, 7 April 1925.

7. *Misr*, 6 May 1925; 11 May 1925; 12 May 1925 (STMM, vol. 17, 276, 316, 330).

8. *Ruz al-Yusuf* [Rose al-Youssef], 17 November 1927, 19.

9. *Al-Kawakib*, February 1951, 69.

10. Habib Zeidan, *Majmu'at al-Aghani al-Sharqiyya* (New York: n.p., n.d.), 330.

11. *Al-Kashkul,* 6 March 1926 (STMM, vol. 16, 509).

12. *Ruz al-Yusuf,* 2 June 1927, 12; Salih Jawdat, *Muluk wa-Sa'alik* (Cairo: al-Nahda al-Misriyya, 1958), 301.

13. *Le Magazine Egyptien,* 17 August 1929, 29–30; 15 March 1930, 31–32.

14. *Ruz al-Yusuf,* 18 March 1930, 16; 8 April 1930, 17; and 29 July 1930.

15. *Al-Sabah,* 16 March 1934, 35.

16. *Al-Sarkha,* 4 November 1930, 18; *al-Masrah,* 31 January 1927, 10.

17. *Ruz al-Yusuf,* 14 January 1930, 20.

18. *Ruz al-Yusuf,* 16 June 1926.

19. Frédéric Lagrange, *Quand l'Egypte se Chantait: Taqāṭīq et chansons légères au début du XXe siècle* (When Egypt serenaded itself: Taqtuqas and light songs at the beginning of the twentieth century), 88 (available at http://mapage.noos.fr/fredlag/taqatiq.pdf, accessed 12 June 2020). For a shorter version of this article, without lyrics of the song "Black Bottom," see Frédéric Lagrange, "Women in the Singing Business, Women in Songs," *History Compass* 6 (2008): 266–50.

20. *Al-Masrah,* 24 January 1927, 3, 8; and 21 February 1927, 16.

21. *Ruz al-Yusuf,* 13 January 1927, 12; *al-Masrah,* 25 July 1927, 6–7.

22. *Al-Naqid,* 10 October 1927, 19; and 17 October 1927, 16.

23. *Al-Naqid,* 10 October 1927, 19; 17 October 1927, 16; and 12 March 1928, 4; *Ruz al-Yusuf,* 29 September 1927, 12.

24. *Ruz al-Yusuf,* 20 October 1927, 13.

25. *Al-Ahram,* 11 August 1928, 5; *Ruz al-Yusuf,* 4 September 1928, 19.

26. *Bulletin de législation et de jurisprudence égyptiennes* (Bulletin of Egyptian legislation and jurisprudence) (Alexandria, 1933), 182–83.

27. Raja Naqqash, ed., *Safahat min Mudhakkirat Najib al-Mahfuz* (Pages from Naguib Mahfouz's memoirs) (Cairo: Markaz al-Ahram, 1998), 88–89.

28. Aran Byrne, trans., *The Non-Fiction Writing of Naguib Mahfouz,* vol. 1 (London: Gingko Library, 2016), 147–48.

CHAPTER 10: ISIS FILMS

1. *Cinéa*, 1 April 1926, 24.

2. *Al-Masrah*, 24 May 1926, 7; 22.

3. *Al-Ahram*, 24 May 1926, p. 5; Youssef Wahbi, *'Ishtu Alf 'Am* (I lived 1,000 years), vol. 1 (Cairo: Dar al- Ma'arif, 1976), picture section.

4. *Al-Masrah*, 31 May 1926, 20–22.

5. *Ruz al-Yusuf* [Rose al-Youssef], 3 February 1927, 14; *al-Masrah*, 31 January 1927, 11.

6. *Al-Masrah*, 21 March 1927, 8.

7. *Ruz al-Yusuf*, 1 December 1927, 21.

8. *Al-Masrah*, 28 March 1927, 7.

9. *Ruz al-Yusuf*, 24 November 1927, 19; *al-Masrah*, 21 March 1927, 7.

10. *Ruz al-Yusuf*, 18 August 1927, 10–11; and 22 December 1927, 22.

11. For example, *al-Naqid*, 17 October 1927, 18.

12. For example, *Ruz al-Yusuf*, 13 October 1927, 14–15.

13. *Al-Naqid*, 5 December 1927, 8.

14. *Al-Sabah*, 30 June 1929, 26 (from Ahmad al-Hadari, *Mawsu'at Tarikh al-Sinima fi Misr* (Encyclopaedia of the history of cinema in Egypt), vol. 1 (Cairo: GEBO, 2019), 287.

15. *Ruz al-Yusuf*, 8 February 1932, 20.

16. *Ruz al-Yusuf*, 11 January 1932, 17.

17. *Manchester Guardian*, 12 September 1923, 12.

18. *L'Egyptienne*, September 1928, 8.

19. Ibid., 5–9.

20. Muhammad Karim, *Mudhakirrat Muhammad Karim* (Memoirs of Muhammad Karim) (Cairo: Akadamiyyat al-Funun, 2006), 172.

21. Pennethorne Hughes, *While Shepheard's Watched* (London: Chatto and Windus, 1949), 57–58.

CHAPTER 11: MADAME BADIA'S CASINO

1. *Al-Ahram*, 20 October 1926, 5.

2. *Al-Dunya al-Musawwara*, 30 November 1930, 23.

3. *Ruz al-Yusuf* [Rose al-Youssef], 14 April 1927, 12–13; 20 October 1927, 12; and 27 October 1927, 16.

4. H. R. Barbor, "An Arab Music-Hall," *Saturday Review*, 30 March 1929, 427–28.

5. *Musical Times*, 1 March 1923, 203–204; *Ruz al-Yusuf*, 29 August 1932, 24.

6. *Daily Boston Globe*, 2 October 1932; *Ruz al-Yusuf*, 31 March 1927, 13.

7. *Ruz al-Yusuf*, 22 February 1932, 22.

8. *Al-Masrah*, 6 December 1926, 13.

9. S. Tamari and I. Nassar, eds., *The Storyteller of Jerusalem: The Life and Times of Wasif Jawhariyyeh, 1904–1948* (Northhampton, MA: Olive Branch Press, 2014), 132–35.

10. *Al-Mahrusa*, 13 April 1923 (STMM, vol. 12, 268–69).

11. *Al-Tiyatru*, December 1924, 20; *al-'Asifa*, 14 May 1933, 19.

12. *Ruz al-Yusuf*, 8 July 1930, 16.

13. *Variety*, 31 March 1937, 68.

14. Nazik Basila, ed., *Mudhakkirat Badia Masabni* (Memoirs of Badia Masabni) (Beirut: Maktabat al-Haya, 1970), 333.

15. *Al-Ahram*, 12 May 1928; *Variety*, 22 August 1928, 5; *The Scotsman*, 15 September 1928, 10.

16. *Zaqzuq wa-Zarifa*, 14 December 1930, 9.

17. *Palestine Post*, 4 July 1933, 2; *Variety*, 6 June 1933, 61.

18. *Le Magazine Egyptien*, 9 May 1931, 26; *al-Sabah*, 4 May 1934; and 11 May 1934, 8.

19. *Al-Ahram*, 1 October 1936, 2.

20. Ibid., 8.

21. *Al-Ahram*, 25 May 1936, 10.

22. *Ruz al-Yusuf*, 1 June 1936, 25.

23. *Al-Ahram*, 7 June 1936, 11; 26 June 1936, 11; and 12 August 1936, 10.

24. *Al-Ahram*, 27 May 1936, 10.

25. Basila, *Mudhakkirat Badia Masabni*, 334–35.

26. *Variety*, 16 March 1938, 21.

27. *Ruz al-Yusuf*, 24 January 1938, 41.

28. *Ruz al-Yusuf*, 25 May 1940, 18; *Chicago Daily Tribune*, 11 January 1942.

29. *Baltimore Sun*, 31 December 1950.

CHAPTER 12: THE SECOND REVOLUTION

1. Edward Said, "Homage to a Belly Dancer," *London Review of Books*, 13 September 1990.

2. "Anglo Egyptian Treaty," *Hansard*, 24 November 1936.

3. Salih Mursi, ed., *Mudhakkirat Kariuka* (Memoirs of Carioca) (Cairo: Nahdat Misr, 2019), 173.

4. Pennethorne Hughes, *While Shepheard's Watched* (London: Chatto and Windus, 1949), 46.

5. Bernard Spencer, "Egyptian Dancer at Shubra," in *Aegean Islands and Other Poems* (London: Editions Poetry London, 1948), 26.

6. Terence Tiller, "Egyptian Dancer," in *The Inward Animal* (London: Hogarth Press, 1943), 31–32.

7. Josephine Baker and Jo Bouillon, *Josephine*, trans. Mariana Fitzpatrick (New York: Harper & Row, 1977), 134.

8. John Eppler, *Operation Condor*, trans. S. Seago (London: McDonald and Jane's, 1977), 190.

9. "El Gorro Magico" (The magic cap), New York State Motion Picture Division, License Application Case Files, Box 1328, File 50663.

10. UK National Archive, FO954/45.

11. *A Report on the Jewish Situation in Egypt* (New York: American Jewish Committee, 1949), 1.

12. *New York Times*, 5 March 1951, 12.

13. *Philadelphia Enquirer*, 17 June 1946, 20.

14. A. W. Sansom, *I Spied Spies* (London: G. G. Harrap, 1965), 253.

15. Marcel Berthier, "Le domaine poétique international du surréalisme" (The international poetic domain of surrealism), *Le Puits de l'Ermite*, March 1978, 80; *Manchester Guardian*, 31 January 1952, 10.

16. *New York Times*, 10 February 1952, 5.

17. *Misr al-Fata*, 25 November 1951, quoted in *al-Ahram*, 13 May 1952.

18. *Manchester Guardian*, 19 August 1952; *Los Angeles Times*, 24 August 1952.

19. *Al-Kawakib*, 12 August 1952.

20. For example, *al-Masrah*, November 1999, 10.

21. *Ruz al-Yusuf* [Rose al-Youssef], 22 March 1954.

22. *Manchester Guardian*, 13 March 1954, 5.

23. Nadia Kamil, *al-Mawluda* (Cairo: al-Karma, 2018), 135.

24. Said, "Homage to a Belly Dancer."

25. *Ebony*, February 1963, 33.

26. *Al-Ahram*, 27 July 1957; *New York Times*, 27 June 1957.

27. *Al-Ahram*, 14 and 15 May 1958; *New Journal & Guide*, 31 May 1958, 18.

28. Aḥmad Ḥamrūsh, *Mujtamaʿ Jamal ʿAbd al-Naṣir* (Cairo: Maktabat Madbūlī, 1984), 252.

29. Nadine El Chaer, "Fifi Abdou as You Have Never Seen Before," *Vogue Arabia*, November 2019.

SOURCES AND
FURTHER READING

In Tahiyya Carioca's obituary, written by Edward Said and published in the *London Review of Books* on 28 October 1999, he commented that her life and death had come to "symbolise the enormous amount of life in that part of the world which goes unrecorded and unpreserved." He went on to lament that "none of the Arab countries I know has proper state archives, public record offices or official libraries," resulting in the "sense of a sprawling, teeming history off the page, out of sight and hearing, beyond reach, largely unrecoverable." This is especially true of Cairo's nightlife, where so much of what happened was kept behind closed doors and almost never officially documented.

Said was right to observe that any attempt to reconstruct the events of this period is hampered by a dearth of historical documents. Many details remain uncertain or unresolved, but a search outside the archives can help bring to life this exciting time in the modern history of Egypt and the Arab world.

WHERE TO BEGIN

Although most of the literature is in Arabic, I have taken care to indicate where English-language sources are available. For those wanting to further explore Cairo (and the entertainments) of this period, here are the best starting points in English:

Ziad Fahmy, *Ordinary Egyptians: Creating the Modern Nation Through Popular Culture* (Stanford, CA: Stanford University Press, 2011).

Carmen Gitre, *Acting Egyptian: Theatre, Identity, and Popular Culture in Cairo, 1869–1930* (Austin: University of Texas Press, 2019).

Karin van Nieuwkerk, *"A Trade Like Any Other": Female Singers and Dancers in Egypt* (Austin: University of Texas Press, 2008).

Virginia Danielson, *The Voice of Egypt: Umm Kulthum, Arabic Song, and Egyptian Society in the Twentieth Century* (Chicago: University of Chicago Press, 1997).

For those interested in hearing some of the music discussed, the AMAR foundation in Beirut has remastered and rereleased a lot of music from the period. Samples can be found on their website: https://www.amar-foundation.org/. The compilation by Amira Mitchell, *Women of Egypt 1924–1931: Pioneers of Stardom and Fame* (London: Topic Records, 2006), also features a number of the artists discussed in this book.

Heather D. Ward, *Egyptian Belly Dance in Transition: The Raqs Sharqi Revolution 1890–1930* (Jefferson, NC: McFarland, 2018), is a good place for more information on the world of dance in Cairo. The website shira.net, run by a belly dancer and instructor, has a rich historical section. Ismail Fayed has written several articles on dance for the website madamasr.com, such as "Notes on Belly Dance."

Major sources I have drawn on are memoirs of the stars from the 1920s and 1930s, many of which were published during the 1950s, 1960s, and 1970s. Some of these were written by the subjects themselves, others were told through a series of interviews with journalists and later written up (many first appeared in the theatrical press in several instalments and only later were compiled for publication). Biographies of featured women are included in the notes to their own chapters. Following are some of the most important memoirs by men:

Najib al-Rihani, *Mudhakkirat Najib al-Rihani* (Cairo: Dar al-Hilal, 1959).

Sha'ban Yusuf, ed., *Najib al-Rihani: Mudhakkirat Majhula* (Cairo: Battana, 2017).

Youssef Wahbi [Yusuf Wahbi], *'Ishtu Alf 'Am* (Cairo: al-Maʿarif, 1973–77), 3 vols.

George Abyad [Jurj Abyad], *al-Masrah al-Misri fi miʾat 'Am* (Cairo: al-Maʿarif, 1970).

Badie Khayri [Badiʿ Khayri], *Mudhakkirat Badiʿ Khayri: 45 Sana Taht Adwaʾ al-Masrah*, ed. Muḥammad Rifʿat (Beirut: Dar al-Thaqafa (n.d., 1960s).

The other key source of information about this period is the contemporary press. I have made extensive use of magazines such as *Ruz al-Yusuf*, *al-Masrah* (later *al-Naqid*), *al-Musawwar*, *al-Tiyatru*, *al-Sarkha*, the daily newspaper *al-Ahram*, and more. The National Theatre in Cairo has published an invaluable anthology of Arabic articles about the theatre covering the period from 1876 to 1925: *Silsilat Tawthiq al-Masrah al-Misri* (Cairo: Markaz al-Qawmi li-l-Masrah, 1997–2021). (See STMM in the notes to this book.) Several digitised press archives have been useful, including (but not limited to) al-Sharekh archive, the online holdings of the Centre d'Études Alexandrines (CEAlex), Jrayed: Arabic Newspapers of Ottoman and Mandate Palestine, Proquest, Gallica, and more.

The world of Egyptian entertainment—perhaps all entertainment—is filled with gossip, exaggerated anecdotes, and myth; it is part of the atmosphere. The stories people told about themselves and the tales printed in the press were often infused with hyperbole, contradiction, and even some fantasy. It has been difficult to identify the "hard facts" among the rumours, and in many cases it would be missing the point to try. If a star from the twenties and thirties remembered an event in a particular way, or if contemporary newspapers printed a salacious anecdote whose literal truth is dubious, those narratives are an important part of the bigger story, and I have tried to include them (and often indicated my doubts). I have, however, tried to avoid any fables that have grown up around these personalities and subsequently gained a life of their own long after the events concerned took place.

Speakers of French or Arabic might be interested to read Lamia Ziadé, *Ô nuit, ô mes yeux: Le Caire/Beyrouth/Damas/Jérusalem* (Paris: P.O.L., 2015), an illustrated book covering the same period.

Secondary literature that has helped me throughout the book includes

Mona Ghandour, *Sultanat al-Shasha* (Beirut: Riad el-Rayyes, 2005); Karin van Nieuwkerk, *A Trade Like Any Other* (Austin: University of Texas Press, 1995); and many works by Sayyid 'Ali Isma'il, in particular *Masirat al-Masrah fi Misr, 1900–1935* (Cairo: General Egyptian Book Organization, 2003). More works used for specific chapters are highlighted in the following sections.

This is not a book about mainstream or literary Egyptian feminism, but the literature on that subject is rich. Recommendations include, for example, Marilyn Booth, *May Her Likes Be Multiplied* (Berkeley: University of California Press, 2001); and Margot Badran and Miriam Cooke, eds., *Opening the Gates: An Anthology of Arab Feminist Writing* (Bloomington: Indiana University Press, 2004).

A good summary of the politics of the 1920s and 1930s is Afaf Lutfi al-Sayyid-Marsot, *Egypt's Liberal Experiment, 1922–1936* (Berkeley: University of California Press, 1977).

SOURCES BY CHAPTER

Chapter 1: "Pardon Me, I'm Drunk"

Translations of Ibn Daniyal's shadow plays have been published in Safi Mahmoud Mahfouz and Martin Carlson, eds., *The Ibn Dāniyāl Trilogy* (New York: Martin E. Segal Theatre Center Publications, 2013). Summaries of the later shadow plays can be found (in Arabic) in Ahmad Taymur Basha, *Khayal al-Zill wa-al-lu'ab wa-al-tamathil 'and al-'Arab* (Cairo: Dar al-Kitab al-Arabi, 1957). Forthcoming at the time of writing is Li Guo, *Arabic Shadow Theatre 1300–1900* (Leiden: Brill, 2020).

Philip Sadgrove, *The Egyptian Theatre in the Nineteenth Century* (Reading, UK: Ithaca, 1996), is a mine of information about James Sanua and early Egyptian theatre (and the source of information revealing that no plays were performed after the British invasion of Egypt until 1884). Also important are Muhammad Yusuf Najm, *al-Masrahiyya fi-l-Adab al-'Arabi al-Hadith, 1847–1914* (Beirut: Dar Bayrut, 1956); and Adam Mestyan, *Arab Patriotism: The Ideology and Culture of Power in Late Ottoman Egypt* (Princeton, NJ: Princeton University Press, 2017). Mestyan's article, "Arabic Theatre in Early

Khedivial Culture, 1868–1872: James Sanua Revisited," *International Journal of Middle East Studies* 46, no. 1 (2014): 117–37, is a detailed look at the sources available to those interested in James Sanua's life.

For a longer history of Ezbekiyya, see Doris Behrens-Abouseif, *Azbakiyya and Its Environs from Azbak to Ismāʿīl: 1476–1879* (Cairo: French Institute for Oriental Archaeology [IFAO], 1985). The novelisation of Shafiqa's life, by Galil al-Bindari, is *Shafiqa al-Qibtiyya* (Cairo: Author, 1962). Muhammad Duwarah also includes a detailed entry on her life in *Daʾirat Maʿarif al-Shaʿb* (People's encyclopaedia), vol. 3 (Cairo: Matabiʿ al-Shaʿb, 1959), 220–24.

For more on the Shimi secret police files, see Alon Tam's 2018 PhD dissertation at the University of Pennsylvania: *Cairo's Coffeehouses in the Late Nineteenth and Early Twentieth Centuries: An Urban and Socio-Political History*.

Chapter 2: From Queen of Tarab to Prima Donna

Mounira al-Mahdiyya never published her memoirs, though many magazines (*al-Masrah* in particular) ran articles about her early life. The most comprehensive biography of her is by Ratiba al-Hifni, *al-Sultana Munira al-Mahdiyya* (Cairo: Shuruq, 2001).

Many of C. R. Ashbee's papers are in the archives of King's College Cambridge.

For the accounts of nineteenth- and twentieth-century Arabic music and its recording business, I am particularly indebted to A. J. Racy for both his book, *Making Music in the Arab World*, and his PhD dissertation; and to Frédéric Lagrange, especially for his 1994 dissertation *Musiciens et Poètes en Egypte au Temps de la Nahda* (Musicians and poets in Egypt at the time of Nahda).

For the history of Egyptian blackface, see, especially, Eve Troutt Powell, *A Different Shade of Colonialism: Egypt, Great Britain, and the Mastery of the Sudan* (Berkeley: University of California Press, 2003).

Chapter 3: "Come On Sisters, Let's Go Hand in Hand to Demand Our Freedom"

For the history of Ezbekiyya's red-light district, see Francesca Biancani, *Sex*

Work in Colonial Egypt (London: I. B. Tauris, 2018). Her work also led me to the archives of Suppression of the Traffic in Persons; other volumes in the London School of Economics Women's Library had short accounts of the lives of some of Ezbekiyya's sex workers.

Ziyad Fahmi's *Ordinary Egyptians* (Stanford, CA: Stanford University Press, 2011) is a detailed account of the popular protests in 1919 Egypt. Beth Baron's *Egypt as a Woman: Nationalism, Gender and Politics* (Berkeley: University of California Press, 2005) has a chapter on the women's demonstration, which in turn points readers to John D. Mcintyre, *The Boycott of the Milner Mission: A Study in Egyptian Nationalism* (New York: P. Lang, 1985), as a good attempt to disentangle the often contradictory evidence about the women's protest(s) of 1919.

Descriptions of the actors' protests can be found in Badie Khayri's memoirs and an article in *Akhir Sa'a* magazine from March 1935, reproduced by Sayyid 'Ali Isma'il in the magazine *Masrahna*, 27 May 2019, 28. I am assuming that Rose al-Youssef's account of a protest is from the same event, though there could have been two (or more) different actors' protests.

Chapter 4: Dance of Freedom
Accounts of Egypt by Billy Brooks and George Duncan were serialised in the *Chicago Defender* sporadically from 16 July 1921 to 13 September 1924.

Donald Malcolm Reid, "Political Assassination in Egypt," *International Journal of African Historical Studies* vol. 15, no. 5 (1981): 625–51 is a good summary of political violence in the early twentieth century.

Frédéric Lagrange's thesis is again a good resource, as is his article "Women in the Singing Business, Women in Song," *History Compass* 7, no. 1 (2009): 226–50.

For the dancers in the Columbian Exhibition, see chapter 7 of Marilyn Booth, *Classes of Ladies of Cloistered Spaces* (Edinburgh: Edinburgh University Press, 2015). On the American aftermath, see Donna Carlton, *Looking for Little Egypt* (Bloomington, IN: Author, 2002).

Lucie Ryzova, "Boys, Girls and Kodaks: Peer-Albums and Middle-Class Personhood in Mid-Twentieth-Century Egypt," *Middle Eastern Journal of Cultural Communication* 8, nos. 2–3 (2015): 215–55, is a good discussion of transvestism and the role of photography in the construction of gender in twentieth-century Egypt. Heba Farid and the Naima al-Misriyya Project have done a lot of work rediscovering the important story of Naima al-Misriyya's career.

Chapter 5: "If I Were Not a Woman, I'd Want to Be One"
Much of Rose al-Youssef's life story is told in her memoirs. Rose al-Youssef [Ruz al-Yusuf], *Dhikriyyat* (Cairo: Kitab Ruz al-Yusuf, 1953). Many other sources on her life are also available.

Over the past ten years, Rashad Kamil has done a huge amount of work: republishing anthologies of Rose al-Youssef's articles, old issues of her newspapers, and her autobiographical writing. Rose al-Youssef's journalistic articles, collected as *Maqalati al-Sahafiyya* (Cairo: Rose al-Youssef, 2017), and a series of memoirs she wrote about her career at the magazine in 1937, *Min Dhikriyyati al-Sahafiyya* (Cairo: Rose al-Youssef, 2016), provide important information about this period of her life.

Cynthia Gray-Ware Metcalf's 2008 PhD dissertation at the University of Virginia, *From Morality Play to Celebrity: Women, Gender and Performing Modernity in Egypt: c. 1850–1939*, contains as much detailed information about Rose al-Youssef's personal life as seemingly possible, some of it based on interviews with Rose's family. This (as well as interviews in the 2002 documentary by Mohamed Kamel El Kalioubi, *Usturat Ruz al-Yusuf—La Lègende de Rose al-Youssef*) is the major source of information about Rose's early life and her relationship with her first husband, Mohammed Abd al-Quddus. Metcalf also raises the spectre of prostitution that may hang over Rose's early life, though it cannot be confirmed.

An early Arabic biography of Rose al-Youssef by Ibrahim 'Abduh, *Ruz al-Yusuf: Sira wa-sahifa* (Cairo: Mu'assasat Sijil al-'Arab, 1961), is a little shaky on the early dates of her career but is a valuable source for her later journalism, including an appendix that documents every issue of *Rose al-Youssef* that was banned and includes the reasons for its prohibition.

The action of this chapter is otherwise largely drawn from the contemporary press and Rose's own memoirs: Ruz al-Yusuf, *Dhikriyyat* (noted earlier in this section). Details about the establishment of Ramses Theatre are mostly from Youssef Wahbi's memoirs, which are also noted earlier. The story about

Rose's death comes from an article by Ahmed Baha al-Din in *Ruz al-Yusuf*, 14 April 1958, reprinted in Rashad Kamil's *Ruz al-Yusuf Sayyida Hurra Mus-taqila dhat al-Siyada*, 43–46. Other slight variations exist, including one by Ihsan Abd al-Quddus in the 2010 edition of Rose's memoirs, *Dhikriyyat*.

Chapter 6: Sarah Bernhardt of the East

In the 1960s and early 1970s, Fatima Rushdi published four separate sets of memoirs. Three were in book form: *Kafahi fi-l-Masrah wa-l-Sinima* (Cairo: al-Maʿarif, 1971); *Fatima Rushdi bayn al-Hubb wa-l-Fann* (Cairo: Saʿdi wa Shandi, 1971); and Muhammad Rifʿat, ed., *Mudhakkirat Fatima Rushdi: Sara Birnar al-Sharq* (Beirut: Dar al-Thaqafa [n.d., 1960s]).

Another of Fatima's memoirs was serialised in *al-Masrah* magazine beginning in October 1964. She also talks about her life in a book she wrote about Aziz Eid: *al-Fannan ʿAziz ʿId* (Cairo: GEBO, 1984).

The chapter on Fatima in Muna Ghandur's *Sultanat al-Shasha* (Beirut: Riad El-Rayyes Books, 2005) has some useful details and sources.

Chapter 7: The Singer, the Baby, and the Bey

Fatima Sirri's account of events was serialised in *al-Masrah* from 20 December 1926 to 25 April 1927. Other details about her case and its aftermath were published in *Rose al-Youssef*, *al-Sarkha*, *al-Ahram*, and many other places.

Nehad Selaiha's attempts to follow up on the story can be found in Nihad Sulayha, *al-Marʾa bayn al-Fann wa-l-Hubb wa-l-Zawaj* (Cairo: al-ʿAyn, 2008).

Chapter 8: Star of the East

A huge number of books have been written about Oum Kalthoum. The two autobiographical works available are Muhammad Shuʿayr, ed., *Mudhakkirat al-Anisa Umm Kulthum* (Cairo: Akhbar al-Yawm, 2018) and Maḥmud ʿAwad (and Umm Kulthum), *Umm Kulthum Allati La Yaʿrifuha Aḥad* (Cairo: Akh-bar al-Yawm, 1969). Most of those listed have been published in English; see Elizabeth Warnock Fernea and Basima Qattan Bezirgan, eds., *Middle East-ern Muslim Women Speak* (Austin: University of Texas Press, 1977).

Virginia Danielson's *The Voice of Egypt* is the only full-length biography of Oum Kalthoum available in English. In Arabic, there are many biographies about her. I found this helpful: Ratiba al-Hifni, *Umm Kulthum: Muʿ-jizat al-Ghina al-ʿArabi* (Cairo: Shuruq, 1994).

Ahmed Rami tells his version of his feelings for Oum Kalthoum in *Mud-hakkirat Ahmad Rami wa-qissat hubbihi li-Umm Kulthum* (Beirut: Maktabat al-ʿAsriyya, 1979).

Laura Lohman, *Umm Kulthum: Artistic Agency and the Shaping of an Arab Legend 1967–2007* (Middletown, CT: Wesleyan University Press, 2010), discusses the rumours of her lesbianism, as does Musa Shadidi, *Jinsaniyyat Umm Kulthum* (Amman: Amjad, 2019). Neither writer thinks the details of Oum Kalthoum's sexuality are themselves important; instead, they are more interested in what the rumours say about her place in Egyptian culture.

Heather Sharkey's chapter in Israel Gershoni and Meir Hatina, eds., *Narrating the Nile: Politics, Cultures, Identities* (Boulder, CO: Lynne Rienner, 2008), discusses the American University in Cairo scandal at length, suggesting that part of the problem was the use of Ewart Hall for religious services at the time.

Chapter 9: "Come On, Tough Guy, Play the Game"
For my description of Zar in this chapter, I am indebted to Hager El Hadidi, *Zar: Spirit Possession, Music, and Healing Rituals in Egypt* (Cairo: AUC Press, 2016). This is a good study of tradition, with a useful bibliography.

Chapter 10: Isis Films
Many books have been written about Egyptian film. Two good introductions are Muhammad Awad and Sahar Hammuda, eds., *The Birth of the Seventh Art in Alexandria* (Alexandria: Bibliotheca Alexandrina, 2007); and Magda Wassef, ed., *Egypte: 100 ans de Cinema* (Paris: Institut du Monde Arabe, 1995).

Prints of early films are extremely hard to find. Where I have not been able to see a film or read a plot summary in the press, I have largely relied on the new 2019 GEBO edition of Ahmad al-Hadari, *Tarikh al-Sinima fi Misr* (Cairo: Nadi al-Sinima, 1989), to fill in the gaps. It was particularly useful in discussing the films *The Tragedy of Life*, *Daughter of the Nile*, and *The Victims*.

A good discussion of Youssef Wahbi's *Children of the Rich* can be found in Ifdal Elsaket, "Sound and Desire: Race, Gender, and Insult in Egypt's First Talkie," *International Journal of Mideast Studies* 51, no. 2 (2019): 203–32.

Aziza Amir's memoirs were serialised in *Rose al-Youssef,* issues 108–111 (3–24 January 1928). Muna Ghandur's *Sultanat al-Shasha* (noted earlier) has a chapter on both Aziza Amir and Bahiga Hafez.

Chapter 11: Madame Badia's Casino

Basila Nazik, ed., *Mudhakkirat Badi'a Masabni* (Beirut: Maktabat al-Haya [n.d., 1960s]) contains a huge amount of detail about Badia's early life and the betrayals in her career (though the betrayals may be somewhat exaggerated). There is also some discussion in both of Naguib al-Rihani's memoirs of their marriage.

The cases of both Imtithal Fawzi and Ayousha Nabil are covered in Shaun T. Lopez, "The Dangers of Dancing: The Media and Morality in 1930s Egypt," *Comparative Studies of South Asia, Africa and the Middle East* 24, no. 1 (2004): 97–105. In describing Fawzi's murder and the scandal surrounding it, I have primarily relied on the accounts in *al-Ahram* that appeared after the murder (23 May–1 June 1936) and during the trial (30 September–9 October 1936). I have tended to follow the account given at the trial by the owner of the Bosphore (*al-Ahram,* 30 September 1936) rather than newspaper reports at the time. Other details come from *Ruz al-Yusuf* and *al-Musawwar.* The Kit Kat Club and its triumphal arch are described in Gabriel Dardaud, *Trente ans au bord du Nil* [Thirty years by the Nile] (Paris: Lieu Commun, 1987).

Chapter 12: The Second Revolution

Tahiyya Carioca's memoirs, serialised in the press in the 1970s, were recently republished in Salih Mursi, ed., *Mudhakkirat Kariuka* (Cairo: Nahdat Misr, 2019). This is the primary source of information about her early life. Her birth date is a subject of debate. The memoirs say 1921; others say 1915. I have said "around 1920" based partly on the memoirs and partly on her immigration records to the United States, which say she was twenty-seven years old in 1946.

Ahmed Hussein, *Mudhakkirat Ahmad Husayn, ra'is Misr al-Fatah* (Cairo: GEBO, 2007), tells the story of his foray into acting as well as the criminal proceedings against him following the Cairo fire. Most of my information about the members of the Partisans of Peace comes from Nadia Kamil, *al-Mawluda* (Cairo: al-Karma, 2018).

For a more in-depth discussion of the wartime community in Cairo, see Artemis Cooper, *Cairo in the War, 1939–1945* (London: H. Hamilton, 1989). The stories of Eppler's spy ring are detailed in A. W. Samson, *I Spied Spies* (London: G. G. Harrap, 1965), as is the story of the policeman on the Casino Badia terrace who helped start the Cairo riots. For more on Egypt's Jewish community, see, for example, Gudrun Krämer, *The Jews in Modern Egypt, 1914–1952* (Seattle: University of Washington Press, 1989); and Joel Beinin, *The Dispersion of Egyptian Jewry* (Berkeley: University of California Press, 1998). For more on Doria Shafik, see Cynthia Nelson, *Doria Shafik, Egyptian Feminist: A Woman Apart* (Cairo: American University in Cairo Press, 1996).

Rufus S. Lewter's story is told in R. C. Lewter, *To Freedom Born: The R. C. Lewter Jr., M.D. Story* (Pittsburgh: Dorrance, 2002).

INDEX